UNIVERSAL SUBGOALING AND CHUNKING

**THE KLUWER INTERNATIONAL SERIES
IN ENGINEERING AND COMPUTER SCIENCE**

KNOWLEDGE REPRESENTATION, LEARNING
AND EXPERT SYSTEMS

Consulting Editor

Tom M. Mitchell

UNIVERSAL SUBGOALING AND CHUNKING

The Automatic Generation and Learning of Goal Hierarchies

by

John Laird
Xerox Palo Alto Research Center
Palo Alto, California

Paul Rosenbloom
Stanford University
Palo Alto, California

Allen Newell
Carnegie-Mellon University
Pittsburgh, Pennsylvania

KLUWER ACADEMIC PUBLISHERS
Boston/Dordrecht/Lancaster

Distributors for North America:
Kluwer Academic Publishers
101 Philip Drive
Assinippi Park
Norwell, MA 02061

Distributors for the UK and Ireland:
Kluwer Academic Publishers
MTP Press Limited
Falcon House, Queen Square
Lancaster LA1 1RN, UNITED KINGDOM

Distributors for all other countries:
Kluwer Academic Publishers Group
Distribution Centre
Post Office Box 322
3300 AH Dordrecht, THE NETHERLANDS

Library of Congress Cataloging-in-Publication Data

Laird, John, 1954–
  Universal subgoaling and chunking.

  (Kluwer international series in engineering and
computer science. Knowledge representation, learning,
and expert systems)
  Bibliography: p.
  Includes indexes.
  1. Artificial intelligence. 2. programming (Electronic
computers) 3. Computer architecture. I. Rosenbloom,
Paul S. II. Newell, Allen. III. Title. IV. Series.
Q335.L33 1986   006.3   86–2778
ISBN 0–89838–213–0

Printed in the United States of America

Second Printing, 1987

CONTENTS

PREFACE

Rarely do research paths diverge and converge as neatly and productively as the paths exemplified by the two efforts contained in this book. The story behind these researches is worth recounting.

The story, as far as I'm concerned, starts back in the Fall of 1976, when John Laird and Paul Rosenbloom, as new graduate students in computer science at Carnegie-Mellon University, joined the Instructible Production System (IPS) project (Rychener, Forgy, Langley, McDermott, Newell, Ramakrishna, 1977; Rychener & Newell, 1978). In those days, production systems were either small or special or both (Newell, 1973; Shortliffe, 1976). Mike Rychener had just completed his thesis (Rychener, 1976), showing how production systems could effectively and perspicuously program the full array of artificial intelligence (AI) systems, by creating versions of *Student* (done in an earlier study, Rychener 1975), *EPAM*, *GPS*, King-Pawn-King endgames, a toy-blocks problem solver, and a natural-language input system that connected to the blocks-world system. However, these production systems still contained only a few hundred rules. It was clear to several of us at CMU that it was important to produce a system with a large number of productions — a thousand was a useful initial target. The view, then as now, was that productions were a way of holding large amounts of knowledge in accessible form, and that they became an interesting model of intelligence only if they could be envisioned as having thousands upon thousands (millions?) of productions rules. Having settled the basic issue of scope (production systems constituted a generally practical programming scheme for AI systems), it was now time to go after size.

Thus, a project got started, informally called the Large Production System project. This settled little about the direction of the project, of course. Gradually, the group homed in on the task of instructing a production system from the outside — the system was to be grown, not programmed. This approach embodied a particular strategy for how to obtain a large production system, by having the system assimilate one externally given production after another. A key constraint was that each new production must be added without the system or user knowing about already existing productions. When the memory of productions became large enough, processing considerations would preclude looking at the existing memory, in any event; so it seemed important to accept this constraint from the beginning. With the selection of this task, the project became known as the Instructible Production System (IPS) project. (This new name served also to avoid the charge, made more than once, that we cared only about size and not about what the system would actually do — a typical American project!) John Laird and Paul Rosenbloom came into this project about a year and a half after it had gotten started, and after it had acquired its new name. Both were motivated by an assessment that production systems were an important organizational scheme for intelligence. Both also had a deep attraction to the view that one could and should be interested simultaneously in human and artificial intelligence — the quintessential cognitive-science orientation.

The actual outcome of the IPS project was hardly something to rave about. No really instructible production systems were ever produced. (The few working systems never got very far off the ground.) The project disbanded after a couple of years and the people involved all went somewhat separate ways, although all remained associated with production systems in some fashion. In fact, there were a few direct lessons, which Mike Rychener presented to the world (Rychener, 1983). However, sometimes direct success is not the proper measure of a project. This is such a case — and beyond all reasonable measure.

The first side effect was the *OPS* series of production-system languages, of which the best known and most widely used is *OPS5* (Forgy, 1981; Brownston, Farrell, Kant & Martin, 1985). The first version was designed by the original members of the Large Production System project, Lanny Forgy, John McDermott, Allen Newell and Mike Rychener (Forgy & McDermott, 1977), as a corporate effort, to be a production system that would remain effective as the size of the rule set grew. It was called the Official Production System to demark it from the other production systems around CMU at the time, *PSG* (Newell & McDermott, 1975) and *Psnlst* (Rychener, 1976; Vol. I, Chap II), and to give it a neutral designation as the one the project would use. It made use of the *Rete* network implementation technology that Lanny Forgy had developed for his thesis (Forgy, 1979). This first side effect has been enough, all by itself, to justify the original project.

The second side effect was the development of the expert-system effort at CMU, and in particular the development of *R1*, nee *XCON* (McDermott, 1982). The task of building an AI system to help with the configuration task was, in fact, initiated from the outside by Sam Fuller, of Digital Equipment Corporation. Fuller had earlier been a faculty member in the Computer Science Department at CMU and maintained many ties with the department including, as it happened, several individuals associated with the IPS project. The project had already begun to retreat from its original aims when this new opportunity came up and John McDermott took hold of this new direction with a vengeance. This side effect too has been enough, all by itself, to justify the original project (Bachant & McDermott, 1984).

There are other side effects as well — Mike Rychener has become one of the agents (if I can describe it so) for moving expert systems into engineering design (Rychener, 1985). Perhaps it is the same everywhere by now, but I no longer even keep track of the people or the projects working in applied artificial intelligence in CMU's engineering school. Certainly the Computer Science Department, which is the continued home of all the research we are talking about here, has no exclusive license on this area and may not even account for the majority of the expert-system activity at CMU.

Recounting the IPS project provides the context for tracking the two research efforts of the present book. With the demise of the project, each followed a separate course. The courses were not isolated from each other. Laird and Rosenbloom were the closest of friends and exchanged notes continually, and I was a common thesis advisor on both efforts. Still, the research paths were quite distinct and they need to be traced separately. Let me start with Rosenbloom's path. It was the one most different from the IPS project and thus provides the proper emphasis of a break with the past.

Enter an entirely external impulse. Stu Card and Tom Moran of Xerox Palo Alto Research Center (PARC), along with myself, had been working throughout the seventies on creating an applied psychology of human-computer interaction (for the story of that research, see Card, Moran & Newell, 1983). We were particularly focused on quantitative laws of human processing that could provide the foundations of engineering models of human interaction. Fitts' Law (Fitts, 1954), which describes how long it takes a user to move (say) a cursor from one part of the screen to another target area, is one such robust law (it is linear in the logarithm of the ratio of the distance to the size of the target area). Another one is the Power Law of Practice, which states that the time to do a repetitive task decreases as a power of the number of times the task has been practiced. The power law of practice has been known for a long time (Snoddy, 1926), although mostly in the context of perceptual-motor skills. Human-computer interaction, although a cognitive task, is also a skilled task and practice is particularly important to it. (Indeed, a common explanation of why people seem never to agree that one programming language is better than another is that sufficient practice with any language makes it seem superior to the practiced user.)

Thus, I was mildly interested in the power law of practice and whether it could be applied to cognitive skills in human-computer interaction. Then, in mid 1979, John Anderson approached me about giving a paper at the upcoming Carnegie Cognitive Symposium (the 16th instance of an annual affair), whose theme was to be the acquisition of cognitive skills. Casting about for a topic, I decided to make it an excuse for looking into the scope of the power law of practice, as well as trying to understand how it fit into a cognitive view of skill such as we had been developing on computer text editing. I deliberately corralled Paul Rosenbloom into helping me with this. He had spent the prior year at San Diego studying psychology and, with the IPS project no longer going, he was casting around for an appropriate new direction.

The result of this effort was Newell & Rosenbloom (1981), which revealed, by drawing on widely scattered work, that the power law applied to any deliberate task — perceptual, motor or cognitive. That raised the question of its explanation in acute form, and we explored the several possibilities. In the background was a proposition I first heard from Herb Simon (1955) in the context of the Zipf distribution (which describes a common law for word frequencies, city sizes, income distributions, and even more) that a ubiquitous phenomenon cannot arise out of aspects specific to each occurrence of the phenomenon, but must depend on something pervasive and elementary that is common. A well-known example is the normal distribution, which arises whenever many independent increments add randomly. Thus, some extremely general structural feature of cognition must be behind the power law of practice. We thought we found it in the well-known psychological phenomenon of *chunking*, whereby a human builds up the organization of memory by assembling collections of existing chunks into larger chunks, each chunk being a description of part of the situation. We proposed in the paper a general theory of learning by chunking, which could explain both the power law of practice and why it would be ubiquitous.

The success of this conference-paper venture set Rosenbloom and myself off on a long trail of investigation, which eventually led to the thesis which is his major contribution to this book. The original chunking theory is cast in quite general form. It posits that chunking occurs continuously with experience; that it obeys some general laws for improving performance; and that the ensemble of tasks being practiced has certain general features. Then it shows that a law of practice emerges with the same shape as the power law. Such a macroscopic explanation leaves many questions unanswered. In particular, it does not actually specify the mechanisms that produce the law, nor does it indicate whether any structural feature of the human cognitive architecture is thereby revealed. This latter issue of discovering the properties of the cognitive architecture was never very far from center stage with us. For me personally it predates by far the history being recounted here (Newell, 1973; Newell, 1980a) and for Rosenbloom it was one of the driving forces behind his interest in production systems. While out at San Diego, Rosenbloom had in fact developed a production-system cognitive architecture, *Xaps*, to explore the differences between the activation-based ideas then beginning to be explored in psychology and the purely symbolic production systems such as *OPS*. Thus, even though our investigation of practice was initiated by the concern for models of human-computer interaction, and made its first progress by the analysis of data on human behavior, the focus of the research shifted to discovering production-system architectures that would exhibit chunking in the appropriate way. This of course is exactly the way of cognitive science — moving freely back and forth between the data-oriented methods of psychology and the system-oriented methods of artificial intelligence.

We can now suspend recounting the path of Rosenbloom's research. It had moved sharply away from the instructible production system path. The thesis itself provides the appropriate next chapter, although it elides somewhat that an initial chunking scheme was built with the activation-based *Xaps2* (Rosenbloom & Newell, 1982), before moving back to a purely symbolic architecture (*Xaps3*) of the studies of the thesis. Let us now return to pick up the path of John Laird's research. This requires some additional context.

How to represent tasks has been a long-standing issue in artificial intelligence, with major options defining distinguishable strands of research in the field. Tasks are to be posed as theorems to be proved; or simply as data structures with algorithms or methods to be applied; or as plans to be instantiated; or as heuristic spaces to be searched. This last option — also called the *problem-space* representation — goes back to the early sixties when it became clear that searching was central to any difficult problem (Feigenbaum & Feldman, 1963). My own research with Herb Simon has always been squarely in this problem-space tradition, where we contributed first to showing the importance of search in artificial intelligence (Newell, Shaw & Simon, 1957; Newell & Ernst, 1965), and then to showing that search plays a similar central role in human problem solving (Newell & Simon, 1972).

The development of production systems is responsive to a separate issue in artificial intelligence, though one of equally long standing, namely, how to represent the intended behavior of the problem solver, i.e., its methods and procedures. For instance, the title of Rychener's thesis was *Production systems as a programming language for artificial intelligence applications*. Thus, the IPS project had adopted the standard procedural framework — the instructions to be given to an IPS were essentially goals and specific domain-dependent methods for accomplishing these goals. Indeed, the very notion of instruction implies becoming sufficiently knowledgeable so that problem solving is no longer necessary. In any event, these two strands of research — task representation and procedure representation — co-existed and ran along side by side in the CMU environment, each focused primarily on a separate aspect of the total problem of intelligent behavior.

John Laird and I began to devote energy to putting the two together — putting problem spaces into production systems. Of course, one could program problem spaces in a production system — Rychener (1976) had shown that was in fact a good way of doing business. But that was just the standard relation of systems to the languages used to program them. We were seeking a more intimate connection. The trigger for this was the developing conviction that all tasks should be represented as search in a problem space. Everyone believed that heuristic search was to be used for difficult tasks, but everyone equally believed that procedural representations were to be used for routine tasks. Indeed, the paradigm shift in artificial intelligence that some people claimed to see in the mid-seventies (Goldstein & Papert, 1977) was away from search entirely and toward knowledge, i.e., toward having enough knowledge to avoid searching. This general view supported the separation of work on problem spaces and work on production systems, because there were clear domains (namely, routine tasks) where procedures were necessary and search was absent. Even within the work on problem spaces this separation was made: operators were viewed as tasks for which routine procedures were available. However, by the late seventies I had gradually become convinced that a single uniform representation should be used for all tasks — routine and problematic alike — a proposition put forth as the *problem-space hypothesis* (Newell, 1980b).

If problem spaces were all, then it was important to be clear on what problem spaces really were — they had to be adequate to cover all forms of processing and all forms of tasks. A standard approach in computer science to such an issue is to develop a programming language or programming system to encapsulate the notions involved. Using the first-year graduate course in artificial intelligence as an excuse, Laird and I developed a Lisp-based problem-space system for student exercises, which we called *TEX*, for Task, EXerciser. As often happens, *TEX* never shaped up enough to help the class; but it did help us think in terms of a problem-solving architecture. Along the way, we developed a list of some forty key questions that needed to be answered in order to define problem spaces adequately — although, again, the list never saw the light of published day (Laird & Newell, 1981). The issues were not just those of basic definitions and organization. An integral part of the problem-space hypothesis was that methods that were important in artificial intelligence had natural representations as searches in problem spaces. So Laird also pursued reformulating as collections of problem spaces the planning schemes used in artificial intelligence: *GPS-Planning, Abstrips, Noah, Assembly-line balancer,* etc. (Laird, 1981).

I emphasize the focussing of research on problem spaces to make clear that the paths of research had diverged and that the specific goals of the IPS project had been suspended (though hardly abandoned, for in such a close knit research arena, all concerns remain within reach). By the time we turned to the proper goals of Laird's thesis research it was to put problem spaces into production systems in an architecture. The criterion was to produce an effective engine for research, in which we could implement real problem-solving systems. Ever since we had fired up the IPS project we had production systems of adequate power (in *OPS*), but we had not obtained an effective organization that allowed us to go beyond what Rychener had done in his thesis. (John McDermott, of course, starting with *R1,* developed a highly successful line of expert systems that avoided the requirement for additional architectural organization beyond the production system.)

The story of Laird's contribution to this book has now been brought almost to where it can be left to the thesis itself to elucidate. Almost, but not quite. For a series of transformations occurred in our view of the architecture, and the thesis only presents the final result. The first of these is symbolized by the *universal weak method* and the second by *universal subgoaling.* The latter is the topic of the thesis, but the former is worth filling in here.

The universal weak method has distal roots in the view that some basic methods of very general character (such as hill climbing and means-ends analysis, and referred to generally as the weak methods) play a special role in artificial intelligence (Newell, 1969). But proximally it is grounded in the IPS project. A major cause of our failure to be able to instruct a production system from scratch seemed to be that the methods given to the IPS to accomplish an initial sequence of tasks rarely were adequate to perform the next task. Actually, the immediate symptom was often that no productions would fire at all and the IPS would simply halt. Here is a simplified model of the situation. The IPS faced a large space of task situations. Each acquired method provided coverage for a small region of this space. However, the methods provided by instruction were like mere dots in this space, so that new tasks hardly ever hit where there was a dot. In short, the mosaic of methods provided insufficient coverage. The failures of the IPSs stand in apparent contrast to the success of many artificial intelligence systems. However, the latter are designed with both the task and the methods selected at the same time, so they were effectively coordinated by the designer when they were created. An IPS was constrained so that each new task was to be an independent increment, which simply had to build on what happened to be there from prior instruction (which had not been planned for this particular task). Once the methods had been dense enough, the strategy might have worked, but it didn't work for getting started from a kernel system.

What was needed, Laird and I reasoned toward the end of the IPS project, were some methods that provide very wide coverage, so that if no specific methods would work, these at least would be there. Not surprisingly, the methods in question were the so called weak methods. In trying to give the IPS the weak methods as default resources, it was necessary to face how to select the appropriate one. Gradually, we discovered how to write a single method (a single collection of productions) that would effect whichever weak method was appropriate. This exercise lay dormant as the research paths separated out from the IPS project. But as a problem-space architecture embedded in production systems began to take shape in 1982 (by then called *Soar*), the exercise provided the understanding that the architecture was not just a framework within which to write methods easily. Rather, it could be structured to realize all the weak methods in a transparent and perspicuous way — in what we then labeled the universal weak method (Laird & Newell, 1983).

The story to this point tells of a common beginning in the IPS project for the research of this book, and how the strands then separated, each to yield its own distinct research. This is an interesting story, especially since it reveals an additional fallout from the IPS project in Laird's work. However, the interest increases (doubles? squares?) when it transpires that these two research efforts merge together again in an immensely fruitful way. This is symbolized by the third small chapter at the end, *Towards chunking as a general learning mechanism*. Its title might just as well have been *Chunking in Soar*, which would then have told the total story in three words, given the prior history as laid out here. Even so, this coming together is worth some additional final words. It is an example of simultaneous deliberation and serendipity, and it ultimately justifies putting these two researches in a single volume as well as tying off the consequences of the IPS project.

Both Laird and Rosenbloom have always been in the game of discovering the ultimate nature of the architecture of cognition and both have always refused to separate artificial intelligence concerns from psychological concerns, while recognizing tactically that research often pursues now one and now the other. The two researches in this book deal with distinct aspects of the cognitive architecture. But it was clear to Laird and Rosenbloom all along that the separation of the two efforts was artificial, though driven by the dictates of distinct sources of knowledge for the research — the power law of practice versus problem spaces in production systems. (The separation was not driven by any requirement to produce separate theses efforts.) We gradually formed a pact that, once the theses were completed, we would forge a single research effort to pursue *Soar* as a general architecture for intelligence. (It almost goes without saying that it would be aimed ultimately at both natural and artificial intelligence.) This *Soar* research team was officially formed in the summer of 1983, when Rosenbloom finished his work (although Laird still had several more months to go). Part of the expectation was to be able to move into *Soar* what we had learned about learning in the chunking studies. For myself, I took that as a long-range commitment — for it didn't seem to me ripe to undertake it immediately. Both Laird and Rosenbloom took the issue as much more pressing.

Nevertheless, in the fall of 1983, with our state of knowledge being the sum of the two theses in this book, we proceeded simply to ask what should be done next to push *Soar* ahead. As a symbol of integration, we agreed that Laird would push on learning aspects and that Rosenbloom would push on problem-solving aspects — an exact switch from the prior specialization and perhaps a reflection of their each having felt a little constrained by their theses topics.

On the problem-solving side, we wanted to tackle something substantial, to see if *Soar* was suitable for complex tasks. John McDermott suggested that we take on the task of *R1*. We had claimed that *Soar* would be good as a knowledge-intensive system, but had only done toy problems with it to date. Thus, McDermott's suggestion was more in the nature of a challenge — that we should cash in our promissory note. That seemed like an interesting path, especially since copying existing systems provides a lot of information — not actually copying them, of course, but doing the same task with the same knowledge, so that the performances should be identical. Thus, Rosenbloom took up this task, with interesting results (Rosenbloom, Laird, McDermott, Newell & Orciuch, 1985). Note that this turn of events is another reconvergence of the separate strands that grew out of the IPS project. (Indeed, it can be added that *Soar* is realized within a modified *OPS5*.)

Laird proceeded down the path of moving chunking into *Soar*. We had already brought up a *Soar* version of an induction scheme called *Version spaces* (Mitchell, 1978), although it did not provide much insight into doing learning generally in *Soar*. Following the copying strategy, we figured to first bring up some version of chunking working on the elementary choice-reaction tasks that had been used in Rosenbloom's thesis, and then to consider how to generalize and extend the chunking to a more general scheme within *Soar*.

It was not to be that way. Instead, in one of those great leaps that all researchers dream about, a completely general scheme of chunking was incorporated in *Soar* in a matter of a day or two, which thereupon worked and led immediately to the results exhibited in the final part of this book. I remember this event well, precisely because I had a before-after snapshot of it. In a meeting on a Monday, we agreed that John Laird would begin actively to bring up a version in the narrow copying sense. I was then out of town and returned home Thursday to a message that chunking was working (as of Wednesday, 12 January 1984) — and on the Eight Puzzle, rather than the little choice-reaction tasks of Rosenbloom's thesis. As usual, one should not make too much of this creation story. We had been thinking about the task for a very long time and from multiple points of view. Furthermore, it took some pushing and hauling to get the chunking to work on *R1-Soar* and on Tic-Tac-Toe, most of which involved refining the definitions of the conditions and actions for a newly built chunk.

Even so, this event marked a turning point for the *Soar* project, as well as for the story of this Preface. From this point on, the two paths of research in this book merged back together to become a single path (Laird, Rosenbloom, Newell, 1985). From now on, there is no separate consideration of problem solving and learning. *Soar* is a problem solver that learns whenever it solves problems. It is a learner whose characteristics depend entirely on the problem solving it does; and the learning it does while attempting a problem plays an integral role in that very problem-solving attempt. Learning and problem solving enter into each other everywhere we turn, and as we observe how the now-joined research effort is proceeding, their integration seems continually to increase.

Allen Newell

References

Bachant, J. & McDermott, J. R1 revisited: Four years in the trenches. *AI Magazine*, 1984, *5*, 21-32.

Brownston, L., Farrell, R., Kant, E. & Martin, N. *Programming Expert Systems in OPS5*. Reading, MA: Addison-Wesley, 1985.

Card, S., Moran, T. P. & Newell, A. *The Psychology of Human-Computer Interaction*. Hillsdale, NJ: Erlbaum, 1983.

Feigenbaum, E. A. & Feldman, J. (Eds.). *Computers and Thought*. New York: McGraw-Hill, 1963.

Fitts, P. M. The information capacity of the human motor system in controlling amplitude of movement. *Journal of Experimental Psychology*, 1954, *47*, 381-391.

Forgy, C. L. *On the Efficient Implementation of Production Systems*. Doctoral dissertation, Carnegie-Mellon University, 1979.

Forgy, C. L. *OPS5 User's Manual* (Tech. Rep.). Computer Science Department, Carnegie-Mellon University, July 1981.

Forgy, C. L. & McDermott, J. OPS, a domain-independent production system language. In *Proceedings Fifth International Joint Computer Conference*. Cambridge MA: MIT AI Laboratory, 1977.

Goldstein, I., & Papert, S. Artificial intelligence, language and the study of knowledge. *Cognitive Science*, 1977, *1*, 84-124.

Laird, J. Planning as Problem Spaces. Computer Science Department, Carnegie-Mellon University (unpublished). 1981.

Laird, J. & Newell, A. What is a Problem Space: A list of issues. Computer Science Department, Carnegie-Mellon University (unpublished). 1981.

Laird, J. & Newell, A. *A Universal Weak Method* (Tech. Rep.). Computer Science Department, Carnegie-Mellon University, June 1983.

Laird, J. E., Rosenbloom, P. S. & Newell, A. Chunking in *Soar:* The anatomy of a general learning mechanism. *Machine Learning*, 1985, Vol. *1*. (in press; also available as CMU CSD Technical Report, Nov 1985).

McDermott, J. R1: A rule based configurer of computer systems. *Artificial Intelligence*, 1982, *19*, 39-88.

Mitchell, T. M. *Version Spaces: An approach to concept learning*. Doctoral dissertation, Stanford University, 1978.

Newell, A. Heuristic programming: Ill-structured problems. In Aronofsky, J. (Ed.), *Progress in Operations Research, III*. New York: Wiley, 1969.

Newell, A. Production systems: Models of control structures. In Chase, W. C. (Ed.), *Visual Information Processing*. New York: Academic Press, 1973.

Newell, A. Harpy, production systems and human cognition. In Cole, R. (Ed.), *Perception and Production of Fluent Speech*. Hillsdale, NJ: Erlbaum,

1980.

Newell, A. Reasoning, problem solving and decision processes: The problem space as a fundamental category. In R. Nickerson (Ed.), *Attention and Performance VIII*. Hillsdale, NJ: Erlbaum, 1980.

Newell, A., & Ernst, G. The search for generality. In Kalenich, W. A. (Ed.), *Proceedings of IFIP Congress 65*. Washington, DC: Spartan, 1965.

Newell, A., & McDermott, J. *PSG Manual (rev. ed)* (Tech. Rep.). Computer Science Department, Carnegie-Mellon University, 1975.

Newell, A. & Rosenbloom, P. Mechanisms of skill acquisition and the law of practice. In Anderson, J. A. (Ed.), *Learning and Cognition*. Hillsdale, NJ: Erlbaum, 1981.

Newell, A. & Simon, H. A. *Human Problem Solving*. Englewood Cliffs: Prentice-Hall, 1972.

Newell, A., Shaw, J. C. & Simon, H. A. Empirical explorations of the Logic Theory Machine: A case study in heuristics. In *Proceedings of the 1957 Western Joint Computer Conference*. Western Joint Computer Conference, 1957. (Reprinted in Feigenbaum, E. & Feldman, J. (Eds.) *Computers and Thought*, New York: McGraw-Hill, 1963).

Rosenbloom, P. S. & Newell, A. *Learning by chunking: A production-system model of practice* (Tech. Rep.). Computer Science Department, Carnegie-Mellon University, Oct 1982.

Rosenbloom, P. S., Laird, J. E., McDermott, J., Newell, A. & Orciuch, E. R1-Soar: An experiment in knowledge-intensive programming in a problem solving architecture. *IEEE Transactions on Pattern Analysis and Machine Intelligence*, 1985, *7*, 561-569. (also available in *Two Soar Studies*, CMU CSD Technical Report, Jan 1985; and in *Proceedings of the IEEE Workshop on Principles of Knowledge-Based Systems*, IEEE Computer Society, Dec 1984).

Rychener, M. D. *The Studnt Production System: A study of encoding knowledge in production systems* (Tech. Rep.). Computer Science Department, Carnegie-Mellon University, October 1975.

Rychener, M. D. *Production systems as a programming langauge for artificial intelligence applications* (Tech. Rep.). Computer Science Department, Carnegie-Mellon University, 1976.

Rychener, M. D. The instructible production system: A retrospective analysis. In Michalski, R. S., Carbonell, J. G. & Mitchell, T. M. (Eds.), *Machine Learning: An artificial intelligence approach*. Palo Alto, CA: Tioga, 1983.

Rychener, M. D. Expert systems for engineering design. *Expert Systems*, 1985, *2*, 30-44.

Rychener, M. D. & Newell, A. An instructible production system: Basic design issues. In Waterman, D. A. & Hayes-Roth, F. (Eds.), *Pattern-Directed In-*

ference Systems. New York: Academic Press, 1978.

Rychener, M. D., Forgy, C. L., Langley, P., McDermott, J., Newell, A., Ramak-
rishna, K. Problems in building an instructible production system. In
*Proceedings of the Fifth International Joint Conference on Artificial
Intelligence.* Cambridge, MA: MIT, 1977.

Shortliffe, E. H.   *Computer-based Medical Consultations: MYCIN.*   New York:
American Elsevier, 1976.

Simon, H. A. On a class of skew distributions. *Biometrika,* 1955, *52,* 425-440.

Snoddy, G. S. Learning and stability. *Journal of Applied Psychology,* 1926, *10,*
1-36.

PART I

UNIVERSAL SUBGOALING

John E. Laird

1 INTRODUCTION

The objective of our research is to develop architectures for general intelligence. One mark of intelligence is rationality, that is, an intelligent agent (implemented in some architecture) uses its knowledge to control its own behavior to achieve its goals by deciding what problems to work on, what formulation of a problem to use, and what actions to take to solve a problem (Newell, 1982). The structure of the underlying architecture is critical in determining whether or not an agent is able to behave rationally and bring knowledge to bear when it is appropriate. The aim of this paper is to develop an architecture so that all aspects of problem-solving in an intelligent agent can be controlled by whatever knowledge is available to the agent.

In Artificial Intelligence (AI), *methods* have been the dominate organization for control knowledge. A method can be implemented procedurally using the standard programming language constructs of AI languages (Hewitt, 1971). For example, the steepest-ascent hill climbing method explores a set of actions to take at a given point, then chooses the best, based on some evaluation function. Following the selection of the best alternative, the method recurs, once again trying out new alternatives and selecting the best. This method encodes the knowledge that we should select between alternative actions based on the evaluation of the results they produce. Figure 1-1 gives a procedural representation of this method as presented in Rich (1983). In this example, as in standard programming languages, behavior is determined by the ordered sequence of the statements along with conditionals, loops and gotos. Although methods are effective representations of control knowledge, they partition the knowledge so that only the knowledge encoded in a single method (the method selected for the current task) can be used at one time. If a piece of knowledge is to be used in many methods, it must be replicated. In an intelligent agent this is a problem since the agent is always learning new knowledge that may be relevant to many different methods. In standard programming languages, it is difficult to identify and modify all the methods that can make use of new knowledge. In addition, if

1. Generate the first proposed solution in the same way as would be done in the generate-and-test procedure. See if it is a solution. If so, quit. Else continue.
2. From this solution, apply some number of applicable rules to generate a new set of proposed solutions.
3. For each element of the set do the following:

   a. Send it to the test function. If it is a solution, quit.
   b. If not, see if it is the closest to a solution of any of the elements test so far. If it is, remember it. If it is not, forget it.

4. Take the best element found above and use it as the next proposed solution. This step corresponds to a move through the problem space in the direction that appears to be leading the most quickly toward a goal.
5. Go back to step 2.

Figure 1-1: Programming representation of steepest-ascent hill climbing.

two methods are found to be useful for a task, it is difficult to combine them. Usually, a new method must be written that incorporates the knowledge from both methods. In a rational agent, all knowledge should be available whenever it is needed, without outside intervention (such as a programmer rewriting methods). Therefore, we must look for other encodings of control knowledge.

Rule-based systems explicitly designed for *meta-level reasoning* provide an alternative to standard programming languages (Davis, 1980; Genesereth, 1983). For example, in **MRS** (Genesereth, 1983), a problem solver consists of a set of *base* rules that encode a task domain and *meta-rules* (Davis, 1980) that encode knowledge to select which of the base rules to apply. The base rules produce the behavior of the system, and the meta-rules control the behavior. Methods are still encoded in the system, but in a more flexible format. Since the meta-rules for a method are syntactically independent, new rules can be added without rewriting the method.

In previous work, we investigated the representation of the *weak methods* in an architecture similar to **MRS** called **Soar1** (Laird and Newell, 1983a; Laird and Newell, 1983b).[1] The weak methods are those methods that are very general and require little knowledge about the task, such as generate and test, means-

---

[1]*Soar1* was the first in the family of *Soar* architectures. We will use *Soar* as a generic term to refer to the current version of the architecture. Therefore, although the current architecture is the second version, namely *Soar2*, it will be called *Soar* in this document.

ends analysis, depth-first search, hill climbing, and mini-max search. These methods are ubiquitous both in human and AI problem solvers. We proposed that a problem solver does not have a fixed set of weak methods plus a mechanism for selecting a method appropriate to a given task. Instead, a problem solver is organized so that all *directly* available knowledge can be brought to bear on every task. We discovered that many of the weak methods *emerge* from such an organization, with different weak methods arising when different knowledge about a task is available. As more knowledge about a task is added, it directly affects the behavior, improves the problem solving, and sometimes changes the weak method that arises. We called this type of organization a *universal weak method* and in *Soar1* we implemented a universal weak method for those weak methods that do not require subgoals.

The universal weak method consists of the problem-solving knowledge that applies for all methods. With just the universal weak method, the system is able to perform the basic functions of problem solving, although it may require extensive search. *Soar1* was successful in representing the weak methods because we were able to identify the primitive units of knowledge that are used in the weak methods and encode them in independent *method increments*. Each method increment is a rule that related some concept about a task directly to some behavior, so each method increment was used whenever the appropriate concepts were available. Since each method increment was independent, the addition of new knowledge (in the form of new method increments) and the combination of knowledge from different methods happened automatically, without any analysis or modification of prior knowledge.

For example, Figure 1-2 contains schemas of the rules required in *Soar1* to encode the knowledge that gives rise to steepest-ascent hill climbing. For a specific task, the first rule would compute a specific evaluation of unevaluated states. The remaining rules control the selection of the current state based on the evaluation and the acceptability of states. The universal weak method defines the semantics of the concepts such as current state, result, ancestor state, prefer, acceptable and unacceptable. The concepts such as *evaluation* and *better* are task specific and must be instantiated for a given task.

Soar1 has some of the properties we desire for an architecture that supports rational agents. With a universal weak method, the knowledge is not pre-compiled into a specific method, instead, all knowledge about a task comes into play to control the behavior. It is easy to add new knowledge (just by adding new rules) and it is easy to combine methods so that the knowledge from both is used for a task. However, *Soar1* (and similar systems) can only support *limited rationality*, that is, they only use knowledge that is *directly* available to control

1. If the current state is **unevaluated**, compute the **evaluation** of the current state.
2. If the current state is unacceptable and a result has an **evaluation** that is **better** than another result, prefer the first result to the second.
3. If the ancestor state is not unacceptable, prefer the ancestor state to the current state.
4. If the current state is not unacceptable and the ancestor state is unacceptable, make the current state acceptable.

Figure 1-2: *Soar1* representation of steepest-ascent hill climbing.

behavior.[2] Each rule relates concepts about the task directly to behavior, using recognition of the available concepts to determine the appropriate behavior. If the directly available knowledge is either incomplete or inconsistent, a random choice is made. If more knowledge could be made available, either by explicitly attempting the alternatives being considered, by attempting to create an analogy with a prior problem or by examining the decision at a different level of detail, a more informed, and thus more rational decision could be made.

Since *Soar1* was limited to using knowledge that directly available, the knowledge to encode a method had to explicitly control the selection of states and operators so that the concepts required by other rules would be available. In Figure 1-2, rules 2-4 explicitly manipulate the selection of the current state so that the concepts required by the other rules will always be available and will be sufficient for carrying out steepest-ascent hill climbing. If a problem solver could gain access to knowledge not directly available, the encoding of knowledge used for a task might be simplified. In place of the representation of knowledge required by *Soar1*, we would like to encode only knowledge about a task and have it affect behavior when it is appropriate. For example, we would prefer to only encode the knowledge about a task as represented in Figure 1-3.

1. If the current state is **unevaluated**, compute the **evaluation** of the current state.
2. If the **evaluation** of a task operator's result is **better** than that of another task operator, prefer the first task operator to the second.

Figure 1-3: Proposed representation of steepest-ascent hill climbing.

The first rule computes an evaluation for a state and the second embodies the notion that one should select an operator based on the results it produces. We

---

[2]This differs from *bounded rationality* (Simon, 1969), where architectural limitations of an agent (such as the size of immediate memory or the rate of learning) limit the behavior of the agent.

would hope that this knowledge alone would be sufficient to cause a system to behave as if it were using steepest-ascent hill climbing. Not only do these rules seem to embody the knowledge humans make use of, instead of the rules in Figure 1-2 or the procedure in Figure 1-1, they should be easier to learn because of their simplicity.

We do want to use directly available knowledge whenever possible, and only attempt to bring additional knowledge to bear if the directly available knowledge is either incomplete or inconsistent. Direct knowledge is very efficient, and at some point we must stop searching for more knowledge and use what is available. However, we must search for more knowledge whenever the available knowledge is insufficient to make progress in problem solving — a situation we call a *difficulty*. Our aim is to extend the limited rationality of *Soar1* so that whenever a difficulty arises, problem solver treats it as a problem to be solved and creates a subgoal (in some AI circles this would be called a *meta-goal*). Within the subgoal, the agent can reason about its decisions, bringing its full problem-solving abilities to bear to resolve the difficulty. The subgoal provides a context for using knowledge that is inappropriate when attempting the original goal, but is critical to making the required decision. The agent can try different alternatives, searching for more information, and based on the results make an informed decision. The process can recur, so that if limited rationality is insufficient for a decision in a subgoal, another subgoal can be used for that decision. Previous AI systems have relied on subgoals created for specific difficulties in problem solving. *GPS* created subgoals when it was unable to apply operators whose pre-conditions were not satisfied by the current state. Many systems in AI use similar subgoals when they are unable to directly apply an operator (Fikes and Nilsson, 1971; Sacerdoti, 1977; Stefik, 1979). More recently, Wilensky (1983) has used *meta-goals* to reason about conflicts between goals and decide which goal to attempt next.

Although AI programs use subgoals to deal with some of the difficulties that arise while problem-solving, no system has a scheme for creating subgoals for all types of difficulties, and for creating them automatically, independent of the task being attempted. We believe that a problem solver must be able to create subgoals whenever limited rationality fails. It should create subgoals for all difficulties and should do so automatically. We call this ability *universal subgoaling*. Universal subgoaling is universal along many dimensions: full problem solving is available for any decision, it is invoked automatically whenever a difficulty arises, and it can be used for any decision that plays a role in problem solving.

The goal of this research is to develop a problem-solving architecture where all appropriate knowledge is used to control all aspects of problem-solving behavior. The remainder of this chapter lays the groundwork. The next section reviews our prior work on the universal weak method detailing how the knowledge for the weak methods can be encoded so that no explicit representation of the weak methods is required. We wish to retain and extend this property in an architecture that supports universal subgoaling. In the following section, we describe the requirements of universal subgoaling that must be satisfied by the problem-solving architecture and the problem-solving paradigm on which the architecture is based. We will use these requirements to motivate many of the design decisions in our architecture. The final section of this chapter describes one paradigm that satisfies the requirements and will be the basis of our architecture: heuristic search through a problem space.

Chapter 2 provides a detailed description of *Soar*, an architecture which incorporates both a universal weak method and universal subgoaling. We pay particular attention to how *Soar* satisfies the requirements of universal subgoaling. An agent implemented in *Soar* will use limited rationality whenever it is adequate, but when it fails, subgoals will be created automatically to gather knowledge that can be used to control the behavior. This is not the first time capabilities such as these have been proposed. They often come under the heading of reflective problem solving (Davis, 1980; Doyle, 1980; Hayes, 1977; McDermott, 1978; Smith, 1982; Weyhrauch, 1980), that is, problem solving that involves reasoning about problem solving behavior. However, *Soar* is the first implemented architecture that uses universal subgoaling to automatically reflect on the difficulties that arise during problem solving.

The presentation of universal subgoaling is not complete without a demonstration. In Chapter 3 we demonstrate that *Soar*, with universal subgoaling, uses its knowledge rationally to solve problems. We show that the knowledge required to produce the weak methods can be encoded in *Soar*, and that the knowledge is used appropriately. With the addition of universal subgoaling, the set of weak methods that can be encoded is significantly increased, and the knowledge required is actually simplified over the techniques in *Soar1*. The individual units of knowledge can apply whenever needed and they are independent of one another so that they are easily added. In addition, the knowledge used to implement the weak methods leads to a useful taxonomy of the weak methods.

The remaining chapters tie off the loose ends. Chapter 4 provides a discussion of issues that arise during the previous chapters, and Chapter 5 concludes. A glossary is included at the end of the paper that provides definitions of the terms used throughout the paper. Two appendices follow the main body of the paper. The first appendix contains the universal weak method as implemented in *Soar*. The second appendix contains descriptions of the implementations of the weak methods that were demonstrated in Chapter 3.

1.1. A Universal Weak Method

Methods play an important role in organizing knowledge for controlling behavior in a problem solver. Our challenge is to break the knowledge out of the method structure so that it is available for all tasks whenever it is applicable. In this section we review an important class of methods, called the *weak methods*, and describe our previous efforts to encode them so that the knowledge implicit in them is always available.

If a general problem solver wishes to attempt a wide variety of problems, especially novel ones, it must have a repertoire of methods that are extremely general, such as generate and test, depth-first search and hill climbing. These are called the weak methods (Newell, 1969). A weak method makes limited demands for knowledge of the task environment (called its *operational demands*) and can thereby be used in many domains. The limited operational demands of the weak methods sometimes translate into poor performance, that is, they are unable to overcome the combinatorial search of the problem space to achieve the goal.

The weak methods are an important starting point if we wish to investigate the properties of knowledge used in problem solving. They are ubiquitous in AI programs to the point where most problem solving is achieved using weak methods. When large amounts of knowledge are available, AI programs can avoid weak methods by constraining the problem solving to be search-free. Beyond AI programs, it has been hypothesized that the weak methods are the basic methods for all intelligent agents (Newell, 1980). Independent of the validity of this hypothesis, the weak methods represent an important class of knowledge that arises in many tasks. The knowledge encoded in the weak methods is usually the first knowledge about a task that becomes available to a problem solver. Before tackling classes of knowledge that are specific to certain domains, we take up the weak methods.

The goal of our previous work with weak methods (Laird and Newell, 1983a) was that the weak methods should arise out of the structure of the problem solver, the proposed task, and the knowledge the problem solver had about the task. Weak methods should not be organized as a pre-existing discrete set of complete control structures with a process for selecting which one is appropriate on a given occasion. Instead, all available knowledge about the task should control the behavior of the agent. We proposed that the different weak methods arise from the use of different task knowledge, not from the explicit selection of a method. We called the organizational framework that leads to the different weak methods a *universal weak method*. A universal weak method is an organizational scheme for knowledge that produces the appropriate problem-solving behavior given only knowledge of the structure of the task being attempted. If there is little or no task-specific knowledge, the universal weak method provides a default behavior so that the problem can be attempted, although significant search may be required. As task-specific knowledge is added, the search becomes more directed and assumes the characteristics of a weak method.

To derive a universal weak method, we observed that a method consists of a specification of behavior (the knowledge used to control behavior), S, and an interpreter for producing that behavior from S. To achieve the properties of a universal weak method, we seek a factorization of S for a given method M into two parts, $S_u + S_m$, where S_u is the knowledge common to all methods and S_m is unique to M. S_u is the universal weak method. S_m is a set of *method increments* for method M, and contains only task-specific knowledge, that is, knowledge about the goals, problem spaces, states, and operators that are used to solve the problem. When the method increments (S_m) are added the universal weak method (S_u), the resulting behavior of the agent is that of one of the weak methods.

We wished to isolate S_u and include it in the problem solver so that it was available for all problems the agent attempted. Following this, we could then extract knowledge from the task that corresponds to the S_m of a particular method, and add it to the agent. However, to have a successful decomposition of all S's into S_u and S_m, the combination of S_u and S_m must occur quickly and easily during problem solving to yield a well-formed method. In addition, it must be possible to quickly and easily combine a new S_m with those already added to S_u so that all past and present knowledge of the agent is available. The above restrictions preclude the use of bodies of fixed code to make the decisions of the problem solver. Fixed code bodies can not be easily combined, nor can they adapt as new knowledge becomes available. Any successful decomposition must allow all applicable knowledge to be used in the decisions of search control.

Our original decomposition had S_u contain just enough knowledge to exhaustively search a problem space. The method increments (S_m) contained search-control knowledge for computing concepts relevant to the task and search-control knowledge for using these concepts to perform the functions of search control, such as the selection of states and operator. A given S_m referred only to its own concepts and not to other aspects of behavior. The method increments could be combined easily with the universal weak method and other method increments because our architecture was a *production system*. The universal weak method and each method increment consisted of a set of productions. The additive nature of productions are well known and this was directly responsible for being able to meet many of the conditions of decomposition. The conceptual independence of each increment permitted the simple addition of productions to suffice.

Although the original universal weak method was successful as a basis for many weak methods, it could only make use of knowledge that was directly available. However, there is no guarantee that all the agent's domain-knowledge will be directly available, or that available knowledge is complete and consistent. Often, by performing some problem solving, more knowledge can be brought to bear that makes a decision possible. We expect that an agent with little control knowledge about a new domain will be unable to make intelligent decisions. It is for these reasons that we must go beyond our original implementation and investigate universal subgoaling.

1.2. Requirements for Universal Subgoaling

We plan to drive our investigation of universal subgoaling by the constraints it places on the other components of a problem solver. Figure 1-4 breaks down these requirements into two parts: (1) requirements on the problem-solving *paradigm* of the agent; and (2) requirements on the problem-solving *architecture* that implements that paradigm.

A paradigm defines the fundamental organization of problems for an architecture. A paradigm must be general enough so that universal subgoaling can be used in all tasks, not just some special subclass. A paradigm also defines the basic functions that have to be performed to take steps toward solving problems. These primitive functions must be both necessary and sufficient for problem solving. If some are not required for problem solving, then a difficulty in performing one may be optional, and any effort expended to alleviate the difficulty will be wasted. If other functions are needed for problem solving, difficulties in them can block progress from which there is no recovery. The purpose of universal subgoaling is to guarantee that whenever one of the primitive functions cannot be carried out directly, a subgoal will be created that can eventually lead to performing that function if it is in fact possible.

The architecture provides an implementation of the paradigm. It consists of the processes and memory that produce the behavior described by the paradigm. The functions of the paradigm must be realized by sufficiently simple patterns of acts in the architecture, so that failure of these acts can be diagnostic of failure of the functions. Thus, that the architecture embodies notions of problem-solving is critical. In a more standard architecture, the primitive acts (such as jumps, adds, divides, or data movement) are remote from the ultimate goals and behavior of the agent, hence the set of possible difficulties it provides (such as divide by zero or illegal memory reference) are of little use to setting up subgoals.

The problem-solving paradigm.

1. The paradigm must incorporate a general theory of problem solving that covers all types of problems, including those dealing with the internal behavior of the system.
2. The primitive functions of the paradigm must be both necessary and sufficient to make progress in problem solving.

The problem-solving architecture.

1. The architecture must implement the problem-solving paradigm: the basic acts of the architecture must correspond to the basic functions of the paradigm.
2. Architectural difficulties must correspond to difficulties in the basic functions of the paradigm.
3. It must be possible to detect the difficulties in performing the basic acts of the architecture in a task-independent manner.
4. The architecture must create subgoals whenever a difficulty arises.
5. The reasons for the difficulties must be available to diagnosis the subgoal.
6. It must be possible for the subgoal to eliminate the difficulty that caused its creation.

Figure 1-4:   Requirements for universal subgoaling.

The detection of difficulty must be possible in all tasks and the system must respond to the difficulty by creating a subgoal. Merely the creation of a subgoal is not sufficient, the reason for the difficulty must be available to the subgoal, so an appropriate diagnosis can be made. Finally, it must be possible for a subgoal to create new results that can eliminate a difficulty so that problem solving can continue. We are not requiring that every subgoal will actually eliminate every difficulty, only that it is structurally possible for a subgoal to create a result that will eliminate the difficulty.

These requirements can be considered as an extension of the three requirements of a reflective system (Smith, 1982): a model of behavior; the ability to reflect on the behavior without disturbing the processing state; and the ability for the results of reflection to modify the processing state to affect future behavior. The extension arises because reflection is to be automatic and appropriate to the achievement of a goal. These are not critical for reflection in a programming language.

1.3. Problem Spaces

Heuristic search of problem spaces has long been an important paradigm in AI (Newell, 1980; Nilsson, 1971; Nilsson, 1980; Simon, 1983).[3] Within AI, problem spaces have been accepted as the fundamental organization for tasks involving puzzles and problem solving. The case is less clear for tasks that involve creativity, induction, complex decision making, routine or rote behavior, or compiled expert behavior. We will adopt search as central to our paradigm, not only because of its history in AI, but also because of work in human problem solving that suggests that the problem space is the fundamental organizational unit of all human goal-oriented symbolic activity, a hypothesis that is called the *Problem Space Hypothesis* (Newell, 1980; Newell and Simon, 1972).

A problem space consists of *states* and a set of *operators* that generate new states from exisiting states. Problem-space search occurs in the attempt to attain a *goal*. A goal is a symbolic expression that designates a situation or state of affairs to be achieved. Given the problem space hypothesis, a goal is interpreted as finding one of a set of *desired states* in the problem space. The problem solver is at some initial state when a new goal is encountered. The problem solver must find a way of moving from its current state (by applying operators) to a desired state that achieves the current goal. By adopting the problem space hypothesis, we are committed to performing *all* problem solving by searching in a problem space.

1.3.1. Search Control

The primitive functions of the problem space paradigm are called *search-control* functions. There is a fixed set of such functions to be performed in searching a given problem space:

1. Decide on success (the state is a desired state).
2. Decide on failure or suspension (the goal will not be achieved on this attempt).
3. Select a goal.
4. Select a problem space.
5. Select a state from those directly available (if the current state is to be abandoned).
6. Select an operator to apply to the state.

---

[3]General problem-solving paradigms that do not place search at the center of problem solving have been proposed by McCarthy (1968), Sacerdoti (1975), McDermott (1978) and Doyle (1980).

7. Apply the operator to obtain the new state.

A problem solver brings search-control knowledge to bear to perform these functions intelligently. Depending on how much knowledge the problem solver has and how effectively it is employed, the search in the problem space will be narrow and focused, or broad and random.

Search control alone provides only limited rationality. It is computationally limited in making the decisions described above because the computations it performs must be possible without searching a problem space. Otherwise we would have an infinite regression of control (who controls the search of the search-control problem space?). Therefore, performing the functions of search control must be possible without problem solving. This restricts search control to a recognition-like process where the knowledge used to perform these functions is *directly available* and does not have to be generated by searching in a problem space. If extended processing involving search is necessary to make a search-control decision (a complex comparison of the substructure of two states for example), search control must create a subgoal to perform the computation within a problem space and not within search control.

1.3.2. Difficulties

The possibility of a set of difficulties that can be the basis of universal subgoaling arises from the adoption of problem spaces as the problem-solving paradigm. The primitive functions of the paradigm (such as selecting goals, problem spaces, states and operators) are directly related to the behavior that is produced by the agent. All behavior is centered around attaining the current goal, and each function performed by search control is directly related to goal attainment. The inability to perform these functions defines a difficulty. The different ways in which functions can fail defines the set of all difficulties.

By reviewing the processing that is performed by search control and the failures that can occur at each step, we can derive the set of difficulties that are to be handled by a universal subgoaling scheme. Figure 1-5 contains the list of functions of search control and the types of difficulties that can arise in performing each function. There are seven search-control functions, and a difficulty for any of them can arise at any time during problem solving. For all of the decision and selection functions, a difficulty arises if a computation is *inconclusive*. A computation is inconclusive if, within the recognition scheme of search control, it is not possible to discriminate among the choices. This can occur for two reasons. First, if there is a lack of knowledge about the choices, search control will know only that there are candidates, but not which is best. Second, the computations necessary to perform the discrimination may be too complex to be performed within search control.

Search-Control Function	**Difficulty**
Decide on Success	Decision is inconclusive
Decide on Failure	Decision is inconclusive
Select Goal	Decision is inconclusive
Select Problem Space	Decision is inconclusive No problem spaces to select from
Select State	Decision is inconclusive No initial state
Select Operator	Decision is inconclusive No operators
Apply Operator	Operator not applied Incomplete operator Operator inapplicable

Figure 1-5:   Taxonomy of difficulties.

Three difficulties arise because all the search-control functions that involve selections (except goal selection) can fail if there are no candidates to choose from. For example, once a goal and problem space have been selected there must be a state for search control to select. If there is none, problem solving cannot continue. Once an initial state has been selected, search control will always have at least one state to select within the current problem space, so that the only time there are no candidate states is when the initial state is being selected. Note, the one difficulty that must not arise is the difficulty of creating a subgoal. If this also requires a subgoal, an infinite recursion can result. Three other difficulties can arise once the operator has been selected and is to be applied: if the operator can not be applied by search control directly because of the complexity involved in applying the operator, if the operator might be only partially specified and must be further instantiated with the current state, if the operator cannot apply because some of its pre-conditions are not satisfied.

The search-control difficulties form the basis of universal subgoaling. However, these difficulties are not the only problems that can arise in problem solving. The special feature of the search-control difficulties is that their presence blocks problem solving from continuing, and therefore they can be detected. Their elimination (through subgoaling) permits problem solving to continue. We believe that search-control difficulties suffice for *all* problem solving, so that these are the only difficulties that require special consideration. An evaluation of this claim requires an empirical demonstration of the sufficiency on a variety of tasks and methods. In Chapter 3 we provide some evidence for this claim, but we fall short of a complete demonstration.

In this section we have seen that search in problem spaces satisfies the requirements of a problem-solving paradigm for universal subgoaling. Problem spaces are a general representational framework for problem-solving. The basic search control functions provide a primitive partition of the problem-solving process and they provide a set of difficulties that correspond to failure in the problem solving process. We must now propose an architecture that implements this paradigm.

2 THE SOAR ARCHITECTURE

In this chapter we propose a problem-space architecture, called *Soar*, that implements universal subgoaling.[4] Throughout this chapter we will verify that *Soar* satisfies the six requirements for universal subgoaling listed in Figure 1-4. *Soar* is a modification of the *Soar1* architecture (Laird & Newell, 1983b). At appropriate places, we will contrast *Soar* to the *Soar1* architecture.

The first section of this chapter provides a general description of the memory and processing structure of the architecture and demonstrates that *Soar* implements the search-control functions necessary for search in a problem space. The second section discusses our implementation of *Soar* as a production system; the memory structures of *Soar* are represented within working memory and the processing structures are represented as productions. We include an example encoding of a task (the Eight Puzzle) in *Soar*. The third section describes our implementation of universal subgoaling within this architecture. In this section we examine the remaining requirements for universal subgoaling and how they are satisfied by the *Soar* architecture. The fourth section describes how *Soar* supports a universal weak method that includes subgoals. The fifth section brings together the loose-ends, such as deliberate subgoals and the search-control knowledge that is common to a wide variety of tasks. This chapter concludes with a short review of the *Soar* architecture.

---

[4]A more detailed description of *Soar* is available in *The Soar User's Manual* (Laird, 1984).

2.1. Architecture Description

A problem-space architecture consists of a processing structure where the functions of search control are decomposed into a discrete set of actions on a memory structure. The memory structure contains the information that search control will use at each node of the search tree to perform its functions. The processing structure must encode the search-control functions so that they can react to the information in the memory structure. We begin by describing the memory structure, which is based on the different objects used in searching a problem space. We follow this by a description of the processing structure that encodes the functions of search control. Within this section, we describe a *preference* scheme that is the interface between the declarative representation in the memory structure and the procedural representation in the processing structure.

2.1.1. The Memory

The memory (or *stock*) consists of *objects*, their *augmentations*, and a *current context* which contains one *slot* for each type of object involved in search: goals, problem spaces, states and operators. The object occupying the goal slot in the current context is the current goal; the object occupying the problem space slot is the current problem space, and so on. The current context focuses the attention of the processing structure on a single goal, problem space, state and operator. The objects are represented by symbols and each slot in the context either contains an object-symbol or nothing, meaning undefined.

Each of the objects in the current context can be *augmented* with additional information. These augmentations are many-valued relations between sets of objects in the stock. Each augmentation consists of a set of objects in labeled slots and it augments each of the objects it contains. An augmentation can be thought of as a list of attribute-value pairs, where each augmented object is the value of one of the attributes. All the semantics of an object are derived from the set of its augmentations. This inverts the normal representation of an object, making the augmentations the data structures that are manipulated instead of a monolithic description of the object. The augmentations of an object are not contained in a fixed data structure so that there is no fixed number of augmentations. The set of augmentations may change over time.

Figure 2-1 shows an example of the stock during problem solving. Each object is a symbol, such as X34, X55, or X76. The current context is composed of the objects in boxes: X34 is the current goal, X55 is the current problem space, X98 is the current state, and the current operator is undefined. An object does not have an inherent type, and conceivably could be the current state at one point during the search and the current operator at another. However, the augmentations of an object can provide information that defines the slot of the current context (goal, problem-space, state, or operator) where an object will be useful. In Figure 2-1, each augmentation is a group of labeled line segments, representing the attributes, meeting at a circled symbol (such as A1). These augment the objects in the current context (such as X34 and X55 for A1), not the slots (such as current goal or current problem space). The augmentations that are available for an object are completely unrestricted during the life of that object. For example, states may (or may not) be augmented with substructure or an evaluation (in the example state X98 is augmented with evaluation X99). Goals may be augmented with a desired state, as in augmentation A1. Problem spaces may be augmented with their operators (augmentations A4, A5 and A6).

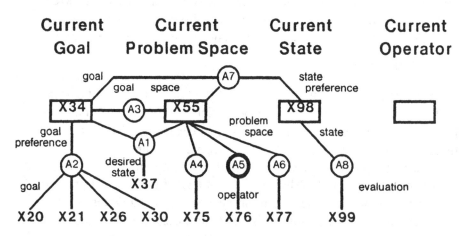

Figure 2-1: Memory structure of *Soar*.

The stock is the directly accessible memory of objects in *Soar* and its structure is necessarily limited by the physical resources of the problem solver. To simplify our analysis of the *Soar1* architecture and the universal weak method, we made an *unlimited memory assumption*, which implied unlimited access to the stock, unlimited capacity of the stock and unlimited reliability of the stock. We continue this assumption in the *Soar* architecture, although we will limit the accessing of objects.

2.1.2. The Processing Structure

A single generic *control act* is available in the architecture to produce behavior: *replacement* of an object in a slot of the current context by another
object from the stock. All the functions of search control are realized by
replacements of one kind or another. When activity for a goal ceases, because of
success, failure or suspension, it can be replaced by a prior goal from the stock.
Returning to a prior state is accomplished by a state in the stock replacing the
current one. An operator is selected by placing it in the current context. A step
in the problem space occurs when the current operator is applied to the current
state to produce a new state. This new state is deposited in the stock and it can
then replace the state in the current context. A subgoal is evoked by replacing
the current goal by the subgoal. Similar replacements set up or change the
problem space. The only search-control function that does not have to be
performed using a replacement is the saving of state. This act is embedded in
the architecture because of the assumption of an infinite memory structure.

2.1.2.1. Initialization

The replacement of an object in one of the slots of the current context may
be followed by the *initialization* of other slots of the context. Two types of
initialization are performed by *Soar*, one that clears invalidated slots, and one
that re-establishes a prior context when a subgoal is terminated.

The first type of initialization is based on the ordering of the slots of the
current context in Figure 2-1. They are ordered from left to right with the
current goal dominating the current problem space, which dominates the state,
which dominates the operator. This dominance occurs because each object in
the current context depends on the ones to its left being established to provide
context for its selection. A problem space is set up in response to a goal; a state
functions only as part of a problem space; and an operator is to be applied at a
state. When the object in a slot is replaced, all those to its right become func-
tionally irrelevant and need to be determined anew. Therefore, after an object
is replaced, all current objects to its right become undefined.

A second type of initialization is required when a subgoal is terminated and
is replaced by its supergoal. Instead of making the rest of the current context
undefined, the current context is replaced with the objects that were current
when the current subgoal was evoked, that is, when the subgoal replaced the
supergoal in the current goal slot. This re-establishes the context for the supergoal when one of its subgoals has terminated. The details of this process are
described in Section 2.3.3.

2.1.2.2. The Elaboration-Decision Cycle

Search-control knowledge is brought to bear by the *Elaboration-Decision cycle*, which involves two distinct phases of processing. The elaboration phase adds augmentations to the current objects. The decision phase determines which object (goal, problem space, state, operator) is to become current, replacing an existing object in the context. Figure 2-2 and the following sections describe the details of the Elaboration-Decision cycle of *Soar*.

The processing cycles of other problem-solving architectures have also been decomposed into two phases where the first phase brings knowledge to bear and the second phase acts on that knowledge. The first phase is a monotonic process that is performed by a theorem prover (McDermott, 1978; Fikes and Nilsson, 1971), a reflection process (Doyle, 1980), a least-commitment process (Stefik, 1979), a pattern matcher (Newell, 1973), or a simulator of a plan (Sacerdoti, 1975). The second phase performs a non-monotonic act based on the knowledge gained during the first. In the second phase, the agent is making a decision that could be wrong. The critical difference between *Soar* and these other architectures is that given the Problem Space Hypothesis, the functions of search control directly correspond to all ways of making progress in problem solving. This correspondence is critical for the successful implementation of universal subgoaling.

Elaboration Phase
Inputs:	Objects and augmentations in the stock, accessed through augmentations of the current context
Result:	Augments current objects
	Monotone increase in information about current objects
Control:	Continue until quiescent

Decision Phase
Inputs:	Objects and augmentations in the stock, accessed through augmentations of the current context
Result:	Vote-for, vote-in, vote-against, or veto of objects in stoc
	Translates augmentations into action
	One new object is selected in the current context
Control:	All voting occurs at the same time

Figure 2-2: The Elaboration-Decision cycle.

2.1.2.3. The Elaboration Phase

The elaboration phase takes objects and augmentations from the stock as input and creates new augmentations of existing objects. The augmentations can include newly created objects (such as new states or new subgoals), but they must also include some existing objects. Elaboration is restricted to accessing objects and augmentations, directly or indirectly, through the augmentations of the current context. Direct access includes the objects of the current context and their augmentations. Indirect access allows the elaboration phase to access augmentations of objects that are augmentations of the current context. Any fixed number of indirect accesses are possible, although in practice no more than three arise. This accessing scheme is a departure from that of *Soar1*. In *Soar1*, any object that was ever in the stock could be accessed independent of its relation to the current context. In *Soar*, all objects in the stock are potentially accessible, however, the path of augmentations to access the object must be known.

Elaboration accomplishes two related functions. First, an object may be augmented with objects that can be useful in problem solving, such as the operators of a problem space or the desired state of a goal. Second, an object may be augmented with additional information that must be explicit given the computationally limited decision phase (see below). The processes of elaborating this knowledge cannot always operate in a single step. Information made explicit by one item of knowledge in search control may enable another item of knowledge to make something else explicit. Thus, successive iterations of elaboration (where many elaborations can happen in one step) are possible, until a state of quiescence is reached.[5]

2.1.2.4. The Decision Phase

The decision phase follows the elaboration phase and converts the symbolized knowledge accumulated by the elaboration phase into behavior by producing a replacement of some object in the current context. Its inputs are the same as the elaboration phases (objects, and augmentations in the stock), but its result is to replace one of the objects in the current context, instead of creating an augmentation. The decision phase is a voting procedure, with the candidates being the objects in the stock. Votes are registered for objects for each slot in the current context. Four types of votes are allowed: vote-for, vote-against,

---

[5]*Soar* provides no guarantee that quiescence will occur. In practice this has never been an issue, but if it does, the architecture could be modified to check for some maximum number of iterations and then terminate the elaboration phase. This may degrade the performance in some cases, but should not create an irrecoverable failure.

vote-in and veto. Vote-for and vote-against each contribute one vote, respectively plus or minus, for their candidate; a veto ensures that the candidate will never win; vote-in ensures that a candidate will win unless it is vetoed. The only outcome is the replacement of an object in the current context; the votes are not encoded in the memory or available to other voters. Hence at voting time, the situation is static and the votes are simply taken and tallied. The winner of a vote for a slot is the unvetoed candidate with the most net votes for that slot. However, given initialization, only the leftmost slot that is changed will survive, all those to its right become undefined. Three outcomes of the voting do not produce a new winner for a slot in the current context: a tie in the voting, no object with a net positive vote, and the winning objects being already in the current context. These outcomes are a part of the basis for universal subgoaling and will be discussed in the Section 2.3.

2.1.2.5. Preferences

The elaboration and decision phases interact by the elaboration phase producing augmentations of objects in the current context and the decision phase converting these augmentations into votes, which in turn cause changes to the current context. In *Soar1*, the elaboration phase produced what we called concepts about the task situation and the decision phase acted on the concepts by testing relations between them and then voting. In *Soar*, the form of the augmentations that are converted to votes is quite constrained and there is a fixed set of decision search-control knowledge that converts these augmentations to votes.

In *Soar*, the augmentations that hold the information that is converted into votes by the decision phase are called *preferences*.[6] Preferences are relational structures that determine a partial ordering of objects for the slots in the current context. When one object is preferred to all other objects for a slot, the decision phase will replace the current object with that object.

Each preference is an augmentation that contains eight slots. Figure 2-3 shows the eight slots that can be defined for each preference: object, object-type, vote-type, compared-to, goal, problem space, state and operator. The object slot contains the name of the object that the preference refers to; X82 in the example. The object-type slot contains the name of the current context slot; goal in Figure 2-3. The vote-type of the preference determines the vote that the object will receive. There are four vote-types of preferences: best, acceptable,

---

[6]Preferences were originally suggested as a basis for general decision making by Allen Newell in an unpublished addendum to his paper on the problem space hypothesis (Newell, 1980). Preferences similar to those used in *Soar* have also been used in the meta-rule work of Genesereth (1983).

reject and worse. A *best*-preference means that it is known that the augmented object is as good an object as can be found for the slot. This type of preference is reserved for cases when the best object can be determined without comparing it to other alternatives. For example, if a winning move in Tic-Tac-Toe is detected, it does not have to be compared to other moves because no other move could be better. An *acceptable*-preference means that the augmented object is a candidate for a position. In Tic-Tac-Toe, all unmarked positions could have acceptable-preferences for the next move. A *reject*-preference is created when an object should not be considered. It would be appropriate to create a reject-preference for a move that ensures a loss in Tic-Tac-Toe. Finally, a *worse*-preference is created when one object is known to be worse than another. A worse-preference also has a *compared-to* slot that contains the name of the better object. The exact semantics of the preferences are defined by the decision search-control knowledge that converts them into votes. We will defer a description of the preference semantics until we present a specific implementation of search control that allows us to state precisely the search-control knowledge.

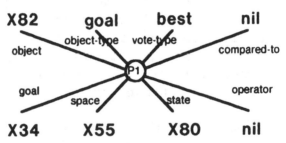

Figure 2-3: The structure of preferences.

The preferences also contain four slots for a goal, problem space, state and operator. These slots specify the current context for which the preference is appropriate. A preference is only valid in a specific context. For example, an operator may be rejected because it has already applied to a state, but the operator should not be rejected for all other states. This was not much of a problem in *Soar1* because we never dealt with cases when the goal or problem space changed. When subgoaling is added, the goal and the problem space change constantly during problem solving so that a state that failed a path constraint for one goal may be quite acceptable given a new goal. Therefore, a preference (of any type) for an object is not universal; it is appropriate only in a specific context. However, in our presentation of specific preferences, the context slots are often omitted. In these cases, it should be assumed that the context slots specify the appropriate current context.

Given this definition of preferences, the preference in Figure 2-3 represents that X82 is a best choice for the goal slot when X34 is the current goal, X55 is the current problem space, X80 is the current state, and the current operator is undefined. In future depictions of preferences, slots that are undefined (such as the operator slot and the compared-to slot in Figure 2-3) will be omitted.

2.1.2.6. Operator Application

In addition to performing the functions of search control, task-specific knowledge must be brought to bear to apply the operators of the current problem space when they are selected. In *Soar1*, there was a phase in addition to elaboration and decision for the application of the current operator to the current state. Operators were essentially black-boxes whose contents could not be examined. This makes it impossible for an agent to deal intelligently with a difficulty in applying the operator. The operator application phase has been eliminated in *Soar*. Application of an operator in *Soar* is done either by elaboration within the current goal or by the operators of a subgoal (namely, the subgoal to apply the operator). When an operator is applied, an acceptable-preference is created that contains the current goal, problem space, state and operator in the context slots and includes a newly created symbol in the object slot, with **state** as the object-type. This new symbol will be the state that is the result of applying the current operator to the current state. The preference that includes the new state provides a data structure that in the future serves as a history of the application of the operator. The creation of the preference is followed by more augmentations that fill in the substructure of the new state.

2.2. Soar as a Production System

Up to this point we have described the memory and processing structure of *Soar* without proposing a specific implementation. In this section we describe how the *Soar* architecture can be implemented as a *production system* (Waterman and Hayes-Roth, 1978). This includes a description of how knowledge in the elaboration and decision phases is encoded as productions and an in-depth discussion of the decision phase, where a fixed set of productions are used to translate the preferences into changes in the current context. We conclude with an example task (the Eight Puzzle) encoded as productions within *Soar*.

Our production system consists of a collection of *productions* of the form:

If C_1 and C_2 and ... and C_n then A

The C_i are *conditions* that examine the current object context and the rest of the stock. The form of the conditions is limited to some class of patterns on the encoding of the objects.[7] A is an *action* that either adds an augmentation to a current object, interacts with the external environment, or contributes to changing an object in the current context by casting a vote. An action can not delete or change an augmentation of an object. A production is *satisfied* if the conjunction of its conditions is satisfied. There can be any number of productions satisfied at a time. All satisfied elaboration productions fire concurrently during the elaboration phase. The votes of all satisfied decision productions are considered during the decision phase. The structure of the architecture (only augmentations, no deletions, etc.) assures that there are no synchronization problems. The production firings are order-invariant within each phase.

There is an underlying search that compares the conditions of the productions to the contents of the stock to determine which productions are satisfied. This is a search to determine the relevant search-control knowledge. This is much less complex than problem solving in general because the knowledge is structured to facilitate efficient, non-combinatoric search. In our case, the knowledge is encoded in productions, and efficient architectures can be built to interpret production systems with a large number of productions.

Soar is implemented as a modification of one such production-system architecture, *Ops5* (Forgy, 1981; Forgy, 1982). The conflict-resolution phase of the *Ops5* interpreter was replaced to implement the Elaboration-Decision cycle of *Soar*. The interpreter simulates parallel execution of elaboration productions, collects and interprets votes of decision productions, detects the difficulties that arise in voting and creates subgoals when difficulties arise. The only conflict-resolution principle is that each instantiation of an elaboration production fires only if the augmentation it is adding is not already present. With these modifications, *Ops5* becomes the *Soar* architecture described above. All productions are either decision or elaboration productions, and these are the only productions in production memory. When presenting productions, we will use abstract descriptions of productions that correspond closely to the original productions. All elements in working memory are either current objects or augmentations. Objects are simple *Ops5* symbols; the slots for current objects are separate working-memory elements; and augmentations (and preferences) are working-memory elements whose attributes are the slot labels.

---

[7] The exact class of patterns is not important, as long as it is similar to those typical of current production systems, which include variables and negated conditions.

2.2.1. Interpreting Preferences in the Decision Phase

In *Soar*, the purpose of the decision phase is to translate preferences into votes which cause changes in the current context. This is possible using the fixed set of decision productions in Figure 2-4. These will be the only decision productions in *Soar*. If other decision productions were allowed, they could vote for objects independently of the preferences in working memory and we would have no guarantee that the final votes reflected the appropriate preferences. Figure 2-4 gives all the decision productions, except those used for subgoal termination which will be described in the section on universal subgoaling to follow.

The decision search-control (in this case a set of productions) defines the semantics of the preferences by translating the different vote-types of preferences into different votes. Each decision production translates a single preference into a vote (sometimes the absence of other preferences is also tested). Remember, the decision productions apply only after all the elaborations settle down, so that the preferences do not instantly determine votes. Once a preference has been created, other elaborations that are sensitive to it may add preferences of their own to support or possibly reject the object of the first preference. A decision production fires only for a given preference when the context described in the preference matches the current context and the vote-type of preference matches the type of vote of the production. The production casts its vote for the object for the slot of the current context specified in the preference. A best-preference is translated to a vote-in, an acceptable-preference is translated into a vote-for, a reject-preference is translated into a veto and a worse-preference is translated into a vote-against. These translations are somewhat complicated by the object-type of preference being considered and the existence of other preferences. The complete details are explained below.

Production D1 handles all acceptable-preferences and translates them into votes for the appropriate object for the appropriate slot. Similarly, D2 handles the best-preferences and translates them into vote-ins. The translation of reject and worse-preferences must be done separately for each slot because of the limited context that is tested for the goal and the state preferences. When a goal is terminated,[8] it should always be rejected, independent of the context. Therefore, in D3, if an object is rejected for the goal slot, it is always vetoed.

---

[8] A goal is terminated when it occurs in a reject-preference and is then vetoed from the current context. A goal may be suspended instead of terminated, simply by voting in another goal without ever vetoing the former goal. Rejection does not imply goal failure — goals that succeed must also be rejected.

D1:   If an object has an acceptable-preference for a slot given the current context, vote for the object for that slot.

D2:   If an object has a best-preference for a slot given the current context, vote-in the object for that slot.

D3:   If an object has a reject-preference for the goal slot, veto the object for the goal slot.

D4:   If an object has a reject-preference for the state slot given the current goal and problem space, veto the object for the state slot.

D5:   If an object has a reject-preference for the problem space or operator slot given the current context, veto the object for that slot.

D6:   If an object has a worse-preference for the goal slot given the current context, and the better object does not have a reject-preference, vote against the worse object for the goal slot.

D7:   If an object has a worse-preference for the problem space, state, or operator slot given the current context, and the better object does not have a reject-preference given the current goal and problem space, vote against the worse object for the state slot.

Figure 2-4: *Soar* decision productions.

Similarly, in **D4**, when a state is rejected, it should be vetoed independent of the current state and operator. However, in **D5**, both the operator and problem space slots receive vetoes only if the complete current context matches the preference. In the case of a worse-preference, the situation is quite similar, except that a worse-preference should be ignored if the object used for comparison has a reject-preference. For goals, the comparison object must not have a reject-preference independent of the current context (**D6**). In the case of problem spaces, states and operators, the comparison object must not have a reject-preference given the current context (**D7**).

In addition to the semantics of the preferences defined by the decision productions, we adopt the convention that there should be only one acceptable-preference for an object for a slot, given a specific context. The *Soar* architecture does not enforce this convention, but all programs implemented in *Soar* obey it.[9] This convention prevents the selection of an object because it has piled up more acceptable-preferences than another object. We want all decisions to be made through the dominance of preferences, not by the number of preferences. An acceptable-preference can be thought of as declaring an object as a candidate for a specific slot, and only through the other preferences is one object determined to be better than another.

In general, the winning object for a slot has a single acceptable-preference and no worse or reject-preferences. It may also have a best-preference. One implicit assumption is that we do not have conflicting worse-preferences and

---

[9]More recent versions of *Soar* enforce this convention.

that a partial ordering of the objects is always possible. For example, we assume that it is never the case that one object is worse than another, and that the second object is also in a preference where it is worse than the first. This is a reasonable assumption in the knowledge-lean tasks we will investigate, but *Soar* can not guarantee that this will not arise in knowledge-rich domains where there is conflicting knowledge. For the present investigation, we will assume that conflicting preferences do not arise. This issue is examined in more detail in Chapter 4.

2.2.2. Encoding a Task in Soar

All knowledge, be it knowledge to select an goal, select an operator, apply an operator, etc., must be encoded as elaboration productions. To implement a task in *Soar*, we must define a set of productions that establish the task (select the goal, problem space, and initial state), and implement the operators of the problem space. In this section, we present an implementation of a simple task called the Eight Puzzle. We start with a description of the task, followed by the productions that establish the goal, problem space and initial state. We present the productions that implement the operators for this task and conclude with an example run of *Soar* using these productions.

2.2.2.1. Eight Puzzle Task Description

In the Eight Puzzle, there are eight numbered movable tiles set in a 3x3 frame. One cell is always empty, making it possible to move an adjacent tile into the empty cell. The problem is to transform one configuration to a second by moving tiles. The states of the problem space are configurations of the numbers 0-8 in a 3x3 grid, where 0 is the empty cell, and 1-8 are the numbered tiles. In our implementation there are twenty-four operators, one for each possible movement of tiles in cells adjacent to each possible empty cell. Other problem spaces with other set of operators are possible.

2.2.2.2. Eight Puzzle Setup Knowledge

Since there is no long-term declarative knowledge in *Soar*, all knowledge concerning the diagnosis of a goal, the selection of the problem space, the creation of the initial state, and the detection of the goal must be contained in productions. Figure 2-5 lists these productions for the Eight Puzzle task. The setup of the current context is achieved by EP1—EP4. Analogous productions exist for any task. They are relatively content free except to establish the appropriate problem space and initial state for the given task. To start problem solving on this task, the current goal is initialized to be eight-puzzle. The productions that suggest the problem spaces and define the initial state are sensitive to the goal symbol, adding preferences for slots in the current context. Production **EP4** augments the eight-puzzle problem space with its operators. This production embodies the knowledge that the operators it suggests belong to the eight-puzzle problem space. Production **EP5** makes acceptable-preferences for applicable operators for the operator slot. For the Eight Puzzle task, the goal is a specific state in the problem space (the *desired* state) and this is added as an augmentation of the goal by production **EP2**. The termination of the goal is detected by the final production, **EP6**, which compares the current state to the desired state. All of these productions are simply added to the decision productions to form the basic knowledge of the task.

EP1:	If the current goal is an Eight Puzzle goal then make an acceptable-preference for eight-puzzle as the current problem space.
EP2:	If the current goal is an Eight Puzzle goal, then augment the goal with a desired state that contains the desired positions of tiles in cells.
EP3:	If the current goal is an Eight Puzzle goal and the current problem space is eight-puzzle and there is no current state, then create an acceptable-preference for a new state, and augment it with the initial positions of tiles in cells.
EP4:	If the current problem space is eight-puzzle, augment the current problem space with the operators of the eight-puzzle problem space.
EP5:	If the current problem space is eight-puzzle and there exists an operator of that problem space that can move a tile into the empty cell of the current state, make an acceptable-preference for that operator at the operator slot.
EP6:	If the current problem space is eight-puzzle and the current state matches the desired state of the current goal in each cell, make a reject-preference for the current goal at the goal slot.

Figure 2-5: Productions for Eight Puzzle task.

2.2.2.3. Task Operators as Productions

To implement the operators of a problem space, more productions must be added. For the Eight Puzzle, we encode the state as a 3x3 grid of cells *[cell (i,j), tile]*, with eight tiles, 1, ... 8, and the 0 tile, indicating the empty cell. There is an operator for each movement of tiles one position in the grid into an adjacent empty cell (there are 24 such moves). Thus, operator $(2,2) \rightarrow (3,2)$ moves the tile in cell (2,2) into the empty cell, which is (3,2). These operators are realized by productions. Once an operator becomes the current operator, the operator is applied by the productions which create a new state and then elaborate that state with the appropriate substructure.

There are many ways to implement operators: as single productions, sets of productions or within subgoals as complete problem spaces. The tasks that were implemented span all of these. One requirement for the representation of operators is that each operator instantiation must be represented by a symbol so that it occur in a preference and be voted into the current context. The second requirement is that the operator produces an acceptable-preference for the state it creates, so that the new state can be considered a candidate for the state slot. The context contained in the preference includes the current operator, so it is only relevant when the current operator has been selected. Under normal processing, the new state will be selected as the current state.

Figure 2-6 contains the productions that apply the operators in the Eight Puzzle task. In this case, each operator in the stock contains augmentations (the empty cell and an adjacent cell to move a tile from) that allow a few operator productions to implement a class of operators. The first production, **EP7**, creates the new state and the preference for it. The next two productions (**EP8**, **EP9**) construct the substructure of the new state by copying or swapping the tiles in the cell positions from the current state.

> **EP7:**   If the current problem space is eight-puzzle and the current state has a blank in the cell that is the to-cell of the current operator, then create an acceptable-preference for a newly created state.
>
> **EP8:**   If the current problem space is eight-puzzle and there is an acceptable-preference for a new state, then copy from the current state each cell that is unchanged by the current operator.
>
> **EP9:**   If the current problem space is eight-puzzle and there is an acceptable-preference for a new state, then that state is augmented with values of the cells from the current state that are changed by the current operator (switching the values of the cells).

Figure 2-6:   Productions for Eight Puzzle operators.

2.2.2.4. Example Trace of Soar on Eight Puzzle

To demonstrate some of the details of the execution of the productions that define a task in *Soar*, we will present a short example of the setup and search of the Eight Puzzle. To perform this demonstration, we include all the productions presented so far: **D1-7** and **EP1-9**. We assume that an Eight Puzzle goal has already selected (EPG1).

Figure 2-7 contains the trace. Each line, representing a single production firing, contains the cycle number, the name of the production and either a short description of the action of the production, or the current context. The productions that have the same cycle number fire in parallel. The cycle number includes an E if it is part of the elaboration phase, and a D if it is part of the decision phase. For the decision phase, many productions may contribute votes, but in this trace only one is important at a time. The trace starts in the Eight Puzzle task where the current goal (called EPG1) is the only object defined.

In the first cycle, the goal is augmented with an acceptable-preference for eight-puzzle for the problem space slot. It is also augmented with a description

Cycle	Production	Action
		Current context: **EPG1**
1E	EP1	Make a problem space preference for eight-puzzle
1E	EP2	Augment EPG1 with desired state: D0001
1D	D1	Current context: **EPG1, eight-puzzle**
2E	EP3	Make a state preference for S0001
2E	EP4	Augment eight-puzzle with its operators: $(1,1) \rightarrow (2,1)$ ...
2D	D1	Current context: **EPG1, eight-puzzle, S0001**
3E	EP5	Make an operator preference for $(2,2) \rightarrow (3,2)$
3E	EP5	Make an operator preference for $(3,3) \rightarrow (3,2)$
3E	EP5	Make an operator preference for $(3,1) \rightarrow (3,2)$
3D	D1	Current context: **EPG1, eight-puzzle, S0001, $(2,2) \rightarrow (3,2)$**
4E1	EP7	Make a state preference for S0002, a new state
4E2	EP8	Augment S0002 with 2 at (1,1)
4E2	EP8	Augment S0002 with 8 at (1,2)
4E2	EP8	Augment S0002 with 3 at (1,3)
4E2	EP8	Augment S0002 with 1 at (2,1)
4E2	EP8	Augment S0002 with 4 at (2,3)
4E2	EP8	Augment S0002 with 7 at (3,1)
4E2	EP8	Augment S0002 with 5 at (3,3)
4E2	EP9	Augment S0002 with at (2,2)
		Augment S0002 with 6 at (3,2)
4D	D1	Current context: **EPG1, eight-puzzle, S0002**
5E	EP5	Make an operator preference for $(1,2) \rightarrow (2,2)$
5E	EP5	Make an operator preference for $(2,1) \rightarrow (2,2)$
5E	EP5	Make an operator preference for $(2,3) \rightarrow (2,2)$
5E	EP5	Make an operator preference for $(3,2) \rightarrow (2,2)$

Figure 2-7: Production trace of Eight Puzzle.

of its desired state, D0001. In the following decision phase, eight-puzzle is selected as the current problem space. In cycle 2, the initial state (S0001) is created with an acceptable-preference for the state slot and the problem space is augmented with its operators. S0001 becomes the current state in the decision phase. Figure 2-8 contains a graphic depiction of the initial state (S0001), the desired state (D0001), and the state that will be created by applying an operator to S0001.

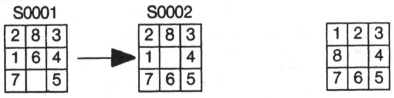

Figure 2-8: Operator application in the Eight Puzzle task.

In cycle 3, production **EP5** creates acceptable-preferences for all of the operators that apply to the current state. These preferences will be translated into votes by **D1** in the decision phase, but the final result will be a tie. As of now we have no way to resolve a tie. This will be handled later by universal subgoaling, so for now we will assume one is chosen at random as was done in *Soar1*. In cycle 4, the operator is applied, first by production **EP7** which creates the preference for a new state (S0002) and then by productions **EP8** and **EP9** which fill in the structure of the new state. Our example concludes with state S0002 being selected as the current state followed by the creation of preferences for the operators that apply to it.

2.3. Universal Subgoaling in Soar

This section describes an implementation of universal subgoaling in *Soar*. Universal subgoaling is based on subgoals that arise out of the difficulties that the agent encounters during problem solving. For universal subgoaling to be successful, these difficulties must be detected in a task independent manner, and they must correspond to difficulties in performing search-control functions. Following the detection of the difficulties, universal subgoaling involves the creation of a subgoal, the selection of the newly created subgoal, problem solving to achieve the subgoal (which can involves the selection of a problem space, states and operators), the termination of the subgoal and the return to the original goal with the results of the subgoal.

2.3.1. Subgoal Detection

Subgoals are created when a difficulty arises in the architecture. Universal subgoaling is the ability of the agent to set up subgoals for *all* possible difficulties that it can face. Although these difficulties can arise in an indefinite number of different contexts, the taxonomy of difficulties must be a small and well-defined set. We gave such a set in Figure 1-5 for the functions required of search control. *Soar* does not explicitly process those functions, but implements them with the Elaboration-Decision cycle. In this section we present the *Soar* difficulties that are the basis of universal subgoaling. They arise from the processing of the Elaboration-Decision cycle. We follow this by a discussion of how these difficulties correspond to the failures of search-control functions.

2.3.1.1. The Soar Difficulties

To make progress in problem solving, *Soar* must replace a current object on each decision phase. We can define a *difficulty* as being those situations when the decision phase can not make a replacement. As observed earlier, there are three situations that lead to difficulties in the decision phase:

1. *No-Change:* There is no-change in the current context during the decision phase.
2. *Tie:* There is a tie in the votes for the winner of an object slot, and all higher-order current objects are unchanged.
3. *All-vetoed:* All the votes for the objects of a type have a net negative total, and all higher-order current objects are unchanged.[10]

Given that the slots in the current context are considered from goal through operator (as ensured by initialization), these three conditions are mutually exclusive so at most one difficulty will arise at a time.

The first difficulty (no-change) arises when the current context is not changed by the voting in the decision phase. A slot in the current context will not change if there are no votes for that slot or if the winning object is already the current object. When these conditions hold for all four slots we have a no-change. Even if an elaboration phase were to follow a no-change difficulty, there would still be no change in the system since the previous elaboration phase ran until quiescence. A no-change difficulty signifies that one of two types of information about the current context is missing. One possibility is that a candidate object needs to be recalled or created, such as a prior state or an initial state of a new problem space. The other possibility is that the current objects must be elaborated with preferences that can be translated into votes by the decision productions. Both of these possibilities can require processing that is too complex for search control. Within a subgoal, construction, retrieval, and evaluation operations can be performed that are outside the limited capabilities of the Elaboration-Decision cycle.

The second difficulty (tie) signifies that search control is unable to discriminate between the objects receiving equal numbers of votes. Given the preference scheme, a tie signifies that no single object dominates the others. A detailed analysis of the substructure of the tieing objects may produce comparisons between objects that can break the tie. Another alternative is to actually select a tieing object and evaluate its ability to make progress toward the goal. As in the no-change difficulty, any of these strategies may require a

---

[10]This difficulty includes the conflicting preferences. See Chapter 4 for a further discussion.

subgoal to resolve the difficulty.

The third difficulty (all-vetoed) signifies that there are no viable candidates for a slot in the current context. This situation can occur when all candidates have been tried and found wanting. A subgoal can be used to decide on a strategy for recovering from the failure. In *Soar*, a fixed strategy was implemented by a set of elaboration productions where the new subgoal and the most recently selected context object are vetoed. Figure 2-9 shows the set of elaboration productions defined to process these failures.

E1: If there is a **vetoed-problem-space** subgoal of the current context, make reject-preferences for the current goal and the subgoal at the goal slot.

E2: If there is a **vetoed-state** subgoal of the current context, make reject-preferences for the current problem space and **vetoed-state** subgoal at their respective slots.

E3: If there is a **vetoed-operator** subgoal of the current context, make reject-preferences for the current state and **vetoed-operator** subgoal at their respective slots.

Figure 2-9: Elaboration productions for handling all-vetoed difficulties.

These productions, **E1-E3**, produce preferences to reject the new subgoal and the object in the current context responsible for the failure. For example, if all the operators receive vetoes because they have already been applied to the current state, a reject-preference will be created for that state. Both the state and the newly created subgoal will be vetoed during the next decision phase.

2.3.1.2. Search-Control Failures as Soar Difficulties

Figure 2-10 shows the correspondence of *Soar* difficulties to the functional failures of search control. If a search-control failure can arise without causing a difficulty in *Soar*, the architecture will be unable to detect the failure, much less find a way to solve it. Our discussion of the correspondence is broken into three parts based on the types of difficulties in *Soar*. First we examine no-change, then ties, and finally those failures that have no corresponding *Soar* difficulty.

The no-change difficulties cover six of the search-control failures. The no-changes are distinguished by the extent to which the current context is defined. In the figure, each no-change difficulty is followed by the right-most object slot that is defined in the current context. Whenever there is a search-control failure because of missing objects (such as when there are no problem spaces, states or operators) a no-change difficulty will occur with the context defined up to that slot. If search control cannot apply an operator for any reason, nothing will happen, and a no-change difficulty will occur with a completely defined context.

When the decision to select an object is inconclusive, a *Soar* tie difficulty occurs. With our preference scheme, every candidate has one acceptable-

Search-Control Function	Search-Control Difficulty	Soar Difficulty
Decide on Success	Inconclusive	None
Decide on Failure	Inconclusive	None
Select Goal	Inconclusive	Tie for goal
Select Problem Space	Inconclusive No candidates	Tie for problem space No-change: goal
Select State	Inconclusive No initial state	Tie for state No-change: problem space
Select Operator	Inconclusive No operators	Tie for operator No-change: state
Apply Operator	Operator not applied Incomplete operator Operator is inapplicable	No-change: complete context No-change: complete context No-change: complete context

Figure 2-10: Search-control failures and *Soar* difficulties.

preference which is translated into a single vote. This will cause a tie unless search control has created more preferences (best, worse, or reject) that distinguish a single candidate and break the tie. If an object is a best choice, or if it dominates all other choices through worse-preferences or reject-preferences, the tie will broken and an object will selected. In these cases, search control has made the decision directly and no search is needed in a subgoal. However, when sufficient preferences are not available to break the tie, search control is unable to perform the selection. Since the elaboration phase runs until it is exhausted, no further search-control knowledge can be brought to bear without a subgoal. Therefore, the preference scheme provides a well-founded decision scheme that guarantees that search control makes a decision if and only if it has sufficient knowledge.

If *Soar* is to be a universal scheme for dealing will all failures that arise in search control, the difficulties for the *Soar* architecture must provide the entire set of functional search-control failures described in Figure 1-5. In fact, two cases appear to be beyond the current universal subgoaling scheme. We are unable to cover the failures that arise when trying to decide whether a goal should be terminated either from success or failure. These two cases will be discussed in Chapter 4.

Just detecting the difficulty in not sufficient. It is also necessary that the subgoals of *Soar* can discriminate between the search-control failures that produce the same *Soar* difficulty and produce relevant results. For example, three different search-control failures produce a no-change difficulty with a complete context. A problem solver must determine whether the difficulty was produced because the operator does not apply, the operator is only partially instantiated, or the operator is too complex to be performed by search control directly. The demonstration that it is possible to distinguish between the different search-control failures will be taken up in Chapter 3.

2.3.2. Subgoal Creation

Once a difficulty is detected, a subgoal must be created to eliminate it. One approach is to use the type of difficulty (tie or no-change) and the type of object where a replacement failed (goal, problem space, state or operator) as a key to index a set of predefined subgoals. This leads to eight types of subgoals (ignoring all-vetoed difficulties, which are processed by productions E1-3). For example, there could be a subgoal to handle no-changes when the context is defined except for the operator, and a different subgoal when there is a tie for the operator slot. We reject this and similar approaches that involve a fixed set of typed subgoals, because they require an immediate classification decision based on limited knowledge. The folly in these approaches is demonstrated by a simple example. Consider the situation where the current context is completely defined and no-change occurs in the decision phase. There are many possible causes of this difficulty: the operator is incompletely defined; applying the operator to the state can not be performed in search control; or the operator does not apply to the current state. Each of these requires a different method and possibly different problem spaces. They must be considered as distinct subgoals. Even for a specific failure, such as the selection of an operator being too complex for search control, many different methods and problem spaces can be used. When we consider that every complex operator may require a different problem space to apply it, we see how difficult it would be to have a prespecified set of goals to handle each of the difficulties that arise from the architecture.

The alternative is to permit the diagnosis of a goal to itself be subject to problem solving. The diagnosis then gradually becomes manifest as the problem solving proceeds, starting with the creation of the subgoal, followed by further augmentations of the goal symbol, the selection of the problem space and possibly the creation of an initial and desired state. Using this approach in *Soar*, a new goal is simply a new symbol and diagnosis occurs both before and after the goal has become the current goal. When a difficulty is detected in the decision phase, a new object is created representing the subgoal to resolve the difficulty. This symbol is included as the object of an acceptable-preference for the goal slot with the objects in the current context. The preference augmentation is also extended to include the objects that tied in the decision phase. This information completely defines the conditions that caused the subgoal, and provides an initial definition of the subgoal. The preference has two purposes: it causes the new goal to be voted in and it defines the context when the goal was created. Following the creation, search-control knowledge performs the rest of the diagnosis using the preference as a source of the context that caused the difficulty. The diagnosis continues as search control selects the subgoal to be the current goal, elaborates it with a problem space, and possibly defines an initial state and desired state or even path constraints. If search control is unable to diagnose the goal so that a problem space and an initial state can be selected, that is another difficulty and a further subgoal will be created to handle it.

In addition to diagnosis, a subgoal must have access to information from the supercontext. *Soar* does not pass explicit parameters down to a subgoal. Instead, the acceptable-preference for the goal is available, and the objects it contains and their augmentations provides the information necessary to diagnosis and solve the subgoal. This is a departure from most current subgoaling schemes that have a set of explicit parameters that are passed down, similar to a procedure call in a standard programming language. This latter approach is not possible in a universal-subgoaling system because the subgoals are not created deliberately. When a subgoal is created, the *Soar* architecture has no way of knowing what information from the current context will be needed in the subgoal to solve it. By avoiding explicit parameters and using the augmentations in the stock, any information that is necessary can be accessed.

To illustrate this process, Figure 2-11 gives a brief trace of the creation and use of a subgoal. Only augmentations and preferences critical to the subgoaling are shown. At time T0, a subgoal has been created because three operators (X75, X76, X77) have tied for the operator slot in the current context. A preference (P2) has been constructed with the new goal object (X82) by the architecture. At time T1, the subgoal replaces the current goal. Once the goal is selected, the behavior of the system proceeds as usual by initializing the rest of the current context. At T1, the goal is augmented with a preference (P3) for a problem space for make selections (SEL) and by T2, SEL has become the current problem space. Preference P4 is created for object X83 to become the current state at T4. SEL would also be elaborated with the operators of the problem space, although they are not shown in this figure. At time T6, X83 has been voted in as the current state and it has been augmented with the operators that caused the tie: X75, X76, X77.

Once the current state is defined, problem solving within the subgoal commences with the selection of an operator to apply to the state. If a difficulty arises at any stage, yet another subgoal will be created automatically to deal with

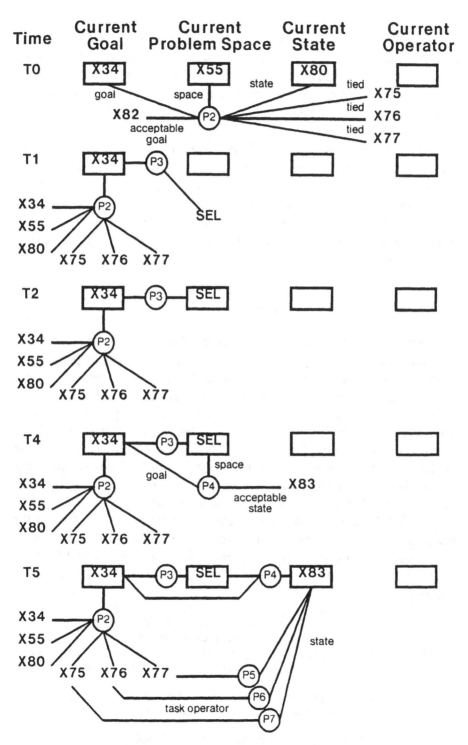

Figure 2-11:   Subgoal creation in *Soar*.

it. For each of these subgoals, problem spaces must either already exist or be created in yet another subgoal using a problem space that actually constructs problem spaces. We have not investigated such a problem space, but at least one such space appears to be necessary for a complete system. Previous work on problem space creation was done in the *UNDERSTAND* project (Hayes and Simon, 1976). We will finesse this issue by including the problem spaces that will be needed by the subgoals that arise.

Within a new subgoal, any productions sensitive to the problem space or goal contribute augmentations that, together with the universal weak method, lead to solving the problem. This is especially important when new subgoals are created because the problem solver may have little or no search-control knowledge relevant to the new goal or problem space. The universal weak method plays an important role in making all relevant knowledge available to attain the goal.

2.3.3. Subgoal Termination

To terminate a subgoal, elaboration productions augment the current goal with a reject-preference so that it will be vetoed. These elaboration productions must be able to detect either the success or failure of the subgoal. Once a subgoal is terminated, the complete context that existed when the subgoal was created (called the *supercontext*, with each object of the supercontext being a *superobject*, e.g., supergoal) must be re-established so that problem solving can continue with the results of the subgoal. The objects from the supercontext are available in the preference that was created for the subgoal. This information is inaccessible to the architecture, so this second type of initialization is performed by decision productions. These are the last three decision productions used in *Soar*: D8, D9 and D10. D8 is sensitive to completed goals, and votes for the goal, problem space and operator of the supercontext. D9 and D10 are used for the re-establishing the state. If the current problem space is different from the superproblem space, the superstate is voted in, otherwise, the current state is retained.

> **D8:** If the current goal has a reject-preference, vote-in the goal, problem space and operator that were current when the current goal was created.
>
> **D9:** If the current goal has a reject-preference, and the current problem space differs from the superproblem space vote-in the state that was current when the current goal was created.
>
> **D10:** If the current goal has a reject-preference, and the current problem space is the same as the superproblem space vote-in the current state.

Figure 2-12: Initialization decision productions.

The purpose of a subgoal is to create structure that can be used in the supergoal. Most current AI subgoaling schemes are similar to subroutines, where the type and number of results must be known when the subgoal is created and a deliberate mechanism passes results back from the subcontext to the super context. Universal subgoaling does not have such a structure, because when the subgoal is created, there is no way of knowing what the results will be. There may be preferences to break ties, or there may be augmentations that will lead to preferences, or there may be a completely new state. However, when the supergoal is reinstated, no explicit return of results is required, since the augmentations and preferences from the subgoal are still available. They will be used immediately by decision productions to alter the results of the voting that caused the difficulty. There is, of course, no guarantee that the preferences built in the subgoal will completely remove the difficulty, in which case another difficulty will be encountered and another subgoal will be created. One exception occurs when the problem space of a subgoal is the same as in the original goal. In this case, the final state of the subgoal is the result. This is handled by initialization production **D10**.

The termination of a subgoal is illustrated in Figure 2-13. This is the same subgoal that was created in Figure 2-11. For this subgoal to be achieved, an object that tied for operator slot must be augmented so that it will receive more votes than the other tieing objects (or the others must be augmented so they receive less). We assume that the problem space of this subgoal has two types of operators. First, there are operators that compare objects and create the required preferences. These operators do not create new states in the SEL space; they just augment the current state. Second, there are operators that select out subsets of the objects that augment the current state based on the preferences they participate in. These operators create new states that have fewer candidate objects. Finally, when a state has only one object, the goal has been achieved. This situation is illustrated at time T24 when an operator preference (16) has been produced involving X77. In addition, X77 is the only task operator linked to the current state (Y23) in the SEL problem space via augmentation 15. At T25, an elaboration production has detected that the subgoal has been achieved and a preference (17) is added so that the current goal will be rejected. At time T26, the original goal and the rest of the current context are restored by decision productions voting them in. Prior to the subgoal, a tie would have resulted at the decision phase. However this time, X27 has been augmented so that it will receive one more vote than the other objects, and it becomes the current operator — the original preferences that produced the tieing votes are not shown. The subgoal has been successful and problem solving continues as before.

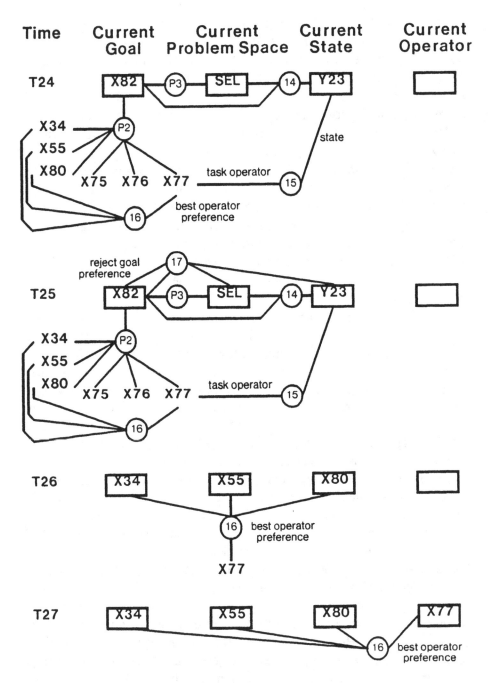

Figure 2-13: Subgoal termination in *Soar*.

2.3.4. Review

In this section we have presented universal subgoaling as it is implemented in *Soar*. This implementation satisfies all of the requirements listed in Figure 1-4. The problem space paradigm we have adopted is a general problem-solving theory that has a set of primitive functions (the search-control functions) that are both necessary and sufficient for making progress in problem solving. *Soar* is an architecture that implements search in problem spaces and it implements the search-control functions through the Elaboration-Decision Cycle. The difficulties that arise in decision scheme (Tie, No-change, All-vetoed) correspond to the failures of search-control functions, and these difficulties can be detected by the architecture. Subgoals are created automatically by the architecture to resolve these difficulties. Within the subgoals, diagnosis and resolution of a difficulty is possible because of the global working memory that allows all subgoals to access and return results via side-effect.

2.4. The Universal Weak Method of Soar

At this point, we have achieved part of the first objective of the thesis: defining an architecture that realizes universal subgoaling. However, universal subgoaling is only a means to an end. Its purpose is to extend the universal weak method of *Soar1* so that knowledge that is not directly available (not explicitly represented in search control) is brought to bear automatically whenever it is needed. In this section we describe a universal weak method for *Soar* that make extensive use of universal subgoaling to automatically search for control knowledge when necessary. In Chapter 4 we will demonstrate how this extends the coverage of weak methods that emerge through the addition of knowledge about the task.

Already, two significant parts of the universal weak method have been presented. First, decision productions **D1-D7** convert preferences into votes that change the current context. Second, decision productions **D8-D10** restore the supercontext when a subgoal is terminated. Together, these decision productions define the semantics of preferences and provide the translation of declarative structure (preferences) into action.

The decision productions alone do not provide a universal weak method. One of the most important attributes of a universal weak method is that it attempts to gather information to control behavior even when there is no search-control knowledge. The definition of the task provides the necessary knowledge for selecting a problem space and an initial state by supplying the acceptable-preferences that are translated into votes by the decision productions. The definition of the task includes the operators of the problem space, so that acceptable-preferences for them can be created. However, in voting for a current operator (as well as the other object slots), the normal situation is that many operators will be possible, and there will not be enough search-control knowledge available to select a single one. A tie will occur, and a subgoal will be created to break the tie. Without a problem space that can break the tie, *Soar* would have to engage in problem solving to create a problem space suitable to the particular tie-breaking task. In fact, the preference scheme we have implemented provides the possibility that a single problem space can be used for all tie difficulties. The preference scheme is a decision system with a well-defined semantics that can be implemented within a problem space.

In this section we present a problem space, called the *selection problem space* that implements the semantics of our decision system. The selection problem space is able to perform computations that are too complex for search control and the decision scheme. Specifically, it can search in order to gain more information about the objects it is considering. The search is performed in subgoals that implement operators of the selection problem space. These are evaluation subgoals, and descriptions of two possible implementations follow the selection problem space. These problem spaces, together with the decision productions, form the universal weak method of *Soar*.

2.4.1. The Selection Problem Space

The selection problem space is selected when the current goal is to break a tie among objects vying for a slot in the current context. A single search-control production can detect such goals and make a preference for the selection problem space. The selection problem space simulates the preference scheme and decision phase of the architecture, but allows search to gain more information to discriminate between objects. Figure 2-14 contains a brief description of the states and operators of the problem space. The states contain the candidate objects from the supercontext, plus preferences for the superobjects given the supercontext. The problem space operators perform three different functions. First, ELIMINATE-WORSE, ELIMINATE-REJECT, SELECT-BEST and RANDOM-PREFERENCE select out subsets of superobjects based on the preferences. Second, EVALUATE either produces an evaluation that allows the creation of a preference between superobjects, or it produces a preference directly. This operator must be task specific, so either productions must exist for evaluating the superobjects of the given task, or a subgoal must perform the evaluation. As we shall see later, many weak methods can be described by the subgoals used to evaluate the superobjects. Finally, COMPARE is used to create a preference where one object is worse than another based on the evaluations created by EVALUATE. The preference is built between the compared objects given the supercontext. This operator must also be task specific, since the basis for comparison of objects differs from task to task. For most tasks, this does not require an operator, but can be performed by task-specific elaboration productions that are sensitive to evaluations of the superobjects.

States   A set of candidate superobjects with or without evaluations.

Operators   ELIMINATE-WORSE: Select all objects that do not have
                                      worse-preferences.

              ELIMINATE-REJECT: Select all objects that do not have
                                      reject-preferences.

              SELECT-BEST: Select the objects with
                                      best-preferences.

              RANDOM-PREFERENCE: Make a preference randomly for
                                      an object.

              EVALUATE: Find a value of a superobject.

              COMPARE: Compare the values of two
                                      superobjects and create a worse-
                                      preference given the supercontext.

Figure 2-14:   Selection problem space description.

Most of the selection problem space operators are implemented with productions that directly apply them when the operators are selected. Productions are also needed to diagnose the goal, select the problem space, detect when the goal is achieved, and select an operator. These productions are shown in Figure 2-15. All except the first three are specific to the selection problem space, while the first three are specific to the subgoal produced because of a tie. This search-control knowledge is independent of the supercontext that led to the selection subgoal.

The first production (SPS1) tests for a tie difficulty and then augments the goal with selection-subgoal. This augmentation simplifies the following productions because they can test for the augmentation instead of the tie difficulty. Production SPS2 detects when the goal is achieved, that is, when the tie has been broken so that the state has only a single superobject. The production makes a reject-preference for the current goal, so that during the following decision phase, decision production D8 will vote in the supercontext and production D3 will veto the current goal. Production SPS3, makes an acceptable-preference for selection and production SPS4 augments selection with **break-ties** so that if there is a tie in operator selection, it will be broken

SPS1:   If the difficulty was a tie, augment the goal with the label **selection-subgoal**.

SPS2:   If the current goal is a **selection-subgoal** and the current state consists of a single superobject, make a reject-preference for the current goal at the goal slot.

SPS3:   If the current goal is a **selection-subgoal**, make an acceptable-preference **selection** at the problem-space slot.

SPS4:   If the current problem space is **selection**, augment the problem space with the label **break-ties**.

SPS5:   If the current problem space is **selection** and the current state is undefined, make an acceptable-preference for the state slot of a new object, consisting of the tieing objects.

SPS6:   If **selection** is the current problem space and a superobject in the current state is marked worse than another superobject in the current state, make an acceptable-preference for ELIMINATE-WORSE.

SPS7:   If **selection** is the current problem space and a superobject in the current state is marked reject, make an acceptable-preference for ELIMINATE-REJECT.

SPS8:   If **selection** is the current problem space and one, but not all of the superobjects in the current state is marked best, make a best-preference for SELECT-BEST.

SPS9:   If **selection** is the current problem space and all of the superobjects in the current state are marked best, make a best-preference for RANDOM-PREFERENCE.

SPS10:   If **selection** is the current problem space and a superobject in the current state is marked acceptable, make an acceptable-preference for RANDOM-PREFERENCE.

SPS11:   If **selection** is the current problem space and a superobject in the current state has no evaluation, make an acceptable-preference for EVALUATE(OBJECT).

SPS12:   If **selection** is the current problem space and there are acceptable preferences for ELIMINATE-REJECT and ELIMINATE-WORSE, make a worse-preference with ELIMINATE-WORSE worse than ELIMINATE-REJECT.

SPS13:   If **selection** is the current problem space and there is an acceptable-preference for EVALUATE and an acceptable-preference for ELIMINATE-REJECT or ELIMINATE-WORSE, make a worse-preference with EVALUATE worse than the other operator.

SPS14:   If **selection** is the current problem space and there is an acceptable-preferences for RANDOM-PREFERENCE and another operator, make a worse-preference where RANDOM-PREFERENCE is worse than other operator.

Figure 2-15:   Selection problem space search-control productions.

randomly by production **E8** of the universal weak method. This is reasonable since the order of tieing operators is not critical. The next production, **SPS5**, creates the initial state by creating a preference for a new symbol in the state slot and augmenting it with the superobjects that tied. The final set of search control creates (productions **SPS6-SPS14**) preferences for the various operators. The first six examine the preferences of the superobjects and add preferences for the operators of the selection problem space. The last three (**SPS12-14**) test the preferences of the operators of the selection problem space, and create new preferences that compare those operators. The result is that if all operators can apply to the state, SELECT-BEST will be selected, followed by ELIMINATE-REJECT, ELIMINATE-WORSE, EVALUATE and finally RANDOM-PREFERENCE.

2.4.2. The Evaluation Subgoal

In the selection problem space, the EVALUATE operator may require a sub-goal to carry out its computation. When an evaluation operator is selected as the current operator, and no productions create a new state (i.e., fail to apply the operator), the decision phase will have no-change, and a subgoal will be created automatically. In this section we will examine two possible problem spaces for this subgoal — one with a new evaluation problem space and the other that uses the original task problem space. Both of these subgoals are restricted to evaluating operators, so they can only be used when the selection problem space is trying to select among a set of superoperators. However, in the next chapter, we will see that these treatments of the evaluation subgoal are the basis for a significant number of weak methods.

2.4.2.1. Subgoal Evaluate1: The Evaluation Problem Space

The first problem space to evaluate task operators (the superoperators of the selection problem space) is the evaluation problem space described in Figure 2-16. This evaluation problem space will be used later to implement mini-max and alpha-beta search. The goal is to create an evaluation of a specific task operator. The states consist of information that can be used to evaluate the task operator. The exact nature of the information used to evaluate the task operator is specific to the task.

States	Information that may lead to an evaluation of the task operator. (This can include the task operator, task state, the state created by applying the operator to the state)

Operators	APPLY:	Apply the task operator to the task state and create a new state (*result*).
	EVALUATE-RESULT:	Statically evaluate the result.
	EVALUATE-OPERATOR:	Evaluate one of the task operators that can be applied to the result.
	COMBINE-EVALUATIONS:	Combine the evaluations into a single value.

Figure 2-16: The evaluation problem space.

The operators of the evaluation problem space gather, combine, and assign evaluations. Some of the evaluations are intermediate results, such as the evaluation of task states or other task operators. Best-preferences or reject-preferences may also be created for the task operator under question, but worse-preferences are only created in the selection problem space where the task operators can be compared to each other. The most direct way of gathering information about the task operator is to apply it to the previously current task state (the APPLY operator). If the resulting state can be statically evaluated it will be done by EVALUATE-RESULT. When EVALUATE-RESULT is inadequate, the operators that apply to the result state can be evaluated by EVALUATE-OPERATOR, which results in a recursive invocation of the evaluate problem space. The evaluations produced by EVALUATE-OPERATOR can then be integrated by COMBINE-EVALUATIONS which creates an evaluation for the result. Many of these operators only augment the current state, so they can be implemented as search-control elaborations instead of operators if the computation is simple enough to be performed by search control directly.

2.4.2.2. Goal-Space Diagrams

In our description of the evaluation problem space, the dependencies between the different subgoal were not crystal clear. We would prefer a concise description that conveyed the basic structure of the problem solving being performed. In previous investigations of problem solving, simple state space graphs (Nilsson, 1971) and problem behavior graphs (Newell and Simon, 1972) were adequate. However, in *Soar* the selection of problem spaces is critical to problem solving. To this end, we have developed a graphical description of the behavior of *Soar* during problem solving. As shown in Figure 3-5, it concentrates on the relationships between goals, subgoals and problem spaces. We call it a *goal-space diagram*, to emphasize the roles of goals and problem spaces in determining the behavior of *Soar*. This type of figure will be used to show the structural relationships between subgoals, problem spaces, states and operators.

Figure 2-17 shows the goal-space diagram for the selection and evaluation problem spaces. The left-most box contains the original task context that leads to the creation of a subgoal when there is a tie in the operator slot. This box contains the task goal (G1), task problem space (P1) and task state (S1). When there is a tie in the operator slot, a subgoal (G2) is produced. The selection problem space (P2) is used with this subgoal. The state of this subgoal (S2) contains the operators that tied in the supergoal; and to gather information about the task operators, the evaluation operator is selected (Q2a), instantiated with a specific operator from the supergoal (Q1n). This leads to a no-change subgoal (G3) and the selection of the evaluation problem space (P3), with the operators listed as Q3a-Q3c. We shall see later that the Apply operator (Q3a) is usually implemented as a subgoal as well, using the original task problem space to apply the task operator to the task state. The operator Q3b evaluates the operators that can be applied to the result (S1b) of applying operator Q1m to S1a. This is computed in an evaluation problem space as well.

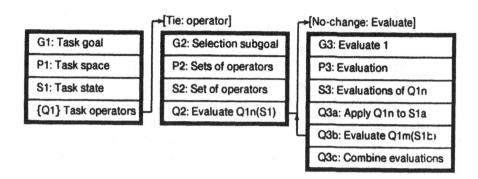

Figure 2-17: The subgoal structure of the evaluation problem space.

2.4.2.3. Subgoal Evaluate2: The Task Problem Space

In the evaluation problem space, the evaluation and application of task operators is performed by operators. This is necessary in the general case where the final evaluation may require a complex combination of other evaluations. In limited cases, these operations can be performed directly as search-control actions in the original task problem space. This is the second alternative for performing the evaluation of a task operator and is described here.

The productions to handle the subgoal directly are presented in Figure 2-18. Within this subgoal, the original task problem space is selected and an operator is evaluated only by the result it produces. There is no complex combination of evaluations from further down in the search tree. We will examine an example where the evaluation of the operator is the evaluation of the task state it produces. This is often called one-step look ahead and it is the steepest ascent hill climbing weak method.

ES1:	If the difficulty was a no-change with EVALUATE(OBJECT) as the current operator, augment the goal with the label **Evaluate-subgoal**.
ES2:	If the current goal is augmented with **Evaluate-subgoal** and the current state has an evaluation, make a reject-preference for the current goal at the goal slot.
ES3:	If the current goal is augmented with **Evaluate-subgoal**, make an acceptable-preference for the super-superproblem space at the problem space slot.
ES4:	If the current goal is augmented with **Evaluate-subgoal**, make an acceptable-preference of the super-superstate for the state slot.
ES5:	A task-specific evaluation of the state.
ES6:	If the current goal is augmented with **Evaluate-subgoal**, make a best-preference for the operator that is associated with the superobject.

Figure 2-18: The search-control knowledge for subgoal Evaluate2.

Once the new goal is voted in, production **ES1** merely augments the goal with a label that the other search-control productions can be sensitive to. Production ES3 makes an acceptable-preference for the task problem space at the problem-space slot. This establishes the task problem space as the current problem space. All search-control knowledge that is specific to this problem space will apply within this subgoal. Once the problem space is defined, productions ES4 and ES6 make the appropriate best-preferences for the task state and the task operator at the state and operator slots. The operator will be applied, and the result will be voted in as the current state. At this point, the state will be augmented by an evaluation ES5 and then production ES2 detects the result, and the goal is achieved. In order to make use of the result produced in this subgoal, there must be a task specific version of production SPS6 that knows to compare the evaluation of the result in order to compare two operators. If no evaluation of the state is possible, search can continue leading to more ties in operator selection and more subgoals, which produces a depth-first search.

Figure 2-19 shows the subgoal structure of this implementation of the evaluation operator. Originally, the task goal, task problem space and task state are selected: G1, P1, and S1 (the left-most box). During the selection of the operator, there is a tie between a set of task operators: {Q1}. This tie leads to the operator-selection subgoal (G2) to break the tie (middle box). The selection problem space (P2) is selected along with the initial state (S2) that contains the tied operators. All of the selection problem space operators plus the evaluate operator are available; however, only the operators used in this discussion are shown in the diagram. Operator Q2a is applied to gather information about one operator at a time, and when selected, causes a no-change difficulty. This leads to the selection of subgoal G3, the original problem space (P1) and state (S1) and the operator ($Q1_n$) being evaluated (right hand box). Once $Q1_n$ has been applied to S1 to produce a result, goal G3 is achieved, and the operator selection goal is re-established. Operator Q2a is reapplied, but instantiated with a new task operator, and this continues until all task operators have been evaluated. They can be compared and preferences can be built that label one worse than another. Operator Q2b then applies and selects out those that are not worse than others. If this leaves a single task operator, the operator selection goal is achieved and the original goal re-instated. If more than one operator remains, the only operator that can apply is RANDOM-PREFERENCE, and it will be selected and applied so that only one task operator remains. Upon returning to the task goal, the tie for operators will be broken, because of preferences added either through comparisons, or by the RANDOM-PREFERENCE operator.

For the Eight Puzzle task, this leads to a search shown in Figure 2-20. The figure traces the states expanded in the Eight Puzzle problem space and shows the distinctive pattern of steepest ascent hill climbing. Note that these states

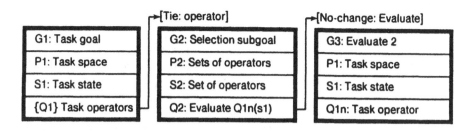

Figure 2-19: The subgoal structure of the second type of evaluation subgoal.

were generated in the attempt to solve many different subgoals and did not result from a single method to achieve a specific goal. Initially, the top configuration is the current state. When there is no way to choose between the operators that can be applied, a subgoal to break the tie is created, and the selection problem space becomes the current problem space. To compare the task operators, each one is evaluated by applying it to the current state and then evaluating the result that is produced. The states are evaluated based on the number of tiles out of position, so the lower the evaluation, the better the state (and the better the operator). The application of each of the task operators produces the three states below the top one. Once these are produced, the selection problem space is able to determine that the operator that produced the one on the left is better than the other two. The search returns to the task problem space and the best operator is selected. Problem solving continues after the operator has been applied and its result has been selected as the current state.

2.4.3. Universal Weak Method Conclusion

We presented the universal weak method for *Soar* as a fixed set of decision productions (**D1-D10**) and the problem spaces and search-control knowledge for selection and evaluation. Whether the *Soar* architecture, together with universal subgoaling, the fixed decision production, and the selection and evaluation problem spaces, form a universal weak method can only be determined empirically. We must see if universal subgoaling and a universal weak method is an adequate structure in which to encode knowledge for a wide variety of tasks. Another test is to encode knowledge about a task in elaboration productions and determine if the resulting behavior corresponds to the weak methods. We must also judge the encodings by the criteria laid down in our initial investigation of a universal weak method (Laird and Newell, 1983a, summarized in Section 1.1). We will perform such an investigation in the next chapter.

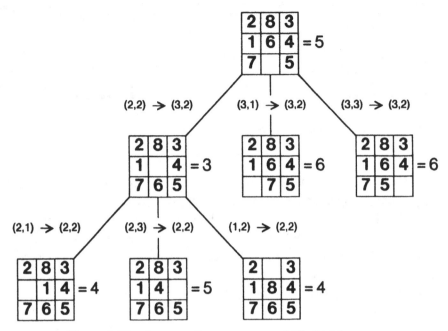

Figure 2-20: A trace of steepest ascent hill climbing.

2.5. The Rest of Soar

In this section we tie up the loose ends of the *Soar* architecture: the implementation of subgoals in *Soar* that are not created automatically and some common search-control knowledge we will find useful in our later demonstrations.

2.5.1. Deliberate Subgoals

Although we have concentrated on subgoals created automatically by the architecture, most problem solvers depend on subgoals created *deliberately* by search control. In *Soar,* the processing of a deliberate subgoal is the same as the processing of goals created by the architecture, except for the act of creation. With deliberate subgoaling, an elaboration production creates a preference that includes the current context and a symbol representing the subgoal. That symbol may or may not be a new symbol. If it is a new symbol, it will also be elaborated with augmentations that allow further diagnosis. If it is not a new symbol, elaboration productions can be sensitive to it directly. In both cases, when the subgoal symbol becomes the current goal, elaboration productions will augment the symbol with sufficient information to completely define the goal and lead to selection of the problem space and initial state, thereby commencing problem solving.

2.5.2. Common Search-Control Knowledge

Figure 2-21 lists elaboration productions that provide knowledge for a wide variety of tasks, but they do not seem universal at this stage. They are included here because they will be used for all tasks in the upcoming demonstration. Production E4 takes a subgoal that was created because of a tie for the current goal and makes a best-preference for it for the goal slot. Without this production, the subgoal will tie with all the other goals that tied, never resolving the tie. Once the goal-tie subgoal becomes the current goal, a problem space can be selected and progress can be made in determining which of the tieing goals should become the current goal. Production E5 rejects operators that have already applied to the current state. Once an operator has been applied to the current state, it has produced its result. Reapplying the same operator will only produce the same result because of the deterministic nature of the operators that are implemented in search control by productions. If probabilistic operators were introduced, the scope of this production could be restricted to problem spaces that have deterministic operators.

E4:	If there is a **goal-tie** subgoal of the current context without a best-preference, make a best-preference for it at the goal slot.
E5:	If an operator of the current problem space has been applied to the current state, make a reject-preference for the operator at the operator slot.
E6:	If there is an **operator-tie** subgoal of the current context, and the problem space is augmented with **break-ties**, make a reject-preference for the subgoal, and randomly make a single acceptable-preference for one of the tied operator at the operator slot.

Figure 2-21: Common elaboration productions.

Production E6 is used to avoid a problem that arises with the addition of universal subgoaling. *Soar* is unable to make a random preference among similar objects. In *Soar1*, a tie in the decision phase was broken randomly. This is quite useful in certain problem spaces where the order of application of operators is irrelevant. However, within *Soar*, a tie causes the creation of a subgoal, and if the subgoal becomes the current goal, there will be an attempt to differentiate among the tieing objects. If no discrimination can be made, one of the tieing objects has to be selected at random by an operator in the subgoal.

This is implemented in *Soar* by a special type of production, called Elaborate-once. On a given elaboration cycle, only one instantiation of an Elaborate-once production will fire, and that instantiation is selected at random. Given this production, an operator can be created that will select from the tieing set and choose one at random. This can be used to make a best-preference for the selected object, and thereby break the tie. This mechanism works fine, but involves a fair amount of overhead to accomplish the simple action of making a random choice.

Production E6 is an implementation of a short-cut of this tie-breaking strategy. When a problem space is augmented with *break-ties*, any subgoal created because of a tie in operator selection will be rejected, and a preference will be made randomly for one of the tieing objects. This production is not really necessary, since if it did not exist a subgoal would be created and the tie would be broken randomly by an operator application in the subgoal. However, it does speed things up and it demonstrates how the mere creation of the sub-goal symbol can be enough to perform an appropriate action.

2.6. Review of Soar

The main result of this chapter has been the description of a problem-solving architecture (*Soar*) that satisfies the requirements for universal subgoaling. This was followed by a presentation of the implementation of a universal weak method in *Soar*. However, the details of the *Soar* architecture has been spread throughout this chapter. It is easy to confuse what type of processing is performed by the architecture, the universal weak method and the productions that are specific to a task. In general, the architecture does very little except create subgoals, the universal weak method translates preferences into votes, and the elaboration productions do the rest. Here we review the architecture.

The two actions of the architecture are (1) adding augmentations to the objects in the current context and (2) replacing an object in one of the slots of the current context. Adding augmentations is the action of the elaboration phase, which is implemented by productions that fire in parallel until quiescence. All task-dependent knowledge is implemented by elaboration productions, all of which are available during every elaboration phase. The elaboration phase is followed by the decision phase, where a fixed set of productions convert preferences into votes for objects to enter the current context. The object that receives the most votes for a given slot replaces the current object in that slot. The slots are processed in order: goal, problem space, state, operator, until the object in the slot changes or a difficulty occurs. Three types of difficulties (no-change, tie, all-vetoed) are recognized by the architecture, which responds by building a preference for a new subgoal. All further processing of the subgoal is determined by the universal weak method and task-specific productions. After a subgoal is created or an object is added to the current context, the cycle continues with the elaboration phase.

3 EMPIRICAL DEMONSTRATION

In this section we provide a demonstration of the *Soar* architecture. The main objective is to demonstrate empirically the universality and rationality of the subgoaling system just defined in conjunction with the universal weak method. However, first we will demonstrate the workability of subgoals in *Soar*. Therefore, the demonstration will consist of the three parts listed below.

1. Encode the necessary search-control knowledge to demonstrate deliberate subgoals. Running tasks with this search-control knowledge should demonstrate all of the mechanisms of subgoaling: subgoal creation, subgoal selection, problem solving in a subgoal, and returning results from the subgoal.
2. Encode the necessary search-control knowledge to demonstrate that *Soar* automatically creates subgoals for all search-control difficulties. This includes a demonstration that every search-control function can be performed within a subgoal created as a result of a difficulty in problem solving (as given in Figure 1-5).
3. Encode a wide variety of search-control knowledge for a variety of tasks where universal subgoaling and the universal weak method are used. For tasks where there is little knowledge, the behavior of the problem solver corresponds to the weak methods. This part of the demonstration consists of encoding a set of weak methods, as search control productions and problem spaces, and then running each weak method on a task and verifying that the behavior of the system constitutes that of the weak method and that the behavior is rational. An important part of this demonstration is verifying that *Soar* maintains the property of the universal weak method and extends it to many of the weak methods not covered in *Soar1*.

These demonstrations must be performed within the context of specific

57

tasks. The encoding of a problem space consists of the productions that implement the operators; the encoding of goal consists of the productions that detect the desired states of the goal as we demonstrated for the Eight Puzzle earlier. Figure 3-1 gives brief descriptions of the seven tasks used for the demonstrations.

Eight Puzzle (EP)

Problem Statement: There are eight numbered movable tiles set in a 3x3 frame. One cell is always empty, making it possible to move an adjacent tile into the empty cell. The problem is to transform one configuration to a second by moving tiles.

States: States are configurations of the numbers 0-8 in a 3x3 grid.

Operators: There are twenty-four operators, one for each possible movement of tiles in cells adjacent to each possible empty cell.

Missionaries and Cannibals (M&C)

Problem Statement: Three missionaries and three cannibals wish to cross a river. Though they can all row, they only have available a small boat that holds two people. The difficulty is that the cannibals are unreliable; if they ever outnumber the missionaries on a river bank, they will kill them. How do they manage the boat trips so that all six get safely to the other side?

States: The states contain the number of missionaries and cannibals on each side of the river and the position of the boat.

Operators: There are ten operators, one for each legal combination of moving missionaries, cannibals, and boat across the river.

Tic-Tac-Toe (TTT)

Problem Statement: There are two players that alternate turns making marks (X or O) in a 3x3 grid. The first player to get three in a row wins.

States: Configurations of X's and O's in a 3x3 grid.

Operators: There are eighteen operators (with a maximum of nine being applicable for a given state): Make a mark of X or O in one of the positions in the grid.

Blocks World (BW)

Problem Statement: There are a set of labeled blocks on a table. They are presented is some initial configuration, such as, block A on top of block B, with an additional block C. The goal is to achieve another configuration, such as, block C on top of block B on top of block A.

States: The states are different configurations of the blocks, represented by assertions, such as (ONTOP A B), meaning block A is on top block B, and (CLEARTOP A), meaning block A has no other blocks on top of it.

Operators: There is one operator: Move a single block, that is clear, from one place (on top a block or the table) to another place (on top a block or the table).

Figure 3-1: Tasks used to demonstrate universal subgoaling.

Labeling Line Drawings (LLD)
Problem Statement: There is a line drawing of 3D objects made of trihedral vertices. The problem is to determine a single, consistent labeling of the lines and junctions as edges and vertices of the 3D objects. (This is the Waltz line labeling task, Waltz 1975 .)
States: The states consist of the drawing with sets of possible labelings of the vertices and edges.
Operators: There is one operator: Mark as inconsistent a vertex labeling if one of its line labelings is not available in one of the adjacent consistent vertex labelings.

Expression Unification (EU)
Problem Statement: There are two expressions, consisting of constants, variables and functions (which can contain expressions). The problem is to determine if the two expressions can be made identical by replacing variables with constants or functions. For example: $(x, F(y, G(y, A)), A)$ and $(z, F(B, G(B, z)), x)$
States: Each state consists pairs of expressions, with partial lists of the replacements for variables, and a pointer into the expressions.
Operators: There are two operators: Replace a variable with a constant or function, and unify two subexpressions.

Sequence Extrapolation (SE)
Problem Statement: There is a sequence of letters that is incomplete. The problem is to complete the sequence. For example: M A B M B C M C D M − − −.
States: Hypotheses of the rules being used to generate the sequence.
Operators: There are two operators: generate a new hypothesis, test a hypothesis.

Figure 3-1: Tasks used to demonstrate universal subgoaling (continued).

Included in the descriptions are a statement of the task, followed by a description of the states and operators that define the problem spaces we chose for the tasks. The tasks are simple tasks, familiar from the AI literature. They include tasks that require extensive search, controlled reasoning, constraint satisfaction and induction. Such tasks are suitable for an initial test of universal subgoaling, being familiar, knowledge-lean and relatively easy to implement. This is not to say they are trivial to solve. These types of tasks are very valuable to AI because they provide paradigmatic examples of difficult problems that occur in many tasks. Three of these tasks (Eight Puzzle, Missionaries and Cannibals, Labeling Line Drawings) were also used in the test of the universal weak method (Laird and Newell, 1983a); the formulations here are identical.

3.1. Deliberate Subgoals

Our demonstration of deliberate subgoals consists of the implementations of a varied set of subgoals, a detailed example of one of these subgoals and a examples of how the *Soar* architecture allows non-standard returns from subgoals.

3.1.1. Five Deliberate Subgoals

The demonstrations of deliberate subgoals use the Blocks World, Eight Puzzle and Missionaries and Cannibals tasks. These are demonstrations of the mechanisms of subgoaling, and not an exhaustive examination of the variety of deliberate subgoals. The problem spaces that are used in the subgoals are either the task problem space or a very simple problem space that often does not require search in order to solve the subgoal. These tasks demonstrate that different types of results can be produced in a subgoal. Figure 3-2 contains a list of the different types of subgoals that were implemented, the results that were produced in the subgoal, and the tasks in which they were implemented.

<u>Deliberate</u> <u>Subgoals</u>	<u>Result</u>	<u>Tasks</u>
Elaborate desired state	Goal augmentations	Blocks world
Test state	State augmentations	Blocks world, Eight Puzzle
Elaborate state	State augmentations	Blocks world, Eight Puzzle
Goal decomposition	New state	Blocks world
Operator subgoaling	New state	Missionaries and Cannibals

Figure 3-2: Deliberate-subgoal demonstration.

The first deliberate subgoal we will discuss elaborates the desired states in the Blocks world task. In the classical formulation of the blocks world task (Sacerdoti, 1977), the desired state is only partially specified. For example, (ONTOP A B) and (ONTOP B C) may be the only propositions used to specify a desired state where A is on B, B is on C, C is on the table and A is clear. If the problem solver is able to deduce that (ONTOP C Table) and (CLEARTOP A) are also true in the desired state, certain strategies like means-ends analysis are much more successful. So, when a Blocks world task is attempted, we can set up the subgoal of elaborating the description of the desired state. Of course, these simple elaborations could be done directly in search control for these examples, but this demonstrates that elaborations can be computed in a subgoal and then used in the original task.

The second subgoal tests the state to determine if it matches the desired state. In both the Blocks world and the Eight Puzzle, this test can be done by a single production. The subgoals test the states component by component, which is much slower, but demonstrates that for complex states in general, a subgoal can test for success when a single production would be impractical. The third subgoal elaborates the current state, either with more substructure, as in the case of the Blocks world, or with an evaluation of the worth of the state, as is the case in the Eight Puzzle. These examples demonstrate that if a necessary computation is too complex for the limited power of search control, a subgoal can be used instead.

The last two subgoals use the task problem space in the subgoal and produce a new state as their result, instead of an augmentation of an existing object. The first type creates a set of subgoals corresponding to the propositions that make up the desired state. In the Blocks world, a desired state consisting of (ONTOP A B) and (ONTOP B C) would be decomposed into two goals, one to achieve (ONTOP A B) and one to achieve (ONTOP B C). Of course, one of the subgoals must be selected first. To avoid creating a tie that would involve additional subgoals, one of the subgoals was arbitrarily augmented with a worse-preference. This type of goal decomposition is an example of AND/OR subgoaling, where the decomposition of the goal into subgoals is the AND part, and the selection of operators to achieve the subgoals is the OR part. We can expect that all of the classic problems of AND/OR goal trees would arise using this scheme. This was not an attempt to solve these problems, just an attempt to demonstrate that one of the classic subgoaling techniques of AI could be easily implemented within *Soar*.

The final deliberate subgoal is operator subgoaling. We will see this again in the demonstration of universal subgoaling. Here, the subgoal is created when search control detects that the current operator will not apply to the current state. The purpose of the subgoal is to create a state so that the selected operator can apply. When these last two subgoals achieve their goals, instead of re-establishing the prior context completely, the current state of the subgoal is maintained and the rest of the context is replaced.

3.1.2. An Extended Example

To demonstrate some of the details of the subgoaling processes, we will present an extended example of the subgoal used to compute the evaluation of a state for the Eight Puzzle. The actual computation performed within the subgoal does not require search, but the creation, initialization, and termination of the goal are typical of all deliberate subgoals. To perform this demonstration, we include all the productions presented so far: D1-10, E1-6, EP1-9. We also add productions EP10-20 as shown in Figure 3-3. These set up the evaluation subgoal (EP-EVAL) and its problem space (EP-SUM) and then carry out the evaluation.

Instead of going through each production, we will describe a trace of the production execution. Figure 3-4 contains the trace. Each line is a single production firing that contains the cycle number, the name of the production, and a short description of the action of the production or the current context.

EP10:   If the current problem space is eight-puzzle and if one non-rejected state has a larger difference than another non-rejected state, create a worse-preference containing the first state.

EP11:   If the current problem space is eight-puzzle, and the current state does not have an difference, create an acceptable-preference for the EP-EVAL subgoal.

EP12:   If the current goal is EP-EVAL, make an acceptable-preference for EP-SUM at the problem-space slot.

EP13:   If the current problem space is EP-SUM, make an acceptable-preference for a new state that contains the superstate and the desired state of the supergoal.

EP14:   If the current problem space is EP-SUM and the superstate differs from the desired state of the supergoal at a given position, augment the current state with a difference of 1 for that position.

EP15:   If the current problem space is EP-SUM and the superstate equals from the desired state of the supergoal at a given position, augment the current state with a difference of 0 for that position.

EP16:   If the current problem space is EP-SUM and the current state has a difference for each position (completely enumerate the set), augment the current state and superstate with a total difference that is the sum of all the differences.

EP17:   If the current goal is EP-EVAL and the current state has a total difference, make a reject-preference for the current goal at the goal slot.

Figure 3-3: Productions for Eight Puzzle state-evaluation subgoal.

The productions that have the same cycle number fire in parallel. For the decision phase, many productions may contribute votes, but we list the one that is most important in determining the final result. The trace starts in the Eight Puzzle task where the current state, S10, has not yet been evaluated, while a prior state, S08, has a difference of 7.

The individual productions are labeled with the number of the cycle they fire on. The cycle number includes a E if it is part of the elaboration phase, and a D if it is part of the decision phase. If there are multiple elaboration phases for a cycle, they are labelled sequentially (as in 4E1, 4E2, ...). In the first cycle, the subgoal is created and then it is selected as the current goal. In cycle 2 and 3, the problem space and initial state are recalled by elaboration productions and then selected. In cycle 4, the individual differences are computed and then totaled. The individual differences and the total differences are augmentations of the current state. The total difference is also an augmentation of the super-state. The difference between a state and the goal is computed to be the total number of cells in the state that differ from the desired state. Therefore, a better state is a state with a smaller difference. Success is determined at 4E3 and the prior context is restored at 4D so that in the final cycle state S10 is compared to S08, and S08 is found to have a larger difference and a worse-preference is created for it.

Figure 3-5 gives a goal-space diagram for the desired-state testing subgoal. The box to the left contains the original task context that leads to the subgoal.

Cycle	Production	Action
		Current context: **EPG1, Eight, S10**
1E	EP11	Create subgoal EP-EVAL
1D	D1	Current context: **EP-EVAL**
2E	EP12	Make EP-SUM p. space preference
2D	D1	Current context: **EP-EVAL, EP-EVAL**
3E	EP13	Make new state S22 a state preference
3D	D1	Current context: **EP-EVAL, EP-EVAL, S22**
4E1	E14	Detect difference at position (1,1)
4E1	E15	Detect no difference at position (1,2)
4E1	E15	Detect no difference at position (1,3)
4E1	E14	Detect difference at position (2,1)
4E1	E14	Detect difference at position (2,2)
4E1	E15	Detect no difference at position (2,3)
4E1	E15	Detect no difference at position (3,1)
4E1	E14	Detect difference at position (3,2)
4E1	E15	Detect no difference at position (3,3)
4E2	E16	Augment S10 with a total difference of 4
4E3	E17	Make a reject-preference for EP-EVAL
4D	D3,D8	Current context: **EPG1, Eight-P, S10**
5E	E10	Make a worse-preference for S08

Figure 3-4: Production trace of state-evaluation subgoal.

This contains the task goal (G1), task problem space (P1) and task state (S1). When there is a new state (such as S1), a deliberate subgoal is produced (G2) and then selected along with its problem space and initial state, as indicated by the arrow and bracketed comment at the top of the box at the right. The problem space for the subgoal computes and combines the differences between a state and its goal.

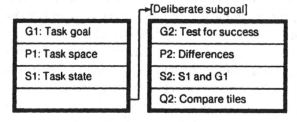

Figure 3-5: The subgoal structure of desired-state testing.

3.1.3. Early Termination of Subgoals

One important type of goal behavior is the early termination of a subgoal, either because a state has been achieved that satisfies a prior goal or because the subgoal is the same as a supergoal. Other types of early termination may arise in problem solving, due to failure in a subgoal, but these two cases of termination are of special interest because they transcend the locality of a single goal and require examining more than one goal at a time. In *Soar*, a limited demonstration of this behavior has been made when the subgoals use the same problem space as the supergoals. Figure 3-6 lists the three types of early termination and the tasks used in the demonstration. For the first two demonstrations, operator subgoaling creates the subgoals, while both operator subgoaling and depth-first search were used in the final demonstration. In the first case, a subgoal is recognized as being equal to a supergoal (not necessarily the immediate supergoal). A single search-control production compares the desired state of the current goal to the desired state of a supergoal, and if they match, the current goal is rejected.

<u>Early Subgoal Termination</u>	<u>Tasks</u>
Detect that a subgoal equals a supergoal	Missionaries and Cannibals
Detect that current state achieves a supergoal (Compare state to all supergoals)	Missionaries and Cannibals Blocks World
Detect that current state achieves a supergoal (Augment subgoals with supergoal tests)	Blocks World Eight Puzzle

Figure 3-6: Tasks implemented to demonstrate early subgoal termination.

In the second two cases of early termination, search control detects that the current state achieves a supergoal. In the first of these, a search-control production must test if the current state matches the desired state of any of the supergoals. If it does, a best-preference is made for that supergoal and a best-preference is made for the current state for the state slot given the context of the supergoal, and the current problem space (which is also the problem space of the supergoal). The unlimited memory assumption makes this possible in *Soar*, but the third alternative allows connections to supergoals when that assumption is removed. In the final case, the descriptions of a supergoal are passed down to subgoals by elaboration productions. This keeps all the relevant information local to a goal instead of requiring that all the supergoals be in working memory and that there be a production that can scan all of them. In contrast, the first two methods require elaboration productions that can test objects (in this case the desired states of supergoals) that may be very distant from the current context.

3.2. Universal Subgoaling

In this section we demonstrate the universality of subgoaling in the *Soar* architecture. In Figure 2-10, we gave the correspondence between the failures of search control and the *Soar* difficulties. In Figure 3-7 we show the same correspondence, but include the tasks that were used to demonstrate that *Soar* produced the correct subgoals and that results could be produced that would eliminate the difficulty. Some of the implementations were truncated, in that an incomplete problem space was implemented to perform the function. In these cases, there were search-control productions that immediately produced the correct result when the subgoal became current. These have no effect on the demonstration.

S-C Function	S-C Difficulty	*Soar* Difficulty	Tasks
Decide on success	Inconclusive	None	None
Decide on failure	Inconclusive	None	None
Select goal	Inconclusive	Tie for goal	Blocks World
Select problem space	Inconclusive	Tie for problem space	Eight Puzzle
	No candidates	No-change goal	Eight Puzzle
Select state	Inconclusive	Tie for state	Eight Puzzle
	No initial state	No-change space	Eight Puzzle
Select operator	Inconclusive	Tie for operator	EP, TTT, MC
	No operators	No-change state	EP, BW
Apply Operator	Not applied	No-change operator	TTT, SE, LLD
	Incomplete operator	No-change operator	Eight Puzzle
	Not applicable	No-change operator	BW, MC, EP

Figure 3-7: Universality demonstration of subgoals.

The processing in the subgoals corresponds to common problem-solving operations that exist as special (nongoal) mechanisms in most AI programs. A tie for the goal slot requires reasoning about the next goal, which, as we will discuss later, can lead to agendas, planning, and metaplanning. The creation of the initial state in a subgoal leads to problem spaces that must interpret a description of a problem and translate it into the current problem space. When there are no operators available (in the Eight Puzzle for example), a subgoal generates operators for the current state, and a second subgoal *instantiates* the operators once they are selected. Ties for the operators result in subgoals that *evaluate* states, compute *differences* between states and goals and then select the operators based on the differences. In *Soar*, all of these types of problem solving arise from subgoals without the special mechanisms that are required in current AI systems.

For each of these tasks, either a problem space must already exist that can be used to solve the subgoals or one must be created within another subgoal. For the no-change demonstrations, search-control productions recognize the subgoals and create preferences for problem spaces and initial states. There may be an arbitrary number of problem spaces that can be used to solve these subgoals. Therefore, it is unlikely that a fixed set of problem spaces can be used for all problems that a general problem solver will encounter. However, the selection problem space can be used whenever a tie exists, for any slot of the current context.

3.3. The Weak Methods

Although the previous section demonstrated that *Soar* can create subgoals for the difficulties in problem solving, it does not demonstrate how this leads to knowledge being brought to bear when appropriate so that useful behavior is generated. In *Soar1* we took the knowledge implicit in the subgoal-free weak methods as our challenge. In *Soar* we extend the challenge to include the knowledge in weak methods that require subgoals. We must demonstrate that we can encode the weak methods so that the knowledge is not locked into a method, but instead, all knowledge is used when it is needed, especially knowledge that requires subgoaling to be made available. The advantages of such an encoding are that a system uses all of its knowledge for all of its tasks so that it is not tied to fixed behavior that is unresponsive to new tasks.

First, we will demonstrate that *Soar* significantly extends the number of weak methods that can be encoded. We will examine the method increments that define each weak method and evaluate our implementation of the weak methods based on four criteria from our implementation of *Soar1*. Not only can we encode method knowledge, but our encodings provide a taxonomy of the weak methods. We have discovered that the many of the weak methods share common method increments and subgoals, providing a structure of the weak methods.

3.3.1. The Weak Methods of Soar

Using the tasks described in Figure 3-1, seventeen different weak methods were investigated. Figure 3-8 gives descriptions of these weak methods. We have attempted to include the most common weak methods used in AI. This does not include all weak methods, since the weak methods are possibly an infinite set, generated from different increments of search-control knowledge. This does includes all of the major weak methods implemented in *Soar1* with our subgoals (marked with *[Soar1]* in the figure) except Best-First Search, Modified Best-First Search, A* and Breadth-First Search. These four methods will be discussed later. The weak methods we have included range from the simplest (requiring little or no search-control knowledge) to some of the most complex (requiring extensive search-control knowledge). In future discussions we will refer to two groups of methods: PD* and Mini-Max*. PD* includes progressive deepening, modified progressive deepening and B*(PD). Mini-Max* includes mini-max and all methods that follow it in Figure 3-8.

Operator Subgoaling (OSG). If an operator cannot be applied to a position, then set up a subgoal of finding a position (starting from the current position) at which the operator can be applied. Implemented for Eight Puzzle, Missionaries and Cannibals, and Blocks World.

Unification (UN). Given two patterns containing variables and functions with variables, find the most general unifying expression. Implemented for Expression Unification.

Hypothesize and Match (H&M). Given a set of exemplar of a functions, generate possible function forms and match them to the exemplars. Implemented for Sequence Extrapolation.

Constraint Satisfaction (CS). There are a set of constraints on a set of variables. An assignment of values to variables must be found that satisfy the constraints. In Waltz Labeling, the possible values a variable are explicitly represented and then the constraints are applied to these values to restrict the values of neighboring variables. This process recurs through all variables until no changes are made in the values of any variable. Implemented for Labeling Line Drawings. *[Soar1]*

Generate and Test (GT). Generate candidate solutions and test each one; terminate when found. Implemented for Eight Puzzle. *[Soar1]*

Depth-First Search (DFS). To find an object in a space generated by operators, do a heuristic search but always move from the deepest position that still has some untried operators. Implemented for Eight Puzzle. *[Soar1]*

Figure 3-8: Weak methods.

Simple Hill Climbing (SHC). To find a maximum point in a space, consider the next moves (operators) from a given position and select the first one that increases the value. Implemented for Eight Puzzle. [*Soar1*]

Steepest Ascent Hill Climbing (SAHC). To find a maximum point in a space, consider the next moves (operators) from a given position and select the one that makes the largest advance. Implemented for Eight Puzzle. [*Soar1*]

Means-Ends Analysis (MEA). Make the next move that best reduces the difference between the current state and the desired state. Implemented for Eight Puzzle, Missionaries and Cannibals, and Blocks World. [*Soar1*]

Progressive Deepening (PD). Rework the analysis of a move repeatedly, going over old ground more carefully, exploring new side branches, and extending the search deeper until new information is discovered. Implemented for Tic-Tac-Toe.

Modified Progressive Deepening (MPD). Same as Progressive Deepening, except that whenever the search is extended, all possible moves are examined. Implemented for Tic-Tac-Toe.

B* (Progressive Deepening). Same as Progressive Deepening, except that optimistic and pessimistic values are used to evaluate each move. (This is not a proof procedure as are B* and Mini-Max.) Implemented for Tic-Tac-Toe.

Mini-Max (MM). To find the best next move in a perfect-information, two-player game, exhaustively try out all moves of each player, and find the line of play that provides the best final result, assuming each player always chooses the best possible move. Implemented for Tic-Tac-Toe.

Depth-Bounded Mini-Max (DPMM). Same as Mini-Max, except there is a prespecified bound on the depth of search. Implemented for Tic-Tac-Toe.

Alpha-Beta (AB). Same as Depth-Bounded Mini-Max, except that the search is not exhausted. Lines of play are ignored because they can do no better than a previously examined set of moves. Implemented for Tic-Tac-Toe.

Iterative Deepening (ID). Similar to Alpha-Beta, except the search begins with a search to depth 1, then iterates through the depths til it reaches a depth limit. The results for each depth of search are used to order the operator selection of the search at the next depth. Implemented for Tic-Tac-Toe.

B* (Mini-Max). A proof procedure similar to Alpha-Beta, except each state has an optimistic and pessimistic value. See Berliner, 1979 for details. Implemented for Tic-Tac-Toe.

Figure 3-8: Weak methods (continued).

The descriptions of the weak methods include the names of the tasks used each method. As is evident from the figure, only a single task was used to demonstrate most weak methods. In our demonstration of *Soar1*, the extension of a method to multiple tasks was always trivial, so that the concentration here is on the number of methods demonstrated instead of the number of tasks for each method.

In contrast to the weak methods in *Soar1*, the weak methods in *Soar* do not arise from the search of a single problem space to obtain a single goal. The pattern of search behavior that characterizes each weak method arises from a search of the task problem space by the subgoals that are generated during problem solving. Steepest ascent hill climbing was an example of this earlier, where the one-step look-ahead occurs in a subgoal that is attempting to evaluate a task operator.

To produce the methods of Figure 3-8, a task is implemented in *Soar* and search-control knowledge about the task, in the form of productions, is added. A weak method arises because certain task-specific search-control knowledge has been added. Given the universal weak method of *Soar* (S_u), each weak method can be defined by the method increments that contain the task-specific knowledge: S_m. However, the subgoals that naturally arise during problem solving are important contributions to the behavior of *Soar* and therefore the generation of weak methods. Since the selection and evaluation problem spaces are part of the universal weak method (S_u) of *Soar*, the new search-control knowledge is sometimes applied in these problem spaces while attempting a subgoal. For some methods, the structure of the task requires problem spaces that implement complex operators of the top task problem space (Hypothesize and Match). These additional problem spaces are not search-control knowledge, but are a part of the implementation of the task.

Appendix B contains the complete listing of the method increments for all weak methods together with the goal-space diagrams that describe the subgoals that arise during problem solving using the methods. In the following section we will examine some of the method increments to understand the structure of the weak methods.

3.3.2. The Structure of the Weak Methods

Since each method arises from the addition of a small amount of new task-dependent knowledge, we expect that many methods share common search control. Certain knowledge should be applicable to many methods, and as the knowledge becomes more specialized, fewer methods will share it. Figure 3-9 shows the hierarchical structure of the weak methods represented in *Soar*. The common knowledge forms the trunk of a tree, with branches occurring when there is different task structure or knowledge available, making each leaf in the tree a different weak method. This structure arises because of shared search-control knowledge, and shared subgoals.

To understand this structure, we will examine the weak methods with respect to the task knowledge and subgoal structure they share. We will start at

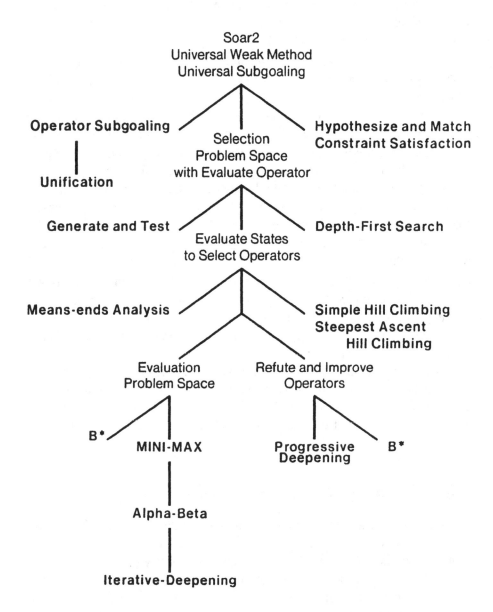

Figure 3-9: Structure of Weak Methods.

the top of the tree, where there is the least amount of task-specific knowledge, and work left to right and top to bottom, where the methods become specialized with more task-specific knowledge. Our discussion will be based on the subgoal structures that arise from these methods. Surprisingly, only four subgoal configurations account for *all* of the weak methods we have implemented. Therefore our discussion will come in four parts.

3.3.2.1. Operator-Subgoaling Weak Methods

Operator subgoaling and unification split off to the left at the top of Figure 3-9 and have the goal-space diagram in Figure 3-10. Operator subgoaling arises when the current context is completely defined and there is no-change because the operator can not apply. The subgoal searches for a state where the operator can be applied.

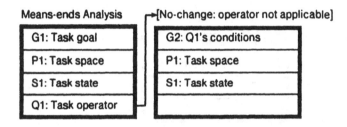

Figure 3-10: Goal-space diagram for operator subgoaling and unification.

There must be task knowledge so that a new desired state can be created that contains the condition of the operator as well as the knowledge to initialize the problem space and state correctly. Unification is a specialization of this method where the task operators (or at least the actions performed by the operators) are specific to the method. Figure 3-11 contains the productions that define operator subgoaling.

Operator Subgoaling

Goal: If the current goal is a no-change goal, where the task operator's **conditions** were not **satisfied** by the task state, **convert** the **form** of the task operator's **condition** into the desired state.

Problem Space: If the current goal is a no-change goal, where the task operator's **conditions** were not **satisfied** by the task state, make an acceptable-preference for task problem space at the problem-space slot.

State: If the current goal is a no-change goal, where the task operator's **conditions** were not **satisfied** by the task state and the state is undefined, make an acceptable-preference for the superstate at the state slot.

Figure 3-11: Method Increments for Operator Subgoaling.

3.3.2.2. Apply-Operator Weak Methods

The methods that split to the right at the top level of Figure 3-9 correspond to Figure 3-12. This subgoal structure arises when an operator can not be executed by search control directly so that a subgoal is required to apply the task operator to the task state. The problem space for this subgoal implements the task operator. The weak methods in our demonstration that required such a subgoal were constraint satisfaction and hypothesize and match. In hypothesize and match, this subgoal structure is inherent because the top problem space is attempting to find the best hypothesis to fit a set of data. This is a search through the space of hypotheses. One of the operators of this space tests a hypothesis. This requires search of another problem space and produces the subgoal structure in Figure 3-12. A second subgoal arises (not shown in Figure 3-12) to implement an operator in the sub-problem space.

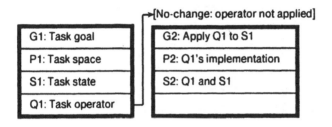

Figure 3-12:   Goal-space diagram for Hypothesize and Match
                           and Constraint Satisfaction.

In constraint satisfaction, one of the operators of the task problem space is to determine the values of a variable that do not violate a neighboring constraint. This computation requires searching through the values and testing each one. In *Soar*, this requires a subgoal because the computation is outside the computational limits of search control. As these two tasks demonstrate, this subgoal structure arises when the implementation of an operator exceeds the processing power of search control by requiring either search or complex processing (even though that processing may be routine).

3.3.2.3. Operator-Selection Weak Methods: Evaluate2

The next set of the weak methods emerge when there is a tie for the operator slot. This is a basic problem for any intelligent system: trying to decide what to do next. These methods make use of the selection problem space with the evaluation operator as shown in Figure 3-13. The method increments for some of the weak methods with this structure are listed in Figure 3-14.

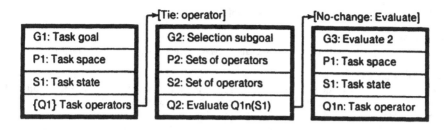

Figure 3-13:   Goal-space diagram for Generate and Test, Depth-First Search,
Simple Hill Climbing, Steepest Ascent Hill Climbing,
Means-ends Analysis, Progressive Deepening,
Modified Progressive Deepening, and B* (PD).

Generate and test and depth-first search split off first in Figure 3-9. Both of these arise from task structure. In generate and test, all newly generated states are terminal states. In depth-first search, the only terminal states can be evaluated. This type of evaluation is only in terms of success or failure and does not allow the comparison of intermediate states. In depth-first search, a tie may arise when the operator is selected in the evaluation subgoal. This will create a selection subgoal, which produces the standard recursion of depth-first search. Means-ends analysis also shares this diagram, although it applies the evaluation operator directly in the selection problem space by using the difference between the task state and its goal to evaluate the operators.

In Figure 3-9, the next set of common search-control knowledge consists of being able to evaluate a state, and the knowledge that task operators can be compared by the evaluation of their results. Note, this does not require that the same evaluation function is used in all tasks. The evaluation function is specific to the task problem spaces, but the knowledge that it can be used is available to all tasks because it is in the selection problem space. This produces the hill climbing methods, and with the addition of refute and improve operators, the progressive deepening family of methods. In B*(PD), the evaluations are actually ranges instead of point values, but the subgoal structure is retained.

3.3.2.4. Operator-Selection Weak Methods: Evaluate1

The tree continues down as additional search-control knowledge is added: a special evaluation problem space for mini-max and its descendents (which are differentiated by the type of evaluation used and whether the depth of the search is considered). Figure 3-15 contains the structure for mini-max and alpha-beta (with its variants) as well as B*(mini-max). As in the previous diagram, the exact nature of the operators in the selection and evaluation sub-

Generate and Test
Task Structure: All new states are terminal states.

Depth-First Search
Task Structure: Only terminal states can be *evaluated* (as either success or no-success).

Simple Hill Climbing
Operator: If the *value* of a task operator's result is *better* than the state it was applied
                           to, make a best-preference for the task operator.
Task Structure: Must be able to *evaluate* all states.

Steepest Ascent Hill Climbing
Operator: If the *value* of a task operator's result is *worse* than result of another task
                           operator's result, make a worse-preference with the first task operator worse
                           than the second.
Task Structure: Must be able to *evaluate* all states.

Means-Ends Analysis
Selection Operator: *compute-difference:* Compute the *differences* between the superstate and the
                           desired state.
Selection Operator: *rank-differences: Rank* the *differences.*
State: If a task operator can *reduce* higher ranked differences than another task
                           operator, make a worse-preference with the second worse than the first.

Figure 3-14: Method increments for selection problem space: Evaluate2.

goals changes when an evaluation has multiple values as in B*, but the subgoal
(and problem space) structure remains the same. Figure 3-16 contains the
method increments for mini-max, the simplest of these methods. Essentially,
mini-max will arise if the problem solver knows how to combine the evaluations
of its opponent, use the evaluation of a state to compare operators, and can
evaluate its terminal states.

The last two diagrams (Figures 3-13 and 3-15) use the two different evaluation subgoals. When implementing tasks that require a subgoal to evaluate task
operators, there is a choice between the two evaluation subgoals discussed earlier. As pointed out at that time, using a separate evaluation problem space
(Evaluate 1) is the most general option and it can be used whenever the other
one is needed. However, the first one (Evaluate 2) is much simpler and is quite
adequate for many evaluations. In the demonstration, each was used when it
was most appropriate.

3.3.3. Analysis of the Weak Methods

Based on the data provided by these weak methods we can briefly analyze
the weak methods. Three areas of interest are: the types of difficulties and
problem spaces that arise in the weak methods; the origin of new weak
methods; and the weak methods that were not covered in our demonstration.

Only a small subset of all *Soar* difficulties arise in this demonstration of the

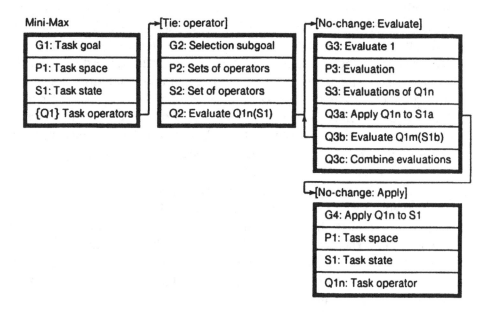

Figure 3-15: Goal-space diagram for Mini-Max*.

Mini-Max Search

Selection Operator:	*combine-evaluations:* Take ***best task-operator value*** that applies to the result, ***invert*** it, and assign it to result.
Operator:	If the result of an operator has a ***worse value*** than another, make a worse-preference for the first operator.
Task Structure:	Terminal states can be evaluate (as in depth-first search).

Figure 3-16: Method increments for selection problem space: Evaluate1.

weak methods. For every method except operator subgoaling, unification, and means-ends analysis, a no-change difficulty arises when an operator is selected because the operator requires a problem space. In operator subgoaling and unification, the only difficulty is also a no-change difficulty with an operator selected; but the selected operator will not apply to the current state, so the subgoal must produce a state that allows the operator to apply. In means-ends analysis, the only difficulty is a tie for the current operator. Ties for the operator slot occur in every weak method except operator subgoaling, unification, constraint satisfaction and hypothesize and match.

In addition to the small number of difficulties, there are only a small number of problem spaces. The selection and evaluation problem spaces show up in many of the methods. A variant of the evaluation problem space shows up in B* where the goal is to either raise a lower bound or lower an upper bound of the evaluation of an operator. The task problem space shows up in subgoals in three different types of subgoals: to create a state that a task operator can apply to, to perform an evaluation of a task operator, to apply a task operator. The only other problem spaces execute complex operators as in constraint satisfaction and hypothesize and match. These latter problem spaces do not give rise to new weak methods, because the knowledge in these subgoals is completely task specific; they implement task operators so there is no general control knowledge that can be factored out. Within these subgoals, we might find weak methods being used to implement the task operators, but the subgoals themselves do not extend the class of weak methods. This surprising lack of a wide variety of problem spaces suggests that problem-space creation may not be as critical as we first thought, at least for the weak methods.

In Figure 3-9 we found a strict hierarchy in the knowledge used by the weak methods. We might have expected to get a tangled hierarchy where certain methods share knowledge from different parts of the tree instead of the strict hierarchy we have shown. Knowledge about different aspects of the task can be added to improve the search and create new methods. In *Soar* this is possible and was done with many of the different types of task knowledge. However, we find that weak methods are named only when they include knowledge about a new aspect of the task, not a new combination of knowledge used in other methods. A good example of this is the combination of means-ends analysis and operator subgoaling.[11] By adding together the method increments for these two methods, *Soar* is able to problem solve better than with either method alone. However, this is not considered a new method (although it is sometimes assumed in the AI literature that means-ends analysis includes operator subgoaling). This suggests that we will find new weak methods by finding new types of task knowledge (see Korf (1983) for a proposed weak method for learning).

Some methods that appeared in the original demonstration of *Soar1* have not been performed with *Soar*, specifically breadth-first search, best-first search, modified best-first search, and A*. It appears that none of these methods can be generated by the addition of a few increments of search-control knowledge. All of these methods appear to require deliberate processing in a state selection space to create and maintain an ordered list of states available. This is because *Soar* has eliminated the infinite accessing assumption of *Soar1*. A review of the weak methods we have implemented shows that a state is selected in one of two ways. First, in a problem space, the new current state is either a descendent or an ancestor of the current state. Second, the current state changes when a subgoal is terminated, and then the new current state is the state that was cur-

---

[11]Both of these methods originated in *GPS* (Newell and Simon, 1963).

rent when the subgoal was created. In both of these cases, these states are available as augmentations of the current context so that search control does not have to scan through all of the available states. However, in breadth-first search, best-first search, modified best-first search and A*, search control must search through all of the visited states of the problem space to determine the next state. Breadth-first continually selects the oldest state, while the others select the best state according to an evaluation function. All of these methods require unlimited access to all states in the stock. One possibility for bringing these into the realm of *Soar* is to add a problem space that can manage and access the states of a task. In the new problem space, operators would search through the states for the best state (which in breadth-first is the oldest state), thereby providing unlimited access to the stock. The problem space would be used when a subgoal is created to select the next state for the task problem space. The search-control knowledge in this space would determine the basis for judging the "best" state. This knowledge, together with operator-selection knowledge (for modified best-first search), should produce the weak methods missing from our demonstration.

3.3.4. Evaluating the Method Increments of Soar

An important aim of our research is that the knowledge encoded in *Soar* is used whenever it is needed to control behavior. One way to evaluate our current encodings is to determine how well they maintain the universal weak method properties of *Soar1*.

For *Soar1*, we considered a number of conditions that must hold for a satisfactory factorization of the total specifications of behavior (S) into two parts, $S_u + S_m$, where S_u is the knowledge common to all methods and S_m is unique to a specific method, M (Laird and Newell, 1983a):

1. The combination of S_m and S_u must produce well-formed methods. (Neither component need be a method in isolation, although either can be.)

2. S_u should specify a nontrivial process; it is easy enough to produce a factorization if little is factored out.

3. S_m and S_u must be combined during problem solving. It must happen easily and quickly, without complex analysis or synthesis; otherwise it will raise issues either of the homunculus or of efficiency.

4. S_m must be extracted from the task environment during problem solving. It must also happen easily and quickly, without complex analysis; otherwise it will raise issues either of the homunculus or of

efficiency.

Given the differences between the *Soar1* and *Soar* architectures (the fixed decision productions acting on preferences and the addition of universal subgoaling
and the selection problem space) we have no guarantee that all of these conditions still hold.

The first three of these conditions are satisfied by the current decomposition
for the *Soar* architecture as we can see from the method increments for the weak
methods we have implemented. Considering the second condition first, S_u is a
valid method on its own that attempts an exhaustive depth-first search of the
problem space. It may be simple, but it is not trivial. It consists of the basic *Soar*
architecture (which includes the logic for creating subgoals), the universal decision productions, the selection problem space and the evaluation problem space.
Method increments (S_m) are not valid methods on their own; however, they
satisfy the first condition because when they are combined with S_u, they
produce well-formed methods as shown by our earlier demonstration. The third
condition is met because all method increments are productions that are combined with S_u by simply adding them to production memory without any further analysis.

The final condition cannot be determined without an explicit theory as to
how the method increments are extracted from the task environment, e.g., until
a learning component is included that automatically extracts the knowledge for
each method increment from the task environment. An important corollary of
this condition is that all the method increments must be dependent on task-
specific information if they are derived from the task, and not task-independent
control information. If we review the method increments of the methods, we
see that *Soar* does not require any control information to be embedded in its
method increments. However, before examining the methods of *Soar*, we will
review *Soar1* and discover that it does not meet this criteria as well as *Soar*.

In *Soar1*, we proposed that the productions of a method increment could be
broken up into two classes: those that created *concepts* about the task, such as
evaluations of a state, and those that converted these concepts into action, such
as the selection of the state with the best evaluation. The first is realized by
elaboration productions and the other by decision productions. Many of the
concepts that were created and then tested embodied the operational demands
of the method, i.e., the knowledge of the task environment that is required to
carry out the method. The decision productions converted the knowledge embodied in those concepts into action by testing concepts and casting votes. By
observing that all of the productions were involved in either the computation or
testing of concepts, we asserted that all method increments do not specify any
control that is not directly related to the task-environment knowledge that

specifies the weak method.

We claimed in *Soar1* that the method increments did not contain control knowledge. However, not every production tested concepts that could be called operational demands. For example, when steepest ascent hill climbing is implemented without subgoaling, the following search-control knowledge is needed.[12]

SAHC1   If the current state is *unevaluated*, compute the *evaluation* of the current state.

SAHC2   If there is a reject-preference for the current state and a descendent has an *evaluation* that is *worse* than another descendent, make a worse-preference with the first descendent worse than the second.

SAHC3   If there is not a reject-preference for the *ancestor*, make a worse-preference with current state worse than the *ancestor* state.

SAHC4   If there is not a reject-preference for the current state and there is a reject-preference for the *ancestor* state, make an acceptable-preference for the current state.

The first production (SAHC1) computes an evaluation, one of the operational demands of the method. The second (SAHC2) embodies both the knowledge that a comparison of the evaluation of states can be used to select operators, and the method for comparing the evaluations. The other two productions (SAHC3 and SAHC4) test the concepts of ancestor state, worse-preference and reject-preference, but none of these embody any concept relating to the task.

In *Soar*, only elaboration productions appear in the method increments because the preferences restrict the decision productions to a fixed set. Instead of decision productions producing action from the concepts, we have elaboration productions producing preferences. However, the individual productions are still devoid of control knowledge and always either create or test task-specific concepts.

The following search-control knowledge is what must be available in *Soar* to achieve the same steepest ascent hill climbing method.

SAHC1'   If the current state is *unevaluated*, compute the *evaluation* of the current state.

SAHC2'   If the *evaluation* of a task operator's result is *worse* than that of another task operator, make a worse-preference with the first task operator worse than the second.

Neither of these productions test any non-task-specific concepts. The test for an *unevaluated* state, an *evaluation* of a state and whether a state is *worse* than another. Therefore, when steepest ascent hill climbing arises in the universal subgoaling version, only the search-control knowledge that is specific to the task

---

[12]In the original *Soar1*, there was no preference scheme, and most of the productions that implemented a method were decision productions. For this analysis they have been translated into the *Soar* style.

is required. The rest of the method arises from universal subgoaling, the selection and evaluation problem spaces, and search-control knowledge that is specific to the problem spaces (see Figures 2-19 and 2-20). This is true of all of the methods that were originally implemented in *Soar1* and have been re-implemented in *Soar*.[13] In steepest ascent hill climbing, the operational demands are the ability to compare two states and select the best. The knowledge that is eliminated, contained in productions **SAHC3** and **SAHC4**, does not test any concept unique to the task, only concepts common to all tasks, such as ancestor state. These productions are control knowledge devoid of context.

The difference in knowledge is even more dramatic for depth-first search, where the following productions were required in *Soar1:*

DFS1   If the current state does not have a reject-preference, make an acceptable-preference for it.

DFS2   If the current state does have reject-preference, make an acceptable-preference for its ancestor at the state slot.

Within *Soar*, no additional search-control knowledge is required to perform depth-first search. Depth-first search emerges from subgoals created to select the next operator. In the preference subgoal each task operator is evaluated, which is performed in the evaluation problem space. This leads back to the task problem space where the task operator is applied to the original task state, producing a new state that becomes the current state. If this state cannot be evaluated, search control will attempt to select an operator to apply, hoping to gather information. This leads to a tie, and we get the recursive subgoaling that is typical of depth-first search.

3.3.5. Conclusion of Weak Method Demonstration

With the original *Soar1* and universal weak method we were able to implement a set of weak methods, but clearly not all. With the addition of universal subgoaling, we extended the set. The encoding of knowledge allows the knowledge to apply whenever it is relevant, even if search is required. The structure we found in the weak methods demonstrates the additive nature of knowledge in *Soar*. As more knowledge about a task is added, the behavior of *Soar* changes and new weak methods arise. This supports our earlier suggestion (Laird and Newell, 1983a) that the weak methods are not pre-packaged

---

[13]In depth-bounded mini-max, the concept of depth is used. However, it is created and maintained by operators instead of by search-control.

methods, but that they arise from the task knowledge, the structure of the task, and the architecture (with universal subgoaling being a critical component).

4 DISCUSSION

Given the *Soar* architecture and the empirical demonstration of the previous chapter, we are in a position to evaluate the work and its impact. In this chapter we combine the investigation of some unresolved issues with an evaluation and discussion of the impact of universal subgoaling on five general topics: goals, memory management, the preference scheme, production systems, and future work to be performed in this area.

4.1. Goals

A universal subgoaling scheme should be able to detect all problem-solving difficulties and create subgoals to remove them. Figure 3-7 showed that our implementation within *Soar* is unable to detect two of eleven difficulties. In this section we discuss these shortcomings. We also examine how well *Soar* supports more complex goal manipulations than have been demonstrated so far.

4.1.1. The Issue of Subgoal Termination

Soar is unable to detect the two search-control failures that arise from deciding to *terminate* the current goal, either because of success or failure. We propose that this inability arises not from a shortcoming in the architecture, but because the ability to detect this failure conflicts with another important design criteria of a general problem solver.

In *Soar*, the detection of goal termination is usually based on a recognition that a current state is the desired state of the goal. One of the advantages of a production-system architecture is its reactive nature. If a test of a goal can be embedded within the conditions of a single production, the production-system architecture is performing the test on every cycle. The agent does not have to explicitly consider whether the current state satisfies the current goal. Instead, the agent will recognize a solution when it arises. As a result, goal testing is not part of a functional framework of *Soar* and this precludes the ability to detect a difficulty in performing the goal test.

Soar can create subgoals for the failures of the other search-control functions because the functional framework defines a normal mode of processing that will lead to a goal, and *Soar* can detect if this normal mode is interrupted by a change in its global state. *Soar* defines a functional framework within which each of these functions must be performed to make progress in the problem space. When one of these search-control functions is performed, the global state of *Soar* is changed, either by a change in the current context (for selection functions), or by the creation of a new state (for application of an operator).

Testing for the termination of a goal in not part of this scenario in *Soar* because of our desire to avoid a fixed scheme for testing goal termination. Testing for the termination of a goal does not have to be performed to make progress in problem solving. There is no fixed point in the functional framework for testing the termination of a goal. Usually, termination will be tested when a new state is achieved. But sometimes a goal may be terminated without ever creating an initial state. Also, long stretches of states can occur during which it is known that the goal cannot be achieved (even though progress is begin made); goal testing during these stretches is then redundant.

Even if the test for goal termination were a part of the functional framework, the architecture must be able to discriminate between a failure to perform the test and a test for termination where the result is that there should be no termination at this time. When a test is attempted there arc three possible outcomes: the test is performed and the goal is terminated, the test is performed and the goal is not terminated, the test fails to perform. In the last two cases, the global state of *Soar* is unchanged. This makes it impossible to differentiate between a test that failed and the inability to test.

To solve this problem, special components could be added to each state that indicate if goal termination has been tested. At a specific point during problem solving, possibly just before the state votes are counted, the architecture could test those components to determine if the test was made, and if not, create a subgoal. However, the system must be able to represent any type of goal, and some goals may require testing for conditions dependent on objects other than the current state. Therefore, the determination of goal termination can occur at any point during problem solving. For example, as soon as the goal becomes the current goal, sufficient information may become available through elaboration to immediately determine that the goal should be abandoned. In other cases, success or failure may be detected when the current state has a specific attribute, or after a specific operator has been applied to the current state.

Therefore, goals would have to be tested at every step in the processing structure of *Soar*, eliminating the reactive nature of the architecture.

The conclusion of this discussion is that these two design criteria conflict in a general problem solver, such as *Soar*. We must investigate if both of them are necessary. It may be possible that the goal can be tested at every step of problem solving, or that the test for goals are created in such a way that they never fail. These possibilities require further research.

4.1.2. Complex Goal Manipulation

In the current description of *Soar*, the goals are selected depth-first; always selecting either a subgoal or supergoal of the current goal. Many problems require more complex goal manipulation.

When there is a tie for goal selection in *Soar*, a subgoal is created to select the goal. This subgoal allows the system to deliberately consider the goals it has available and select from them. Within this subgoal, the goals can be rated and the best goal can be selected. A demonstration of this was implemented for the Blocks World where two subgoals are compared and a preference is created. Upon returning to the situation that caused the tie, the better goal is selected. This is similar to the meta-planning (Wilensky, 1981) and the agenda mechanisms (Lenat, 1982) of current AI problem solvers. One advantage of the *Soar* scheme is that the tie between a set of goals is just a problem like any other, and it does not require any special mechanisms in the architecture. Since it is a goal, no fixed solution is wired in that is used every time a selection between goals has to be made. Instead, the system can devote all of its problem-solving abilities to the selection of a goal.

Within a subgoal to select a goal, very complex problem spaces can be selected with states that embed the structure of the goal hierarchy. Operators in the problem space can move up and down the goal hierarchy, gathering evaluations of goals. There may also be operators that move across the goal hierarchy by traveling between goals that share common substructure or preferences. By extending this problem space to include operators that can add, delete, or rearrange goals in the hierarchy the problem solving, commonly called *planning*, can be implemented. This is exemplified by Sacerdoti's *NOAH* program (Sacerdoti, 1977). Within *Soar* this would not be a separate type of problem solving, just a special problem space. Although, this type of goal manipulation has not been implemented, *Soar* seems well suited to it.

A second type of planning, often called abstraction planning, was first described in *Planning GPS* (Newell and Simon, 1972) and *Abstrips* (Sacerdoti, 1974). In these systems, planning occurs by solving an abstract problem in a problem space with abstract operators, and then using the solution path to the abstract problem as search control within the original problem space. One approach to this type of planning is to create new problem spaces that are abstractions of the original. Within *Soar* we have not yet investigated how to create new problem spaces so it is unclear how easy this would be to implement. However, another approach is available if the operators of the original problem space are implemented in subgoals.[14] Instead of creating new problem spaces, the original problem space would be used, but when an operator is to be applied in a subgoal, the subgoal only performs an abstraction of it. A complete solution could be created this way and then the history of operator application could be used as a plan to solve the problem in the original problem space.

4.2. Memory Management

We have assumed an unlimited memory capacity for the stock in *Soar*, primarily to simplify the investigation. We cannot live with this assumption if we are going to tackle substantial problems, because the stock continues to grow during problem solving. This shows up in *Soar1* by the working memory of the production system growing larger and larger. Unfortunately, the speed of a production system is dependent on the size of its working memory, executing more slowly as working memory grows larger (Forgy, 1979). If we are to have an efficient problem solver, we must find a way to limit the size of working memory. There are two possibilities in *Soar*. We can either include the management of the stock as a search control function and add productions that deliberately remove data from the stock or we can embed a fixed memory management strategy in architecture.

4.2.1. Stock Management by Productions

In *Soar*, elaboration productions can only add new augmentations to objects in the current context. All objects are completely defined by their augmentations, so the only memory to manage is the augmentations. In *Soar*, a new class of productions (called *remove* productions) could manage memory by removing augmentations that are no longer needed. The remove productions could fire in parallel with the elaboration productions, but must be restricted to removing augmentations that do not elaborate objects in the current context.

---

[14]This approach was first suggested by Allen Newell (Newell, 1964).

Without this restriction, infinite loops would develop when an elaboration production is adding a given augmentation to the current context and a remove production constantly removes it. Moreover, the goal hierarchy is represented as a series of augmentations of the current goal and its supergoal; hence, not all augmentations of non-current objects can be removed or the system will lose track of the progress it has made on unfinished goals. As problem solving continues, the number of goals can become unbounded, so remove productions cannot be a complete solution to the problem.

Even though we must look elsewhere for a complete solution, remove productions allow us to demonstrate that for complex subgoaling schemes, we can maintain a fixed size for working memory. Taking the productions for Tic-Tac-Toe with the progressive deepening version of B*, we added twelve remove productions (actually defined as elaboration productions) that removed augmentations of objects from completed subgoals and previously examined states. Figure 4-1 shows the results in terms of the number of production cycles per second and number of production actions per second. When the remove productions are not used, the production system runs slower and slower because the working memory is growing larger and larger. Conversely, the addition of the remove productions keeps the production system running at a constant rate because the working memory is kept at a constant size. The addition of remove productions increases the number of actions per cycle required to perform the same amount of search because the remove productions fire in parallel with other elaboration productions. The most meaningful measure is the number of cycles per second because this reflects the amount of search being performed.

| | Original B* | | With Remove Productions | |
cycles	cycles/sec	actions/sec	cycles/sec	actions/sec
100	3.0	10.6	2.7	12.9
200	1.6	5.3	2.4	11.6
300	1.1	3.5	2.4	11.9
400			2.6	12.4

Figure 4-1: Effect of adding remove productions to *Soar*.

This demonstration shows that problem solving in *Soar* is not strongly dependent on the infinite memory assumption.

4.2.2. Memory Management by the Architecture

Even with remove productions, working memory can gradually grow arbitrarily large with data from suspended goals. An alternative strategy is to save the information in search control as elaboration productions. For instance, the working memory of the production systems could be restricted to the current context and their augmentations. Whenever the context changes, the architecture could automatically delete all augmentations that do not involve current objects. At the same time, the architecture could build elaboration productions that would reconstruct those augmentations when the appropriate context is re-established. The goal hierarchy is then saved in production memory instead of working memory. Of course, this is only an advantage if increasing production memory does not markedly increase the time it takes to determine the conflict set. Current work in production system architectures (Gupta and Forgy, 1983; Forgy, 1979) suggests that the execution speed of a production system can be independent of the number of productions, while no such possibility is seen for the size of working memory. This suggestion for maintaining a fixed size working memory has not been implemented and requires further research.

4.3. Preferences

In *Soar*, a fixed set of decision productions with the associated preference scheme replaces the decision productions in *Soar1*. The preference scheme has been presented as one of the basic components of *Soar* without any justification. In this section we examine the reasons for the preference scheme and one problem with it.

4.3.1. Justification for Preferences

The preference scheme we are using has the obvious advantage that it allows search control to reason about a declarative representation of the information that will cause changes in the current context. With the addition of universal subgoaling, a preference scheme is important for two other reasons. First, preferences provide the communication medium between a problem space where a difficulty arises and the subgoal created to solve the difficulty. Second, the preference scheme provides a decision scheme whose difficulties correspond to the failures of search control.

With the introduction of universal subgoaling, *Soar* must be able to transmit information between a goal and its subgoals. In typical programs this is done with a fixed set of parameters and results. *Soar* passes information by augmenting the objects involved, such as the subgoal when it is created. Preferences play a crucial role in this scheme, first by providing a representation of the information that leads to the difficulty, and second because the creation of a preference in a subgoal can be its result. Without preferences, the information responsible for the difficulty is not available because it is encoded in the conditions of decision productions, so that subgoals are unable to reason about why a difficulty arose. In *Soar*, the preferences that lead to a difficulty are available in the subgoal. In addition, preferences are required for passing back results. Without preferences, a tie-subgoal is unable to make augmentations that would modify the votes for objects so the tie would be broken when the original context is re-established. Since the conditions of the decision productions are unavailable, it is impossible for the subgoal to produce a result that it could guarantee was correctly interpreted. In *Soar*, the preferences are the only data structure that the decision productions are sensitive to, so that a preference created in the subgoal will directly affect the selection of objects in the original goal.

The second advantage of the preference scheme is that the difficulties that arise in the voting scheme correspond to the failures of search control when a decision is inconclusive. Without a preference scheme, there is no guarantee that a tie in the voting corresponds to a failure. In *Soar1*, a tie could arise even if one object was better than another by having an additional decision production that voted many times for the worse object. With the preference scheme of *Soar*, a tie will occur whenever there is not a clear preference (which is when search control is unable to make the decision), and a tie will not occur whenever there is a clear preference (the decision can be made by search control, and a subgoal would be of no help).

4.3.2. Conflicting Preferences

In *Soar*, the search-control knowledge is assumed to be internally consistent. We have been concerned with the knowledge-lean end of the problem-solving spectrum, where any knowledge the system has should be available in making search control decision. However, in a system that has large amounts of heuristic search-control knowledge it is possible that some of it conflicts. This would show up in *Soar* as conflicts in the preferences for selecting objects for the current context, specifically as conflicting worse-preferences.

As the preference scheme is currently implemented, it is possible for one object to be a worse choice than another while at the same time the second is a worse choice than the first. In *Soar*, both objects will receive a vote-against and will not win. However, both preferences cannot be correct, and one should be nullified. Although it is currently not implemented, the *Soar* architecture could detect these conflicts and create subgoals to deal with them. However, there appears to be only one option available in *Soar* to break the conflict and that involves rejecting one of the objects under consideration. Adding a reject-preference breaks the conflicts because worse-preference for the non-rejected object will be ignored (all worse-preferences are ignored if the object in the compared slot receives a reject). This method of breaking the conflict relies on rejecting an object when it would seem more appropriate to eliminate one of the preferences. Once an object is rejected, it can never become current in the current context, even if the other object is later rejected. This is an area for future work in *Soar*.

4.4. Production Systems

In addition to being a problem-space architecture, *Soar* is a production-system architecture. In this section we examine the impact of universal subgoaling and problem spaces on production systems. Problem spaces and universal subgoaling have affected the design of the underlying architecture in two areas: the structure of working memory and the conflict resolution strategy.

4.4.1. Conflict Resolution

Most production-system architectures compare the conditions of productions to the contents of working memory and determine the set of *production instantiations* (the matches of working memory to individual productions) that are satisfied. This set is called the *conflict set* and *conflict resolution* is the process of selecting a subset (usually one) of these productions to fire. The rationale for selecting only a subset is that the actions of different productions may conflict, leaving working memory in either an indeterminate state or with conflicting data. Conflict resolution is performed by a fixed mechanism that tests features such as the recency of working memory elements. In *Soar*, we want all of the available knowledge to apply on each cycle. Since elaborations are monotonic, the actions of the productions can not conflict. When there is a selection, as in the selection of an operator or state, it is not made by a fixed procedure like conflict resolution, but by all available search control as implemented in productions. When the recognition power of the productions is too weak, universal subgoaling allows the selection to become a problem itself. This leads us to abandon conflict resolution for our production system architecture, except to inhibit the firing of productions whose results already exist in working memory.

4.4.2. Working Memory Representation

Soar is a modified version of the *Ops5* production system language. *Soar* uses the *Ops5* working memory elements to represent the augmentations that make up its memory. Each *Ops5* working memory element consists of a set of attribute-value pairs. The general *Ops5* philosophy is that each working memory element is a separate object with the values of the attributes defining all of its properties. The obvious implementation for *Soar* objects is a separate working memory element for each object. This and other object-centered implementations fail, because an object in *Soar* is defined by the roles it plays in augmentations, which cannot be represented by simple attribute-values. For example, in means-ends analysis, the current state is compared to the desired state and if they are not equal, a difference is created. This difference cannot be placed as an attribute of the state or goal object description because the state might have be compared to many different goals and a goal will surely be compared to many different states. Instead, the difference must be an augmentation of both of the state and the goal. Hence, in *Ops5* it must be represented as a separate working memory element.

4.5. Future Work

Our *Soar* implementation of universal subgoaling suggests future research in a number of areas.

1. For *Soar* to be a complete architecture, we must eliminate the infinite memory assumption by incorporating a memory management scheme.
2. We have demonstrated the *Soar* architecture with universal subgoaling for many weak methods and a set of relatively simple tasks. These tasks are excellent for developing and testing untried theories of problem solving, but we should also test the architecture on tasks with other properties, that is, tasks that are from different parts of the space of tasks. Some tasks may require large amounts of knowledge and corresponding complex methods.
3. Several specific problem spaces should be investigated to determine how well they can be represented in *Soar*. For example, a planning

space that includes goal hierarchies as states in a problem space should be possible within *Soar*. An analogy or problem reformulation problem space could be implemented to make contact with one of the other areas of research in AI.

4. We have not explored the relationship between universal subgoaling and deliberate subgoals. We do not understand the origin of deliberate subgoals nor the origin of the search-control knowledge necessary to determine the termination of a goal. Recent experiments with *Soar* suggest that our universal subgoaling scheme may make deliberate subgoals unnecessary (Laird & Newell, 1984; Rosenbloom, Laird, McDermott & Newell, 1984).

5. We do not understand the origin of problem spaces. They may be constructed explicitly by special problem spaces, or new problem spaces may evolve from old problem spaces through some automatic learning mechanism. Both of these options should be explored.

6. As should be obvious from the previous point, a learning component needs to be added to *Soar*. The *Soar* architecture should be well suited to learning. Individual pieces of knowledge do not have to be integrated into a complex control structure. Given the universal weak method, new knowledge helps constrain the search without complex analysis or synthesis. One type of learning that seems well suited to the *Soar* architecture in "chunking", where the processing in subgoals is "chunked" into productions so that in the future the answer is known directly without problem solving in the subgoal (Rosenbloom & Newell, 1983). Originally a problem solver will use universal subgoaling to deal with difficulties that arise, but as learning progresses, the difficulties are avoided by the use of learned search-control knowledge. This approach has lead to some encouraging results described in Part III.

7. Finally, we can consider designing a production system architecture to service *Soar*. Currently, *Soar* is grafted on top of *Ops5*. This has worked well as an experimental vehicle, but the differences between *Soar* and *Ops5* seem significant enough that a specially designed architecture could simplify the representation of productions and working memory in *Soar* and greatly increase the efficiency of *Soar*.

5 CONCLUSION

The immediate goal of this research has been to construct a problem-solving architecture that implements universal subgoaling so that rational problem solving is possible. This has been successful to a large extent and in this chapter we summarize the work and review the original hypotheses that were the basis of this work.

The long-term goal of our research is to develop an architecture for a generally intelligent problem solver. We chose problem spaces as the basic organizational framework of the problem-solving architecture. In previous work, we implemented a universal weak method that provides the ability to perform as any weak method (Laird & Newell, 1983b). In this work we have concentrated on another aspect of problem solving that we considered critical to a general problem solver: universal subgoaling. Universal subgoaling is the ability of a problem solver to treat any difficulty that arises during problem solving as a problem in itself. The problem solver is able to bring its full problem-solving ability to bear to alleviate these difficulties. The problem solver never has to rely on fixed bodies of code that are unresponsive to changes in the environment or the problem solver's knowledge of the environment. All of its knowledge is brought to bear when necessary.

Universal subgoaling allows a system to reason about its own decisions when it is unable to make them directly. Universal subgoaling requires a closed set of difficulties that can arise during problem solving. We have shown that our problem-space architecture, *Soar*, defines such a set. These difficulties are produced by failures of the decision phase, and they are universal because they are common to all tasks and cover the failures of search control. Given this set of difficulties, *Soar* produces new goals that can be selected for problem solving. We have demonstrated that *Soar* produces these goals under the appropriate circumstances and that the mechanisms for initiating and terminating these goals work correctly. We concluded our demonstration of universal subgoaling by showing that the searches that naturally emerge from subgoaling correspond to a broad class of the weak methods. Our universal subgoaling scheme extends the range of the universal weak method to include methods that require subgoaling. It also simplifies the search-control knowledge that is required for many weak methods by substituting reactive subgoals for control knowledge.

This research has required the integration of five basic hypotheses: (1) problem spaces are the fundamental organizational unit of all goal-directed behavior; (2) production systems are the underlying architecture of cognition; (3) universal subgoaling is a fundamental functional capability of intelligent systems; (4) the weak methods form the basic methods of all intelligent systems; and (5) a single organization (a universal weak method) can give rise to all weak methods. The ability to implement a single system integrating these five ideas provides support for each one individually and as a group. Without problem spaces as the basic organizational unit of all problem solving, we would be unable construct the *Soar* architecture with the small set of search-control functions from which all action must result. The *Soar* architecture, with its preference scheme, provides the small set of difficulties that span all the failures of search control, thereby providing the basis of universal subgoaling. Universal subgoaling and the preference problem space contribute to the generality of the universal weak method. As we showed, the weak methods emerge from the integration of universal subgoaling and problem-space search. When difficulties arise, a subgoal is created to handle them, often resulting in other subgoals that make investigations into the original problem space, producing the characteristic behavior of the weak methods. The weak methods differ only in specific knowledge about the task, such as evaluations of a state. The underlying representation of search control as productions provides the necessary modularity of knowledge that is essential for a representation of weak methods as increments to search control. The recognition character of the productions provides the direct computation needed by search control to perform its duties efficiently, and together with the preference scheme, defines the limits of search-control abilities.

As a separate confirmation of our hypotheses, the resulting structure of the weak methods, based on small increments of knowledge, suggests that the weak methods emerge from the structure of the task, and not as separate, monolithic methods. If this is true, and our demonstration strongly suggests that it is, this provides support for the weak methods as the basic methods of intelligent systems. As more knowledge is added, more specialized methods arise, but the weak methods are always available when there is little knowledge of the task. This success with representing the weak methods supports the concept of universal subgoaling, showing that it plays an important role in the basic methods of intelligent systems.

ACKNOWLEDGMENT

Part I of this book is a reproduction of my Ph.D. thesis in the Department of Computer Science at Carnegie-Mellon University. It is appropriate to acknowledge those people that made my thesis possible.

First and foremost I would like to thank Allen Newell. Through the years he has spent many hours discussing my work with me and reading drafts of my papers. Needless to say, much of this work owes it origins to his ideas. He had the foresight to conceive of the possibility of a universal weak method and universal subgoaling. In addition, he has been both an advisor and a friend. It has been a joy to work with him during my years at Carnegie-Mellon.

I would like to thank my thesis committee: Jaime Carbonell, Jill Larkin, and John McDermott. Each member has helped me improve my thesis by providing important insights and helpful suggestions. I'd also like to thank Paul Rosenbloom for his friendship and our many discussions of my research over the years.

Finally, I'd like to acknowledge the continued support and love of my wife and my family.

GLOSSARY

This section defines the terms used throughout this part of the book.

Augmentation.   An augmentation is a many-valued relation between sets of objects in the stock. For example, a goal, a problem space and a state may partake in an augmentation that signifies that the state is the initial state of the goal given the problem space.

Current Context.   The current context contains one slot for each type of object involved in search: goals, problem spaces, states and operators. The object occupying the goal slot is the current goal; the object occupying the problem space slot is the current problem space slot is the current problem space; and so on.

Decision Phase.   The decision phase is one part of the Elaboration-Decision Cycle. It determines which object (goal, problem space, state, operator) is to become current, replacing an existing object in the context. In *Soar*, the decision phase is implemented by a set of productions that translate preferences into votes. The object receiving the most votes for a slot becomes the new current object for that slot. The same decision productions are used for all subgoals and all problem spaces.

Deliberate Subgoal.   A deliberate subgoal is a subgoal that is created by search control. The system knows (has the search-control knowledge) that a goal should be created at a given point in problem solving.

97

Desired State.

When a goal is attempted within a problem space, the set of the states in the problem space that achieve the goal are called desired states. These states may be represented explicitly in the stock, or search-control may have the knowledge to recognize them directly.

Difficulty.

Within this paper, we restrict the definition of difficulty to be a subset of what is commonly considered a difficulty. Therefore, a difficulty (as defined in this paper) is the inability to carry out the basic steps of problem solving. When the system tries to perform the functions of search control and fails, this is a difficulty. However, if the system performs a search control function that leads it away from a goal, this is not a difficulty (as defined in this paper).

Elaboration Phase.

The elaboration phase is the part of the Elaboration-Decision Cycle that augments objects in the stock. In *Soar* it is implemented by productions that fire in parallel until quiescence. The elaboration productions contain all of the system's knowledge about a task (the operators) and its search-control knowledge.

Goal.

A goal represents the intention to attain some object or state of affairs. A goal does not state what behavior is to be used to attain the desired situation. In *Soar*, a goal's semantics are determined by its augmentations. These may include a desired state for a given problem space.

Method.

A method is a specification of behavior to obtain a goal for a problem solver. In typical AI systems, a method consists of statements from standard programming languages with subgoals added to extend the generality of the method. In *Soar*, methods are realized by collections of elaboration productions in one or more problem spaces.

Method Increment.

A method increment is a piece of knowledge for a method about the task being attempted, but no control knowledge. When a method increment is added to the current search-control knowledge of a problem solver, the behavior of the problem solver should change to reflect the new knowledge.

Object.   There are four types of objects in *Soar*: goals, problem-space, states and operators. An object is a symbol. Its semantics are determined solely by its augmentations.

Operational Demand.   The operational demands of a method are the aspects of a task that must be available for the method to be executed (but not necessary for it to succeed or to be efficient). For example, to carry out hill climbing it must be possible to compare two states to determine which is higher on the evaluation function.

Operator.   The operators of a problem space create a new state when applied to an existing state. Since the states do not pre-exist in the problem solver, operators must be used to generate them. A specific operator may not apply to every state in the problem space. Operators are implemented in *Soar* by elaboration productions or by search in another problem space in a subgoal.

Preference.   A preference is a special type of augmentation that represents information about the appropriateness of an object for a slot in the current context.

Problem Space.   A problem space consists of a set of states and operators. The states of the problem space do not pre-exist, but must be generated by applying operators to other states. A problem in a problem space is an initial state and a set of desired states defined by the goal.

Search Control.   Search control is the process of using knowledge to intelligently perform the functions of search in a problem space. In *Soar*, search-control knowledge is encoded as elaboration productions.

State.   A state of a problem space is a symbolic expression that represents one possible situation in a problem space.

Stock.   The stock is the declarative memory of *Soar* that includes the current context, objects and augmentations.

Subgoal.   A subgoal is a goal that is created while attempting to solve another goal. The subgoal is created either by search-control knowledge (deliberate) or by the architecture.

Universal Subgoaling. Universal subgoaling is the ability of a problem solver to create subgoals whenever difficulties arise that prevent further problem solving progress.

Universal Weak Method. A universal weak method is an organization of a problem solver so that the weak methods emerge from the knowledge the problem solver has of the task instead of through analysis or explicit selection. As knowledge about a task is acquired by the problem solver, its behavior will change so that it corresponds to a different method.

Weak Method.   A weak method is a method that makes limited operational demands and provides a schema for using knowledge about a task.

REFERENCES

Berliner, H. The B* tree search algotithm: a best-first proof procedure. *Artifical Intelligence*, 1979, *12*, 23-40.

Davis, R. Meta-rules: Reasoning about control. *Artificial Intelligence*, 1980, *15*, 179-222.

Doyle, J. *A Model for Deliberation, Action, and Introspection.* Doctoral dissertation, Massachusetts Institute of Technology, May 1980.

Fikes, R. E. and N. J. Nilsson. STRIPS: A new approach to the application of theorem proving to problem solving. *Artificial Intelligence*, 1971, *2*, 189-208.

Forgy, C. L. *On the Efficient Implementation of Production Systems.* Doctoral dissertation, Computer Science Department, Carnegie-Mellon University, 1979.

Forgy, C. L. *OPS5 Manual.* Computer Science Department, Carnegie-Mellon University, 1981.

Forgy, C. L. Rete: A fast algorithm for the many pattern/many object pattern match problem. *Artificial Intelligence*, 1982, *19*, 17-37.

Genesereth, M. An overview of meta-level architecture. In *Proceedings of the Third Annual National Conference on Artificial Intelligence.* AAAI, 1983.

Gupta, A. and Forgy, C. *Measurements on Production Systems* (Tech. Rep.). Computer Science Department, Carnegie-Mellon University, December 1983.

Hayes, P. J. In defence of logic. In *Proceedings of IJCAI-77.* IJCAI, 1977.

Hayes, J. R. and Simon, H. A. Understanding complex task instructions. In Klahr, D. (Ed.), *Cognition and Instruction.* Hillsdale, NJ: Erlbaum, 1976.

Hewitt, C. *Description and Theoretical Analysis (using Schemata) of PLAN-NER: A language for proving theorems and manipulating models in a robot.* Doctoral dissertation, MIT, 1971.

Korf, R. E. *Learning to Solve Problems by Searching for Macro-Operators.*

Doctoral dissertation, Carnegie-Mellon University, July 1983.

Laird, J. E. *The SOAR2 User's Manual.* Computer Science Department, Carnegie-Mellon University, 1984.

Laird, J. E., and Newell, A. *Universal Subgoaling: Summary of Results* (Tech. Rep.). Department of Computer Science, Carnegie-Mellon University, 1984.

Laird, J. E. and Newell, A. *A Universal Weak Method* (Tech. Rep.). Computer Science Department, Carnegie-Mellon University, 1983.

Laird, J. E. and Newell, A. A universal weak method: Summary of results. In *Proceedings of IJCAI-83.* Los Altos, CA: Kaufmann, 1983.

Lenat, D. B. Heuretics: The theoretical and experimental study of heuristic rules. In *Proceedings of the National Conference on Artificial Intelligence.* Kaufmann, 1982.

Lenat, D. B. Eurisko: A program that learns new heuristics and domain concepts. *Artificial Intelligence,* 1983, *21,* 61-98.

McCarthy, J. Programs with common sense. In Minsky, M. (Ed.), *Semantic Information Processing.* Cambridge, MA: MIT Press, 1968.

McDermott, D. Planning and Acting. *Cognitive Science,* 1978, *2,* 71-109.

Newell, A. The possibility of planning languages in man-computer communication. In *Communication Processes.* New York: Pergamon Press, 1964.

Newell, A. Heuristic programming: Ill-structured problems. In Aronofsky, J. (Ed.), *Progress in Operations Research, III.* New York: Wiley, 1969.

Newell, A. Production Systems: Models of Control Structures. In Chase, W. (Ed.), *Visual Information Processing.* New York: Academic, 1973.

Newell, A. Reasoning, problem solving and decision processes: The problem space as a fundamental category. In R. Nickerson (Ed.), *Attention and Performance VIII.* Hillsdale, NJ: Erlbaum, 1980.

Newell, A. The knolwedge level. *Artificial Intelligence,* 1982, *18,* 87-127.

Newell, A. and Simon, H. A. GPS, A program that simulates human thought. In Feigenbaum, E.A. and J. Feldman (Ed.), *Computers and Thought.* New York: McGraw-Hill, 1963.

Newell, A. and Simon, H. A. *Human Problem Solving.* New Jersey: Prentice Hall, 1972.

Nilsson, N. *Problem-solving Methods in Artificial Intelligence.* New York: McGraw-Hill, 1971.

Nilsson, N. *Principles of Artificial Intelligence.* Palo Alto, CA: Tioga, 1980.

Rich, E. *Artificial Intelligence.* New York: McGraw-Hill, 1983.

Rosenbloom, P. S., and Newell, A. The chunking of goal hierarchies: A generalized model of practice. In R. S. Michalski, J. G. Carbonell, & T. M. Mitchell (Eds.), *Proceedings of the 1983 Machine Learning Workshop.* , 1983.

Rosenbloom, P. S., Laird, J. E., McDermott, J., Newell, A., Orciuch, E. *R1-SOAR: An Experiment in Knowledge-Intensive Programming in a Problem-Solving Architecture* (Tech. Rep.). Department of Computer Science, Carnegie-Mellon University, 1984.

Sacerdoti, E. D. Planning in a hierarchy of abstraction spaces. *Artificial Intelligence*, 1974, *5*, 115-135.

Sacerdoti, E.D. The Nonlinear Nature of Plans. In *Proceedings of IJCAI-75*. IJCAI, 1975.

Sacerdoti, E. D. *A Structure for Plans and Behavior*. New York: Elsevier, 1977.

Simon, H. A. *The Sciences of the Artificial*. Cambridge, MA: MIT Press, 1969.

Simon, H. A. Search and reasoning in problem sovling. *Artificial Intelligence*, 1983, *21*, 7-30.

Smith, B. C. *Reflection and Semantics in a Procedural Language* (Tech. Rep.). MIT/LCS/TR-272, Laboratory for Computer Science, MIT, 1982.

Stefik, M. J. *Planning with Constraints*. Doctoral dissertation, Stanford University, Computer Science Department, 1979.

Waltz, D. Understanding line drawings of scenes with shadows. In Winston, P. H. (Ed.), *The Psychology of Computer Vision*. New York: McGraw-Hill, 1975.

Waterman, D. A. and Hayes-Roth, F., (Eds.). *Pattern Directed Inference Systems*. New York: Academic Press, 1978.

Weyhrauch, R. W. Prolegomena to a theory of mechanized formal reasoning. *Artifical Intelligence*, 1980, *13*, 144-170.

Wilensky, R. Meta-planning: representing and using knowledge about planning in problem solving and natural language understanding. *Cognitive Science*, 1981, *5*, 197-233.

Wilensky, R. *Planning and Understanding: A Computational Approach to Human Reasoning*. Reading, MA: Addison-Wesley, 1983.

APPENDIX **A.**
UNIVERSAL WEAK METHOD

A.1. Conventions for all Search Control Descriptions

There are a few type-font conventions that are maintained in all the search-control descriptions in the appendices. All words in **bold-face** are names of either objects (such as the name of a goal, problem space or operator) or fixed symbols that are always available in *Soar* (such as **break-ties**). All words in ***bold-italics*** are task concepts that are specific to the task. These embody the operational demands of a method. For the selection and evaluation problem spaces, some of the operators and search-control knowledge are followed by [TS]. This signifies that *task specific* concepts are being used and that operators or search control must be instantiated for a specific task. In a few methods, two subgoals are quite similar. In these cases, only one subgoal is described in detail.

A.2. Universal Decision and Elaboration Productions

D1:   If an object has an acceptable-preference for a slot given the current context, vote for the object for that slot.

D2:   If an object has a best-preference for a slot given the current context, vote-in the object for that slot.

D3:   If an object has a reject-preference for the goal slot, veto the object for the goal slot.

D4:   If an object has a reject-preference for the state slot given the current goal and problem space, veto the object for the state slot.

D5:   If an object has a reject-preference for the problem space or operator slot given the current context, veto the object for that slot.

D6:   If an object has a worse-preference for the goal slot given the current context, and the better object does not have a reject-preference, vote against the worse object for the goal slot.

D7:   If an object has a worse-preference for the problem space, state, or operator slot given the current context, and the better object does not have a reject-preference given the current goal and problem space, vote against the worse object for the state slot.

D8:   If the current goal has a reject-preference, vote-in the goal, problem space and operator that were current when the current goal was created.

D9:   If the current goal has a reject-preference, and the current problem space differs from the superproblem space vote-in the state that was current when the current goal was created.

D10:   If the current goal has a reject-preference, and the current problem space is the same as the superproblem space vote-in the current state.

E1:   If there is a **vetoed-problem-space** subgoal of the current context, make reject-preferences for the current goal and the subgoal at the goal slot.

E2:   If there is a **vetoed-state** subgoal of the current context, make reject-preferences for the current problem space and **vetoed-state** subgoal at their respective slots.

E3:   If there is a **vetoed-operator** subgoal of the current context, make reject-preferences for the current state and **vetoed-operator** subgoal at their respective slots.

A.3. Common Elaboration Productions

E4:   If there is a **goal-tie** subgoal of the current context without a best-preference, make a best-preference for it at the goal slot.

E5:   If an operator of the current problem space has been applied to the current state, make a reject-preference for the operator at the operator slot.

E6:   If there is an **operator-tie** subgoal of the current context, and the problem space is augmented with **break-ties**, make a reject-preference for the subgoal, and randomly make a single acceptable-preference for one of the tied operator at the operator slot.

A.4. Selection Subgoal

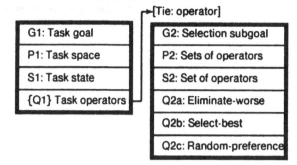

Goal	Selection
States	A set of candidate task objects with evaluations and preferences.
Operators	**eliminate-reject:** eliminate an object that has a *reject* preferences.
	eliminate-worse: eliminate an object that has a worse-preferences than other objects.
	select-best: select the objects that have best-preferences.
	random-preference: make a random preference from the objects.

Search-Control Knowledge

Goal Elaboration	If the difficulty is a tie, mark the goal as **Selection-subgoal**.
Goal Test	If the current state *consists* of a single object, make a reject-preference for the current goal.
Space Selection	If the current goal is **Selection-subgoal**, make an acceptable-preference for **Selection** at the problem space slot.
Space Elaboration	If the current goal is a **Selection-subgoal**, mark the problem space with **break-ties**.
State Selection	If the current problem space is **Selection**, make an acceptable-preference for the objects that tied the state slot.
Operator Selection	If the current problem space is **Selection** and one of the task objects in the current state is marked reject, make an acceptable-preference for **eliminate-reject**.
	If the current problem space is **Selection** and one of the task objects in the current state is marked worse, and the object it is worse than is not marked reject, make an acceptable-preference for **eliminate-worse**.
	If the current problem space is **Selection** and one but not all of the task objects in the current state is marked best and not marked reject, make a best-preference for **select-best**.
	If the current problem space is **Selection** and a task object in the current state is an acceptable-preference, make an acceptable-preference for **random-preference**.
	If the current problem space is **Selection** and there are acceptable-preferences for **eliminate-reject** and **eliminate-worse**, make a worse-preference with **eliminate-worse** worse than **eliminate-reject**.
	If the current problem space is **Selection** and there is an acceptable-preference for **random-preference** at the

operator slot and there an acceptable-preference for another operator and there is not a worse or reject-preference for that operator, make a worse-preference with **random-preference** worse than other operator.

A.5. Evaluate-Operator Subgoal 1

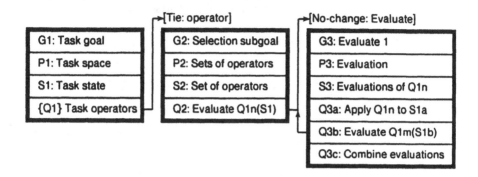

Goal	Selection Subgoal
Operators	**evaluate(q):** evaluate an object (in the following examples this object will always be an operator).

Search-Control Knowledge

	State Elaboration	If the current problem space is **Selection** and the *value* of a task operator's result is *worse* than another, make a worse-preference with the first task operator worse the the second.[TS]
	Operator Selection	If the current problem space is **Selection** and a task operator (q) has no value, make an acceptable-preference for evaluate(q).

Goal	Evaluate-Operator Subgoal 1
States	Information that will lead to an evaluation of the task operator (this includes the task operator, the task state, sometimes the result, and the evaluation of operators that apply to the result).
Operators	**apply:** Apply the task operator to the task state and create a new state (the *result*). (This is performed in the task problem space, but even though it is task dependent, the productions that select it are universal.)
	evaluate-operator: Evaluate one of the task operators that can be applied to the result. (This is performed by an evaluate1 subgoal and, like apply, does not have to be instantiated with task specific information.)
	evaluate-result: Statically evaluate the result. (This is often performed by search control of the task problem space when the **apply** operator is executed.)[TS]
	combine-evaluations: Combine the evaluations produced by **evaluate-operator** to create an evaluation of result.[TS]

Search-Control Knowledge

	Goal Elaboration	If the difficulty is a no-change with **evaluate** as the current operator, mark the goal as **Evaluate-Subgoal1**.
	Goal Test	If the current goal is **Evaluate-Subgoal1** and there is an evaluation of the superoperator, make a reject-preference for the current goal at the goal slot.
	Space Selection	If the current goal is **Evaluate-Subgoal1**, make an acceptable-

preference for the **Evaluation** problem space at the problem space slot.

State Selection   If the current goal is **Evaluate-Subgoal1**, make an acceptable-preference for a state containing the objects from the super-supercontext at the state slot.

A.6. Evaluate-Operator Subgoal 2

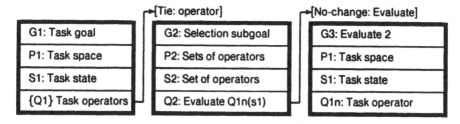

	Goal	Selection Subgoal
Operators		evaluate(q): evaluate an object along a dimension.

Search-Control Knowledge

	State Elaboration	If the current problem space is **Selection** and the task objects are operators and the *value* of a task operator's result is *worse* than another, make a worse-preference with the first task operator worse than the second using the super-context.[TS]
	Operator Selection	If the current problem space is **Selection** and one of the task objects (q) has no value, make an acceptable-preference for **evaluate(q)** at the operator slot.
		If the current problem space is **Selection** and there is acceptable-preference for **evaluate(q)** at the operator slot, and there are acceptable preferences for **eliminate-worse** or **eliminate-reject**, make a worse-preference with **evaluate(q)** worse than one of the other operators
		If the current problem space is **Selection** and **random-preference** is an acceptable-preference for the operator slot, and **evaluate** is an acceptable-preference, make a worse-preference with **random-preference** worse than one of the other operators.

	Goal	Evaluate 2
States		Task states.
Operators		Task operators.

Search-Control Knowledge

	Goal Elaboration	If the difficulty is a no-change with **evaluate** as the current operator, mark the goal as **Evaluate-Subgoal2**.
	Goal Test	If the current goal is **Evaluate-Subgoal2** and there is an evaluation of the operator being evaluated, make a reject-preference for the current goal at the goal slot.
	Space Selection	If the current goal is **Evaluate-Subgoal2**, make an acceptable-preference for the problem space of the operator being evaluated at the problem space slot.
	State Selection	If the current goal is **Evaluate-Subgoal2** and the current state is undefined, make a best-preference for the super-superstate at the state slot.
	State Elaboration	Some state evaluation.[TS]

Operator Selection   If the state is super-superstate, make a best-preference for the operator being evaluated.

APPENDIX **B.**

WEAK METHOD SEARCH CONTROL

B.1. Operator Subgoaling

If an operator cannot be applied to a position, then set up a subgoal of finding a position (starting from the current position) at which the operator can be applied. Implemented for Eight Puzzle, Missionaries and Cannibals, and Blocks World.

Operator Subgoaling   ⊶[No-change: operator not applicable]

G1: Task goal
P1: Task space
S1: Task state
Q1: Task operator

G2: Q1's conditions
P1: Task space
S1: Task state

Search-Control Knowledge

Goal Elaboration   If the current goal is a no-change goal where the task operator's *conditions* were not *satisfied* by the task state, *convert* the *form* of the task operator's *condition* into the desired state.

Space Selection   If the current goal is a no-change goal where the task operator's *conditions* were not *satisfied* by the task state, make an acceptable-preference for the task problem space at the problem space slot.

State Selection   If the current goal is a no-change goal where the task operator's *conditions* were not *satisfied* by the task state, and the state is undefined, make an acceptable-preference for the superstate at the state slot.

B.2. Unification [Match]

Given two patterns containing variables and functions with variables, find the most general unifying expression. Implemented for Expression Unification.

Unification   ┌─▶[No-change: operator not applicable]

G1: Comparison	G2: Unify subexpression
P1: Unify	P1: Unify
S1: Two expressions	S1: Two expressions
Q1a: Unify Varaible	Q1a: Unify Varaible
Q1b: Unify Equal	Q1b: Unify Equal

Goal   **Unify two expressions**

States   A combination of two expressions, a current position, expression-differences, and unifications (replacements).

Operators   **Unify-variable:** Replace all instances of a variable that occurs in the current position of one expression with the sub-expression (possibly atomic) in the other.
                           Unify-equal: Unify two corresponding sub-expressions.

Search-Control Knowledge: Unification is an implementation of operator subgoaling within a specific problem space. Therefore, unification includes all the search-control knowledge from operator subgoaling, instantiated for this particular problem space.

Goal Elaboration   If the current goal is a no-change goal where the **Unify-equal** operator could not apply to two subexpressions of the task state, mark the goal as **Operator-subgoal**, and **Compare-Expressions**.
                           If the goal is **Operator-subgoal**, the desired state is the unification of the two subexpressions that are not equivalent.

Goal Test   If all parts of the two expressions have been unified, make the current goal a reject-preference.

Space Selection   If the current goal is **Compare-Expressions** make **Unification** an acceptable-preference for the problem space.

State Selection   If the current problem space is **Unification**, make the expressions instantiated in the superoperator a state that has an acceptable-preference for the state.

State Elaboration   If the subexpressions at a *position* of the two expressions are not equal, augment the state with an *expression-difference*.

Operator Selection   If there is a variable at a position in an expression, make **unify-variable** an acceptable-preference for the operator slot.

B.3. Hypothesize and Match

Given a set of exemplar of a functions, generate possible function forms and match them to the exemplars. Implemented for Sequence Extrapolation.

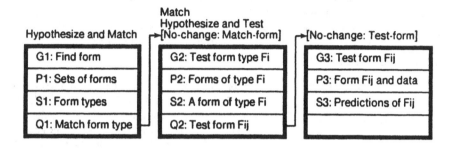

Hypothesize and Match	Match Hypothesize and Test →[No-change: Match-form]	→[No-change: Test-form]
G1: Find form	G2: Test form type Fi	G3: Test form Fij
P1: Sets of forms	P2: Forms of type Fi	P3: Form Fij and data
S1: Form types	S2: A form of type Fi	S3: Predictions of Fij
Q1: Match form type	Q2: Test form Fij	

Goal	**Hypothesize**
States	Form-length: different lengths of forms.
Operators	**generate-next-form**: create a form-length. **match-form**: compare the form-length to the exemplars.

Search-Control Knowledge

Goal Test
If **match-form** *applied successfully*, make the current goal a reject-preference for the goal slot.
If **generate-next-form** *failed*, make the current goal a reject-preference for the goal slot.

State Selection
Form-length is 1.

Operator Selection
If **match-form** *failed*, make **generate-next-form** an acceptable-preference for the operator slot.
If **match-form** has not applied to the current state, make **match-form** an acceptable-preference for the operator slot.

Goal	**Match-Subgoal**
States	Partially specified forms of the specified length.
Operators	**test-form**: compare the form to the exemplars. There are five operators that reduce differences by refining the form: **define-pointer, undefined-pointer, next-syntax, next-pointer, same-pointer**

Search-Control Knowledge

Goal Elaboration
If prior-context was completely defined with **match-form** as the current operator, mark the goal as **Match-Subgoal**.

Goal Test
If a state has no differences after **test-form** applied, make the current goal a reject-preference for the goal slot and mark **match-form** *applied successfully*.
If no operator applies, make the current goal a reject-preference for the goal slot and mark **match-form** *failed*.

State Selection	A form of the specified length.
Operator Selection	If the current state has a *difference*, make the operator that will *reduce* a *difference* an acceptable-preference for the operator slot.
	If **test-form** has not been applied to the current state, make **test-form** an acceptable-preference for the operator slot.

Goal   **Test-Subgoal**

States   A form of the specified length, the exemplars, current values of pointers from the form, the current position in the form and the exemplars.

Operators   **next-datum:** get next exemplar, next position in form.
                      Predict: add the *predictions* of the *form* for the current *position.*

Search-Control Knowledge

Goal Elaboration	If the prior-context was completely defined with **test-form** as the current operator, mark the goal as **Test-Subgoal**
Goal Test	If **next-datum** does not apply and there are no *differences*, make the current goal a reject-preference for the goal slot.
	If there is a *difference*, make the current goal a reject-preference for the goal slot.
State Elaboration	If, for the current *position*, the *prediction* does not match the *exemplar*, augment the state with a *difference*.
State Selection	The form, the exemplars.
Operator Selection	If the current *exemplar* equals the current *prediction*, make **next-datum** a best-preference.

B.4. Waltz Labeling: Constraint Satisfaction

There are a set of constraints on a set of variables. An assignment of values to variables must be found that satisfy the constraints. In Waltz Labeling, the possible values of a variable are explicitly represented and then the constraints are applied to these values to restrict the values of neighboring variables. This process recurs through all variables until no changes are made in the values of any variable. Implemented for Labeling Line Drawings.

Constraint Satisfaction →[No-change: operator not applied]

G1: Task goal	G2: Apply contraint
P1: Task space	P2: Constraint implementation
S1: Task state	S2: S1 and Q1
Q1: Apply constraint	

States   Networks where the nodes are sets of possible *values* (instances) and the links are dependences between the sets (constraints).

Operators   **Restrict Values:** Restrict the *values* of a node to a set of instances.

Test Constraint: Test a constraint between nodes and mark instances that fail it, so they will not be considered in the future. (This is implemented as a no-change subgoal in the given task.)

Search-Control Knowledge

Goal Elaboration	Mark the goal with **break-ties**.
Goal Test	no-change with current operator = nil.
State Selection	Network with no constraints on the possible *values* of the nodes.
State Elaboration	Mark the *values* at a *node* that *fail linked constraints*.

B.5. Generate and Test

Generate candidate solutions and test each one; terminate when found. Implemented for Eight Puzzle.

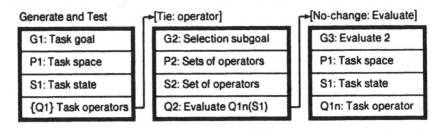

Task Structure   All results are terminal states.

B.6. Depth-First Search

To find an object in a space generated by operators, do a heuristic search but always move from the deepest position that still has some untried operators. Implemented for Eight Puzzle.

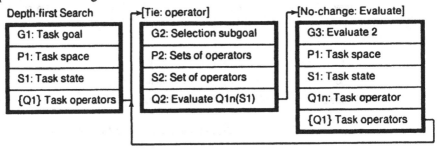

Task Structure   Only terminal states can be *evaluated* (as success or failure).

B.7. Simple Hill Climbing

To find a maximum point in a space, consider the next moves (operators) from a given position and select the first one that increases the value. Implemented for Eight Puzzle.

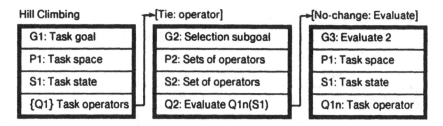

Hill Climbing	[Tie: operator]	[No-change: Evaluate]
G1: Task goal	G2: Selection subgoal	G3: Evaluate 2
P1: Task space	P2: Sets of operators	P1: Task space
S1: Task state	S2: Set of operators	S1: Task state
{Q1} Task operators	Q2: Evaluate Q1n(S1)	Q1n: Task operator

Goal   Selection-subgoal

Search-Control Knowledge

> *State Elaboration*   If the **value** of a task operator's result is **better** than the superstate, make the task operator a best-preference.

Goal   Evaluate-subgoal2

Task Structure   Must be able to **evaluate** all states.

B.8. Steepest Ascent Hill Climbing

To find a maximum point in a space, consider the next moves (operators) from a given position and select the one that makes the largest advance. Implemented for Eight Puzzle.

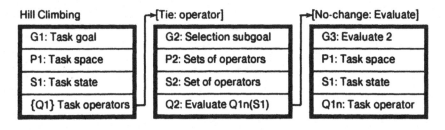

Hill Climbing	[Tie: operator]	[No-change: Evaluate]
G1: Task goal	G2: Selection subgoal	G3: Evaluate 2
P1: Task space	P2: Sets of operators	P1: Task space
S1: Task state	S2: Set of operators	S1: Task state
{Q1} Task operators	Q2: Evaluate Q1n(S1)	Q1n: Task operator

Goal   Selection-subgoal

Search-Control Knowledge

> *State Elaboration*   If the current problem space is **Selection** and the task objects are operators and the **value** of a task operator's result is **worse** than another, make the first task operator a worse-preference

Goal   Evaluate-Subgoal2

Task Structure Must be able *evaluate* all states.

B.9. Means-Ends Analysis

Make the next move that best reduces the difference between the current state and the desired state. Implemented for Eight Puzzle, Missionaries and Cannibals, and Blocks World.

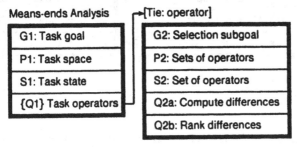

Means-ends Analysis   ┌─[Tie: operator]

G1: Task goal	G2: Selection subgoal
P1: Task space	P2: Sets of operators
S1: Task state	S2: Set of operators
{Q1} Task operators	Q2a: Compute differences
	Q2b: Rank differences

Goal   Selection-subgoal

Operators   compute-difference: Compute the *differences* between the superstate and the desired state.
                    rank-differences: *Rank* the *differences*.

Search-Control Knowledge

State Elaboration   If a task operator can *reduce* higher ranked *differences* than another task operator, make the second a worse-preference for the operator slot of the supercontext.

B.10. Progressive Deepening

Rework the analysis of a move repeatedly, going over old ground more carefully, exploring new side branches, and extending the search deeper until new information is discovered. Implemented for Tic-Tac-Toe.

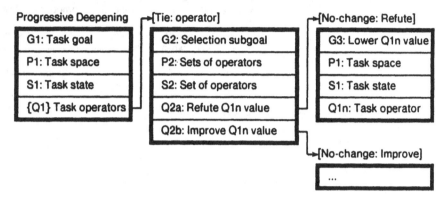

Goal	Selection Subgoal
Operators	**refute:** find a lower value of a task operator. **improve:** find a higher value of a task operator. **ask-user:** ask the user for a preference.

Search-Control Knowledge

	State Elaboration	If the current problem space is **Selection** and the task objects are operators and the *value* of a task operator's result is *worse* than another, make the first task operator a worse-preference
	Operator Selection	If is the *user's move*, make a best-preference for **ask-user**. If there are **select-best** and **ask-user**, mark select-best as a worse-preference. If a task operator (q) has a *non-lose value*, make refute(q) an acceptable-preference. If a task operator (q) has a *non-win value*, make improve(q) an acceptable-preference.

Goal	Refute-Subgoal
States	Task states.
Operators	Task operators.

Search-Control Knowledge

	Goal Elaboration	If the difficulty is a no-change with **refute** as the current operator, mark the goal as **Refute-Subgoal**. If the current goal is a **Refute-Subgoal**, mark the goal with **break-ties**.
	Goal Test	If a the current state is *terminal*, make the current goal a reject-preference for the goal slot. If the *value* of a state is found that is *worse* than the *current value* of the super-taskoperator, make the current goal a

reject-preference for the goal slot.

Space Selection	If the current goal is **Refute-Subgoal**, make the super-superproblem space an acceptable-preference for the problem space slot.
State Selection	If the current goal is **Refute-Subgoal**, make the super-superstate an acceptable-preference for the state slot.
Operator Selection	If the state is the superstate, make the superoperator a best-preference.
	If the state is *same side* as superstate, make the operator that was selected when current value was achieved an acceptable-preference.
	If the state is *opposite side* as superstate, make any operator that was selected previously a worse-preference.

Goal   **Improve-Subgoal** — Similar to **Refute-Subgoal**.

B.11. Modified Progressive Deepening

Same as Progressive Deepening, except that whenever the search is extended, all possible moves are examined. Implemented for Tic-Tac-Toe.

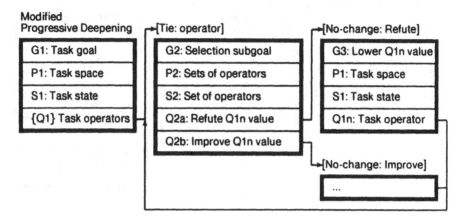

Goal	Selection-subgoal — same as Progressive Deepening
Goal	**Refute-Subgoal & Improve-Subgoal**

Search-Control Knowledge

Goal Elaboration	Goal *is not* augmented with **break-ties**.
Goal Test	If this is not a subgoal of a **Selection-subgoal** of a top-level Tic-tac-toe goal, and a *value* for a task operator is generated, make the current goal a reject-preference for the goal slot.

Task Structure This requires *evaluation* of *non-terminal* states to make a preference of tieing task operators.

B.12. B* (Progressive Deepening)

Same as Progressive Deepening, except that optimistic and pessimistic values are used to evaluate each move. (This is not a proof procedure as are B* and Mini-Max.) Implemented for Tic-Tac-Toe.

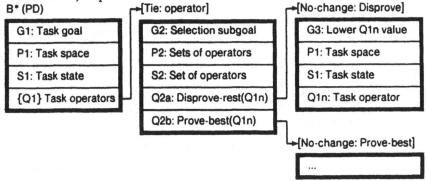

B* (PD)		[Tie: operator]		[No-change: Disprove]
G1: Task goal	→	G2: Selection subgoal	→	G3: Lower Q1n value
P1: Task space		P2: Sets of operators		P1: Task space
S1: Task state		S2: Set of operators		S1: Task state
{Q1} Task operators		Q2a: Disprove-rest(Q1n)		Q1n: Task operator
		Q2b: Prove-best(Q1n)		

[No-change: Prove-best]

...

Goal	Selection-subgoal — Includes all from Progressive Deepening (replacing **refute** with **disprove-rest** and **improve** with **prove-best**) plus the following:
States	They differ from the states defined earlier because each task state has two values: optimistic and pessimistic.
Operators	**disprove-rest:** find a worse optimistic value for an operator. **prove-best:** find a better pessimistic value for an operator. **Search-Control Knowledge**

State Elaboration   If the **optimistic value** of a state is worse than the **pessimistic value** of another state, make the first state a worse-preference for the state slot.

Operator Selection   If a task operator's ($Q1_n$) **pessimistic value** is worse than the **pessimistic value** of another operator, make disprove-rest($Q1_n$) an acceptable-preference.

If the task operator's ($Q1_n$) **optimistic value** is one of the best, make prove-best($Q1_n$) an acceptable-preference.

If there is an acceptable-preference for **disprove-rest** of the operator with the worst **optimistic value**, make that a best-preference.

If there is an acceptable-preference for **prove-best** of the operator with the best **pessimistic value**, make that a best-preference.

Goal	**Disprove-Rest-Subgoal**
States	Task states.
Operators	Task operators.

Search-Control Knowledge

Goal Elaboration   If the difficulty is a no-change with **Disprove-rest** as the current operator, mark the goal as **Disprove-Rest-Subgoal**.

If the current goal is a **Disprove-Rest-Subgoal**, mark the goal

	with **break-ties**.
Goal Test	If the current goal is **Disprove-Rest-Subgoal** and a state has a *point value*, make the current goal a reject-preference for the goal slot.
	If the current goal is **Disprove-Rest-Subgoal** and the *optimistic value* of a state is found that is worse than the current *optimistic value* of the super-taskoperator, make the current goal a reject-preference for the goal slot.
State Elaboration	Augment the state with a *optimistic value* and a *pessimistic value*.
Operator Selection	If the state is superstate, make the superoperator a best-preference.
	If the state is *same side* as superstate, make the operator that was selected when current value was achieved an acceptable-preference.
	If the state is *opposite side* as superstate, make any operator that was selected previously a worse-preference.

Goal   **Prove-Best-Subgoal** — Similar to **Disprove-Rest-Subgoal**.

Note: Must do maxing in subgoals to determine if a value is significant and what state to expand next (possibly similar to MPD). This may lead to a tie when determining which to expand, might have to use a subgoal, which gives a point to return to.

B.13. Mini-Max Search

To find the best next move in a perfect-information, two-player game, exhaustively try out all moves of each player, and find the line of play that provides the best final result, assuming each player always chooses the best possible move. Implemented for Tic-Tac-Toe.

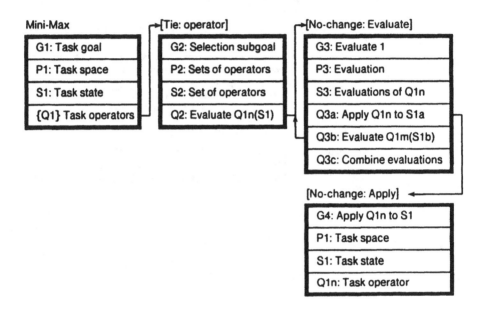

Goal	**Evaluate-Subgoal1**
States	The combination of the result of the task operator and the task state, evaluation of the result, and evaluation of task operators that apply to result.
Operators	**combine-evaluations:** Take *best task operator value* that applies to the result, and assign its *inverse* to result.
Goal	**Apply-Subgoal**
States	Task states
Operators	Task operators

Search-Control Knowledge

Goal Elaboration	If the difficulty is a no-change with **Apply** as the current operator, mark the goal as **Apply-Subgoal**.
Goal Test	If the task operator (with task state) has a result, make the current goal a reject-preference for the goal slot.
State Elaboration	Add *value* of *terminal* states.

B.14. Depth-Bounded Mini-Max Search

Same as Mini-Max, except there is a prespecified bound on the depth of search. Implemented for Tic-Tac-Toe.

Subgoal Structure
    Same as Mini-Max

Goal   Selection-subgoal — Same as Mini-Max, except for the following:
Search-Control Knowledge

            Goal Elaboration   Add a *global depth*.

Goal   Evaluate-Subgoal — Same as Mini-Max, except for the following:
Search-Control Knowledge

            Goal Test   If the *current depth* equals the *global depth* and the result has a *value*, make the current goal a reject-preference for the goal slot.
                                    If the result is a *terminal* state, make the current goal a reject-preference for the goal slot.

            Goal Elaboration   The *current depth* of this goal is the *current depth* of its supergoal plus one.

Goal   Apply-Subgoal — Same as in Mini-Max, except for the following:
Search-Control Knowledge

            State Elaboration   Evaluation of the current state (tied to the current depth).

B.15. Alpha-Beta Search

Same as Depth-Bounded Mini-Max, except that the search is not exhausted. Lines of play are ignored because they can do no better than a previously examined set of moves. Implemented for Tic-Tac-Toe.

Subgoal Structure
    Same as Mini-Max

Goal   Selection-subgoal — Same as Depth-Bounded Mini-Max.

Goal   Evaluate-Subgoal — Includes all of Depth-Bounded Mini-Max, except for the following:
Search-Control Knowledge

            Goal Test   If the *Alpha-value* of the current state is *worse* than the *value* of a task operator, make the current goal a reject-preference for the goal slot.

            State Elaboration   The *Alpha-value* of this state is $-($*Beta-value*$)$ of the super-state.
                                    The $-$*Beta-value* of this state is $-(\text{Max}($*Alpha-value*(superstate) & task operator values$))$.

Goal   **Apply-Subgoal** — Same as Depth-Bounded Mini-Max.

B.16. Iterative Deepening

Similar to Alpha-Beta, except the search begins with a search to depth 1, then iterates through the depths til it reaches a depth limit. The results for each depth of search are used to order the operator selection of the search at the next depth. Implemented for Tic-Tac-Toe.

Subgoal Structure
> Same as Mini-Max

Goal   Selection-subgoal — Same as Alpha-Beta, plus the following:

States   A set of candidate task operators with evaluations, with a **terminal depth**.

Operators   **increase-depth**: increase the current **terminal depth**.

Search-Control Knowledge

> *Goal Elaboration*   Add a **global depth**.

> *State Elaboration*   Remove elaborations not based on depth.
> If the current **terminal depth** equals the **global depth** and the **value** of a task operator is worse than another, make that task operator a worse-preference.

> *Operator Selection*   If a task operator ($Q1_n$) has no **value** for current **terminal depth**, make an acceptable-preference for Evaluate($Q1_n$).
> If q had the **best value** for the previous **terminal depth**, make evaluate($Q1_n$) a best-preference for operator.
> If all task operators have a **value** for the current **terminal depth**, make **increase-depth** a best-preference.

Goal   Evaluate-Subgoal — Includes all of Alpha-Beta, plus the following:

Search-Control Knowledge

> *Operator Selection*   If q had the **best value** for the previous **terminal depth**, make evaluate($Q1_n$) a best-preference for operator.
> If all task operators have a **value** for the current **terminal depth**, make **increase-depth** a best-preference.

Goal   Apply-Subgoal — Same as Alpha-Beta

B.17. B* (Recursive)

A proof procedure similar to Alpha-Beta, except each state has an optimistic and pessimistic value. See Berliner, 1979 for details. Implemented for Tic-Tac-Toe.

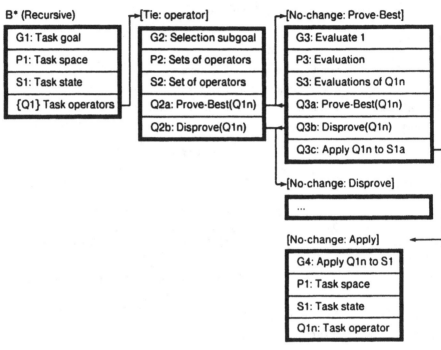

Goal	Selection-subgoal — Includes all from original B*.
Goal	Disprove-Rest-Subgoal
States	Combination of result of the task operator and the task state, evaluation of the result, and evaluation of task operators that apply to result.

Search-Control Knowledge

	Goal Elaboration	If the difficulty is a no-change with **Disprove-Rest** as the current operator, mark the goal as **Disprove-Rest-Subgoal** to change one of the *values* of the task operator.
	Goal Test	If the task operator has a new *optimistic* or *pessimistic value*, make the current goal a reject-preference for the goal slot.
	State Elaboration	Task operators that apply to the result. Evaluations of task operators that apply to the result. Take *best* task operator *optimistic value* that applies to the result, *invert* and assign as *pessimistic value* of task operator of goal. Take *best* task operator *pessimistic value* that applies to the result, *invert* and assign as *optimistic value* of task operator of goal.

Prove-Best-Subgoal

        Similar to Disprove-Rest-Subgoal.

Apply-Subgoal   Same as apply subgoal in original B*.

PART II

THE CHUNKING OF GOAL HIERARCHIES

A Model of Practice and Stimulus-Response Compatibility

Paul S. Rosenbloom

1 INTRODUCTION

How can systems — both natural and artificial — improve their own performance? At least for natural systems (people, for example), we know that *practice* is effective. A system is engaged in practice when it repeatedly performs one, or a set of similar, tasks. Recently, Newell and Rosenbloom (1981) brought together the evidence that there is a ubiquitous law — the *power law of practice* — that characterizes the improvements in human performance during practice. The law states that when human performance is measured in terms of the time to perform a task, it improves as a power-law function of the number of times the task has been performed (called the *trial number*). This result holds over the entire domain of human performance, including both purely perceptual tasks, such as target detection (Neisser, Novick, & Lazar, 1963), and purely cognitive tasks, such as supplying justifications for geometric proofs (Neves & Anderson, 1981) or playing a game of solitaire (Newell & Rosenbloom, 1981).

The ubiquity of the law of practice suggests that it may reflect something in the underlying *cognitive architecture*. The nature of the architecture is of fundamental importance for both Artificial Intelligence and Psychology (in fact, for all of Cognitive Science). It provides the control structure within which thought occurs; determining which computations are easy and inexpensive, and what errors will be made and when. Take the recent flux of work on expert systems such as MYCIN (Shortliffe, 1976) and R1 (McDermott, 1982) for example. Two important ingredients in these systems stem from fundamental work on the cognitive architecture; specifically, the development of *production systems* (Newell & Simon, 1972; Newell, 1973) and *goal-structured problem solving* (Ernst & Newell, 1969; Newell & Simon, 1972).

We use the power-law of practice as a clue to lead us down a (hopefully) fruitful path in our search for the cognitive architecture. This path is well defined because of the paucity of practice models that can produce power-law practice curves (Newell & Rosenbloom, 1981). As a beginning, Newell and

Rosenbloom (1981) developed an abstract model of practice based on the concept of *chunking* — a concept already established to be ubiquitous in human performance — and derived a practice equation from it capable of closely mimicking a power law. We hypothesized that this model formed the basis for the performance improvements brought about by practice. Rosenbloom and Newell (1982a; 1982b) took this one step further by showing how this *chunking theory of learning* could be implemented within a highly parallel, activation-based production system — *Xaps2* — for a 1023-choice reaction-time task (Seibel, 1963). This work established more securely that the theory is a viable model of human practice, by showing how it could actually be applied to a task to produce power-law practice curves. By producing a working system, it also established the theory's viability as a practice mechanism for artificial systems.   In Chapter 2 we review the relevant portions of the Newell and Rosenbloom (1981) and Rosenbloom and Newell (1982a) articles.

The principal weakness of the work done up to that point, was that the implementation was heavily task dependent. Both the representation used for describing the task, and the chunking mechanism itself had built into them knowledge about the specific task and how it should be performed. The mission of the current work is to remove this flaw, by producing generalized, task-independent models of performance and learning.

The first component of the mission — generalizing the model of task performance — is tackled by examining a set of tasks that fall within a neighborhood around the Seibel (1963) task. We have chosen the class of *stimulus-response compatibility*[1] tasks. The area of compatibility is a subdomain of the set of tasks referred to as *reaction-time* tasks. These tasks, which are used widely in psychological experimentation, involve the presentation to a subject of a stimulus display — such as an array of lights, a string of characters on a computer terminal, or a spoken word — for which a specific "correct" response is expected. The response may be spoken, manual — such as pressing a button, pushing a lever, or typing — or something quite different.

From the subject's reaction-time — the time it takes to make the response — and error rate, it is possible to draw conclusions about the nature of his cognitive processing. Stimulus-response compatibility includes those tasks in which there is a clear stimulus display, a clear response apparatus, and a clear rule for relating the two. The main phenomenon is that more complex and/or "counter-intuitive" relationships between stimuli and responses lead to longer reaction times and more errors. Though these tasks are important in their own right — especially in the areas of human factors engineering and man-machine

---

[1]This phrase will often be abbreviated as *S-R compatibility*, or even just *compatibility*.

interaction — no adequate model for the phenomenon currently exists.

In Chapter 3, we discuss in more detail the phenomena of S-R compatibility, and develop a theory for the phenomena — the *algorithmic model of stimulus-response compatibility.* From this theory[2] we can derive both a metric model of stimulus-response compatibility, and the type of task performance-models that are required for the application of the chunking theory. Though created as part of an investigation into practice, the algorithmic model of compatibility stands on its own as one of the contributions of this work.

The compatibility models and the Seibel task are integrated into a single representational framework through the intermediate concept of a *goal hierarchy.* In a goal hierarchy, the root node expresses a desire to do a task. At each level further down in the hierarchy, the goals at the level above are decomposed into a set of smaller goals to be achieved. Decomposition continues until the goals at some level can be achieved directly. This is a common control structure for the kinds of complex problem-solving systems found in artificial intelligence, but this is the first time they have been applied to the domain of reaction-time tasks.

These goal structures provide us with the generalized task representation required as the basis for the second component of this work — the formulation of a task-independent chunking mechanism. Chunking essentially implements a form of store-versus-compute trade-off, in which patterns of parameter values are related to patterns of results — a form of goal-based caching. The second major contribution of this work is the development of this generalized chunking mechanism. Both the goal hierarchies, and the chunking of these hierarchies are discussed in Chapter 4.

The third component of this work is part of a continuing investigation into the nature of the architecture of cognition. We start with an instantiation of our current best theory — production systems — and extend it to handle the new set of results brought forward during the investigations of compatibility and practice. In Chapter 5 we present the *Xaps3* production-system architecture. It is the result of stretching the previous architecture (*Xaps2*) to handle this new material. Parts of it were stretched beyond the breaking point, requiring major modifications to the architecture. The resulting system is considerably simpler than the often baroque *Xaps2* architecture.

In Chapter 6 we present the new results generated from simulations of the practice and compatibility tasks within the new architecture. In addition to generating simulated practice results for the practice task and simulated performance data for the compatibility tasks, the simulation produces simulated prac-

---

[2]We will use the terms *theory* and *model* interchangeably.

tice data for the compatibility tasks. This interaction is the locus of some un-expected results.

The chunking theory, as implemented in this work, provides a model of practice, but it is not intended to handle many of the other interesting aspects of learning. One important component of learning that will not be addressed is initial method acquisition. How does the subject learn how to perform a task the first time he sees it? Practice, as we are using the term here, refers only to the improvements that can be made in an already correct performance program. In order to tackle initial method acquisition, problem-solving behavior must be incorporated into the architecture, and melded with the practice mechanism. This and other miscellaneous topics — such as the relation of this work to earlier models and to other reaction-time phenomena — are discussed in Chapter 7. Instead of making major claims about these phenomena, we will be satisfied with sketching outlines.

Finally, in Chapter 8, we summarize the accomplishments of this work, and where to go from here.

In order to make this work readable for its entire intended audience — both computer scientists and psychologists — those concepts that are unfamiliar to researchers in either field must be explained. This means that the explanations of such concepts as the analysis of algorithms and stimulus-response com-patibility will be redundant for many readers (but not likely for the same readers). Please bear with this in the service of making this work accessible to all.

2 PRACTICE

One aspect of intelligent behavior that we have been studying for several years is *practice*. The current work — a more general implementation of the chunking theory of learning — represents the third in a continuing series of studies of the effects that practice has on performance. These new results are built upon the foundation laid by the two earlier efforts. The first study established that practice curves follow *power-law* functions, and developed a macrotheory of practice — the chunking theory of learning — that predicted power-law-like curves (Newell & Rosenbloom, 1981). The second study started from the macrotheory and implemented it within a production-system architecture for one reaction-time task (Rosenbloom & Newell, 1982a; Rosenbloom & Newell, 1982b). These results are summarized and discussed in the following sections; details can be found in those articles.

2.1. The Power Law of Practice

Performance improves with practice. More precisely, the time to perform a task decreases as a power-law function of the number of times the task has been performed. This basic law — known as the *power law of practice* or the *log-log linear learning law*[3] — has been known since Snoddy (1926). While this law was originally recognized in the domain of motor skills, it has recently become clear that it holds over a much wider range of human tasks — possibly extending to the full range of human performance. Newell and Rosenbloom (1981) brought together the evidence showing this for perceptual-motor skills (Snoddy, 1926; Crossman, 1959), perception (Kolers, 1975; Neisser, Novick, & Lazar, 1963), motor behavior (Card, English & Burr, 1978), elementary decisions (Seibel,

---

[3]Power-law curves plot as straight lines on log-log paper.

1963), memory (Anderson, 1980), routine cognitive skill (Moran, 1980), and problem solving (Neves & Anderson, 1981; Newell & Rosenbloom, 1981).

Practice curves are generated by plotting task performance against trial number. This cannot be done without assuming some specific *measure* of performance. There are many possibilities for such a measure, including such things as quantity produced per unit time and number of errors per trial. The power law of practice is defined in terms of the *time* to perform the task on a trial. It states that the time to perform the task (T) is a power-law function of the trial number (N):

$$T = BN^{-\alpha} \tag{2.1}$$

Figure 2-1 shows the practice curve for one subject in Kolers (1975) study of reading inverted texts. The solid line represents the power-law fit to this data ($r^2 = 0.932$).

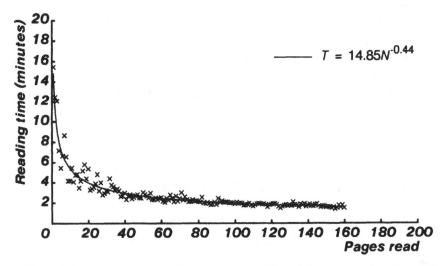

Figure 2-1: Learning to read inverted text. Plotted from the original data for Subject HA (Kolers, 1975).

If Equation 2.1 is transformed by taking the logarithm of both sides, it becomes clear why power-law functions plot as straight lines on log-log paper:

$$\log(T) = \log(B) + (-\alpha)\log(N) \tag{2.2}$$

Figure 2-2 shows the practice curve from Figure 2-1 as plotted on log-log paper. Its linearity is clear.

Figure 2-3 shows a practice curve from a 1023-choice reaction-time

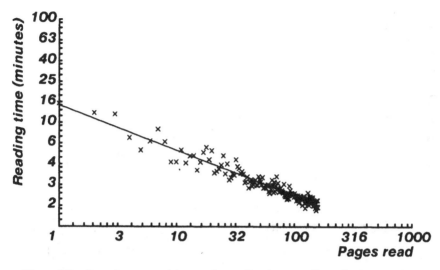

Figure 2-2: Learning to read inverted text (log-log coordinates). Plotted from the original data for Subject HA (Kolers, 1975).

task (Seibel, 1963), plotted on log-log paper. Each data point represents the mean reaction time over a block of 1023 trials. This curve is linear over much of its range, but has deviations at its two ends. These deviations can be removed by using a four-parameter *generalized* power-law function. One of the two new parameters (A) takes into account that the asymptote of learning is likely to be greater than zero. In general, there is a non-zero minimum bound on performance time, determined by basic physiological limitations and/or device limitations — if, for example, the subject must operate a machine. The other added parameter (E) is required because power laws are not translation invariant. Practice occurring before the official beginning of the experiment — even if it consists only of transfer of training from everyday experience — will alter the shape of the curve, unless the effect is explicitly allowed for by the inclusion of this parameter. Augmenting the power-law function by these two parameters yields the following generalized function:

$$T = A + B(N+E)^{-\alpha} \tag{2.3}$$

A generalized power law plots as a straight line on log-log paper once the effects of the asymptote (A) are removed from the time (T), and the effective number of trials prior to the experiment (E) are added to those performed during the experiment (N):

$$\log(T-A) = \log(B) + (-\alpha) \log(N+E) \tag{2.4}$$

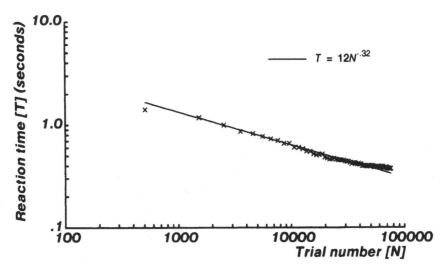

Figure 2-3: Learning in a Ten Finger, 1023 Choice Task (Log-Log coordinates). Plotted from the original data for Subject JK (Seibel, 1963).

Figure 2-4 shows the Seibel data as it is fit by a generalized power-law function. It is now linear over the whole range of trials. As stated earlier, similar fits are found across all dimensions of human performance. Though these fits are impressive, it must be stressed that the power law of practice is only an *empirical* law. The true underlying law must resemble a power law, but it may have a different analytical form.

2.2. The Chunking Theory of Learning

Newell and Rosenbloom (1981) showed that no existing theories of practice were capable of producing power-law practice curves[4]. To rectify this deficiency they created a new theory of practice, called the *chunking theory of learning*. The chunking theory proposes that practice improves performance via the acquisition of knowledge about patterns in the task environment. Implicit in this theory is a model of task performance based on this pattern knowledge. These patterns are called *chunks* (Miller, 1956). The theory thus starts from the *chunking hypothesis*:

- *The Chunking Hypothesis*: A human acquires and organizes

---

[4]See Anderson (1982a, 1983) for a recent alternative model of the power law of practice.

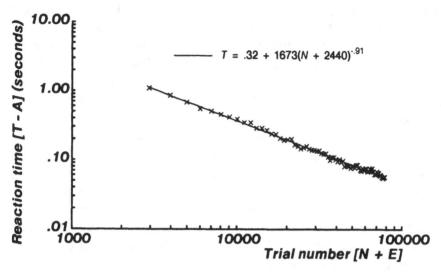

Figure 2-4: Optimal general power law fit to the Seibel data (Log-Log coordinates).

knowledge of the environment by forming and storing expressions, called *chunks*, which are structured collections of the chunks existing at the time of learning.

The existence of chunks implies that memory is hierarchically structured as a lattice (tangled hierarchy, acyclic directed graph, etc.), rooted in a set of preexisting *primitives*. A given chunk can be accessed in a top-down fashion, by *decoding* a chunk of which it is a part, or in a bottom-up fashion, by *encoding* from the parts of the chunk. Encoding is a recognition or parsing process.

The existence of chunks does not need to be justified solely on the basis of the practice curves. Chunks stand on their own as a thoroughly documented component of human performance (Miller, 1956; DeGroot, 1965; Bower & Winzenz, 1969; Johnson, 1972; Chase & Simon, 1973; Chase & Ericsson, 1981). The traditional view of chunks is that they are data structures representing the combination of several items. For example, in one set of classic experiments, Bower and colleagues (Bower, 1972; Bower & Springston, 1970; Bower & Winzenz, 1969) showed that recall of strings of numbers or letters is strongly influenced by the segmentation of the string. If the segmentation corresponds to a previously learned grouping of the items (for example, FBI-PHD-TWA-IBM), performance is better than if it is contradictory (FB-IPH-DTW-AIB-M). These results were interpreted as evidence for segmentation guided chunking of familiar strings. By replacing a string of several letters with a single chunk, the subject's memory load is reduced, allowing more letters to be remembered. At recall time the chunks are decoded to yield the original items to be recalled.

The chunking theory of learning proposes two modifications to this classical view. The first change is to assume that there is not a single symbol (chunk) to which the items are encoded, and from which they can later be decoded. As a simple example, the process of reading the string IBM out loud is more than just the encoding of the three letters into a chunk, followed by the subsequent decoding to the three letters. What needs to be decoded is not the visual representation of IBM, but the articulatory representation — allowing the subject to say IBM.

Based on this consideration, the chunking theory assumes that there are two symbols for each chunk — a *stimulus* symbol and a *response* symbol. The process of using a chunk consists of encoding the stimulus items to the stimulus symbol (a many-one mapping), mapping the stimulus symbol to the response symbol (a one-one mapping), and decoding the response symbol to the response items (a one-many mapping) (Figure 2-5). It is the encoding and decoding processes which are hierarchical. The mapping serves as a point of control at which the choice of response can be made.

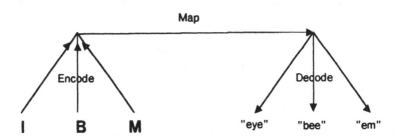

Figure 2-5: A three-part chunk for the articulation of the visual string "IBM".

The second difference between this proposal and the classical view of chunking is that the chunk consists of the three processes (encoding, mapping, and decoding), not just the symbols. This is really just a shift of emphasis, in which chunks are viewed as the processes, rather than just as the results of the processes.

The following performance assumption codifies this notion of chunking, and relates it to the performance of the system.

- *Performance Assumption*: The performance program of the system is coded in terms of high-level chunks, with the time to process a chunk being nearly independent of the size of the chunk[5].

---

[5]This formulation is slightly stronger than the one given in Newell and Rosenbloom (1981).

One possible instantiation of this assumption is that performance consists of serially processing a set of chunks, with the components of each chunk being processed in parallel, or by a fast hierarchical (logarithmic) process. Performance is thus improved by the acquisition of higher-level chunks. Another assumption is needed to tie down this acquisition process:

- *Learning Assumption*: Chunks are learned at a constant rate on average from the relevant patterns of stimuli and responses that occur in the specific environments experienced.

This assumption starts from the view that the human is a time-independent processing mechanism. It processes information the same way one hour as the next, one day as the next — as a function of stored knowledge and learned procedures, but not directly of time. In short, there is not a built-in historical clock. Thus there exists a basic constant rate of chunk acquisition (with respect to time, not trials). This same view underlies the appeal of the *total-time hypothesis* (Cooper & Pantle, 1967).

The learning assumption tells us the rate at which chunks are acquired, but it says nothing about the effectiveness of the newly acquired chunks. Do all chunks improve task performance to the same extent, or does their effectiveness vary? The answer to this question can be found by examining the structure of the task environment. If the patterns in the task environment vary in their frequency of occurrence, then the effectiveness of the chunks for those patterns will also vary. The more frequently a pattern occurs, the more the chunk gains. The final assumption made by the theory is that the task environment does vary in this fashion:

- *Task Structure Assumption*: The probability of recurrence of an environmental pattern decreases as the pattern size increases.

2.3. The Results of Chunking in One Task

Rosenbloom and Newell (1982a; 1982b) further specified, implemented and analyzed the results of the chunking theory in the context of a 1023-choice reaction-time task (Seibel, 1963). This is a perceptual-motor task in which the task environment consists of a stimulus array of ten lights, and a response array of ten buttons in a highly compatible one-one correspondence with the lights, each finger right below a light. On each trial, some of the lights are *On*, and some are *Off*. The subject's task is to respond by pressing the buttons corresponding to the lights that are *On*. Ten lights, with two possible states for each light, yields 2^{10} or 1024 possibilities. The configuration with no lights on is not used, leaving 1023 choices.

Based on an investigation into the structure of the task (four subjects were run informally) the following facts were ascertained and used as a basis for a performance model for the task:

- There is no single *right* control structure for the task. The subjects employed qualitatively different strategies.
- Each subject used predominantly one strategy, but not exclusively.
- The lights were processed in a predominantly left-to-right fashion.
- The number of *On*-lights is a significant component of the reaction time.

The performance model consisted of the following simple iterative algorithm.

> **Focus** a point to the left of the leftmost light.
> **While** there is an *On*-light to the right of the focal point **Do**
> **Locate** the *On*-light.
> **Map** the light location into the location of the button under it.
> **Press** the button.
> **Focus** the right edge of the light.

The model of practice for this task started with this simple model of initial task performance and a chunking mechanism. As experimental trials were processed, chunks were built out of the stimulus and response patterns that were experienced. The stimulus patterns consisted of combinations of lights (both *On* and *Off*), and the response patterns consisted of combinations of button presses. These chunks reduced the response time on later trials by allowing the subject to process a group of lights on each iteration, rather than just a single light.

This scheme was implemented in (and as part of) the *Xaps2* production-system architecture. The performance algorithm was implemented as a set of productions interpreted by the architecture. The chunking mechanism consisted of *Lisp* code built in as part of the architecture (in line with the assumption that learning was a continuous process concurrent with performance). It produced chunks, which were themselves productions.

Each chunk consisted of three productions. The *encoding* production was created from a pair of successively processed stimulus patterns. Its job was to perceive the new stimulus pattern whenever the two subpatterns were in working memory. The *decoding* production was created from the two response patterns corresponding to the stimulus patterns used in the encoding production. It decoded the new response pattern into its two subresponses. The *connection* production was responsible for linking the new stimulus pattern to the appropriate response pattern. Chunking thus consisted of the acquisition of hierarchical encoding and decoding networks (built out of parallel-firing productions) that gradually allowed larger and larger portions of the task to be done in one shot.

Figure 2-6 shows the result of simulating this model for 75 blocks of 1023 trials each[6]. This curve is indeed a power law; it is linear in log-log coordinates over the entire range of trials ($r^2 = 0.993$). A slight wave in the points is still detectable, but the linearity is not significantly improved by resorting to the generalized power law (r^2 is still 0.993).

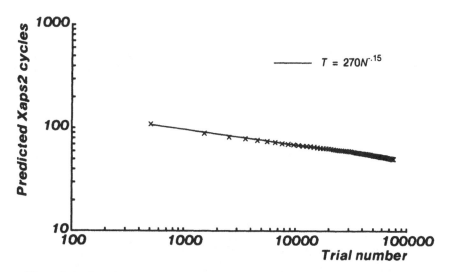

Figure 2-6: Practice curve predicted by the meta-simulation (log-log coordinates). Seventy five data points, each averaged over a block of 1023 trials. The probability of creating a chunk when there is an opportunity is 0.02.

This model produced good results, but it had its problems. The most important was the amount of task dependency built into the system — both in the implementation of the performance model and the chunking theory. The representation of the performance algorithm was based on the processing of a simple, fixed, goal structure that was too inflexible to be extendible. Even more critically, the chunking mechanism had to be designed specifically for the task. The mechanism knew that the lights were spread our horizontally so that lights could be uniquely signified by the horizontal position, with vertical position essentially ignored. It knew that it was to chunk lights and buttons, it knew how

---

[6]These results are actually from a meta-simulation — a more abstract simulation of the production-system model (Rosenbloom & Newell, 1982a).

they were represented, and which ones were being focussed by the performance system.

It proved possible to generalize the task-performance model to other tasks while remaining within the *Xaps2* architecture, but it did not prove possible to make the analogous extensions to the formulation of the chunking mechanism. This problem was solved by the development of the *Xaps3* architecture (Chapter 5). In combination with the performance model described in Chapter 4, all of these task-dependencies disappear.

3 STIMULUS-RESPONSE COMPATIBILITY

As was discussed in Chapter 1, the first step that must be taken in the creation of a general implementation of the chunking theory of learning, is the generalization of the model of task performance. In this chapter, we do exactly this, through the analysis and modeling of performance in a set of related *stimulus-response compatibility* tasks. This excursion into compatibility phenomena is a digression from the primary focus on practice, but it is a necessary step in the development of the chunking model. We will return to the discussion of practice in Chapter 4.

Stimulus-response compatibility deals with the relationship between stimuli and responses. Specifically, how does varying this relationship affect reaction time, errors, and the rate of learning? Consider a concrete example in which there are two buttons, one on top of the other, that can be used to summon either an up-elevator or a down-elevator. In the *compatible* situation, the top button summons the up-elevator and the bottom button summons the down-elevator. In the *incompatible* situation, the relationship is reversed — the top button summons the down-elevator and the bottom button summons the up-elevator. In the compatible situation people are faster, and make fewer errors. These effects are clearly robust, and rather large. The problems encountered in performing in the incompatible situation do not stem from a lack of knowledge about the correct relationship — subjects are told the mapping from stimulus to response at the start — instead, it is a problem in actually performing the mapping.

There are three reasons why compatibility was chosen as the domain in which to investigate generalized performance models. The first reason is that the tasks are closely related to the ten-light, ten-button task employed in the earlier work. They make contact with that task, but stretch the demands on the representation of performance models. The second reason is that the

149

phenomena of compatibility are important in their own right. This is especially
true in the field of human factors engineering, where the relationship between
stimulus displays, and simple manual controls is critical. The third reason is
that, even though the phenomena have been studied since the early fifties, there
is no useful theory of compatibility. Welford (1980) sums up the latter situation
nicely:

> Surprisingly, after more than twenty years' research there is no
> metric for compatibility that transcends particular experimental con-
> ditions. (p. 99)

In this chapter, we present some compatibility results, discuss the
phenomena and existing explanatory notions, and present a cross-experimental
metric model of compatibility (in terms of performance models for the tasks).
We wrap up with a discussion of those other stimulus-response compatibility
sub-phenomena and experiments not directly addressed in the remainder of this
chapter.

3.1. The Phenomena

Consider the position of a subject in a typical reaction-time experiment. On
each trial of the experiment, the subject is presented with a stimulus display —
of a visual, auditory, or kinesthetic nature — containing some set of information, from which he must determine the proper response — usually requiring
a vocalization or some manipulation by the hands or fingers. A single *condition*
of the experiment will define a set of possible stimulus displays (the *stimulus
environment*), a set of possible responses (the *response environment*), and the
mapping of the stimulus displays into the responses.

In a stimulus-response compatibility experiment, the conditions are varied
so as to evaluate the relationship between the mapping and performance —
reaction time, errors, and learning rate. It was known by the early fifties (Fitts &
Seeger, 1953) that the stimulus and response environments could not be treated
independently. It is the interaction between the two, as defined by the mapping, that is critical. The simplest illustration of this can be found in tasks where
the *task environment* — the combination of the stimulus and response environments — does not vary across conditions. Only the mapping varies.

In one such experiment, reported by Duncan (1977), the stimulus environment consisted of an oscilloscope on which a vertical line could appear in one of
four horizontal positions (top part of Figure 3-1). The response environment
consisted of a set of four buttons, lying under the fore and middle fingers of the

subject's hands (bottom part of the figure). On each trial of the task, one of the lines would appear on the oscilloscope, and the subject was to press the appropriate button. There were three conditions in the experiment, each of which specified a different mapping of line position to button. In the *corresponding* condition (Figure 3-1a), each line was mapped to the button below it. In the *opposite* condition (Figure 3-1b), each line was mapped to the opposite button — the first line to the last button, the second line to the third button, the third line to the second button, and the last line to the first button. In the remaining *mixed* condition (Figure 3-1c), half of the combinations (either the inner two or the outer two) were defined to be corresponding, and the other half were defined to be opposite[7].

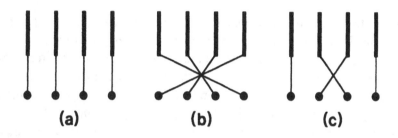

Figure 3-1: The three compatibility conditions in Duncan (1977): (a) corresponding, (b) opposite, and (c) mixed.

Table 3-1 shows the reaction times for the three conditions. This data represents one point in practice — the sixth experimental run — from the learning curves presented in Duncan (1977). The entire learning curves can be found in Figure 6-19.

Though the mixed condition is only a single condition, each trial is either corresponding or opposite. Therefore, the data has been partitioned to reflect this split. The main thing to notice at the moment is that though the task environment remains unchanged, manipulating the mapping yields differences in the time it takes to perform the task. The corresponding trials are consistently faster than the opposite trials, and the trials in the mixed condition are slower than the analogous ones in the non-mixed (pure) conditions. The pure-corresponding condition is compatible, while the others are incompatible.

Even when the task environment is modified across conditions, by changing

----

[7]Duncan actually employed both mixed conditions, one in which the inner two lights were corresponding, and one in which the outer two were. For the results that we are interested in, these two conditions can be combined into one.

	Corresponding	Opposite
Pure	411	461
Mixed	485	539

Table 3-1: Mean reaction times (msec) for the sixth experimental run in Duncan (1977).

either the stimulus or the response environment, it is the mapping that accounts for most of the variance. For example, Fitts & Seeger (1953) reported a nine condition experiment in which three stimulus environments were crossed with three response environments. Table 3-2 shows the apparatuses used to define these environments, as well as the mean reaction-times for the nine conditions. Stimulus apparatus S_A contains eight lights at the 45° points of a circle. On each trial in which it is used, exactly one light goes on. Stimulus apparatuses S_B and S_C both contain four lights. On each trial, either one light comes on, or a pair of adjacent lights (with respect to the circle) comes on. With apparatus S_B, the four lights are at the 90° points of a circle. With apparatus S_C, the display is twice as wide, the horizontal lights in one half, and the vertical lights in the other. Adjacency for apparatus S_C is defined as if the lights were still in the circle of apparatus S_B. The light on the far left is "at" -90°, the middle light is "at" 90°, the top-right light is "at" 0°, and the bottom-right light is at 180°.

The three response apparatuses are defined analogously to the stimulus ones. In response apparatus R_A, there is a lever that can be pushed towards any of the eight 45° angles. When used in conjunction with S_A, the lever is pushed in the direction of the light. With S_B and S_C, if one light is on, the lever is pushed in that direction; if two lights are on, then the lever is pushed towards the mean of the two angles. For example, if the right and top lights (which actually appear in the middle and top-right of the display, respectively) in apparatus S_C are on, then the lever should be pushed at a 45° angle. Response apparatus R_B allows the lever to be pushed at only 90° angles. When it is used with either stimulus apparatus S_B or S_C, the lever is pushed in each direction specified by an on light. This may require the lever to be pushed either once or twice. When used with stimulus array S_A, the lever is pushed once if the light is at a multiple of 90°, and twice otherwise, at an angular displacement of $+45°$ and $-45°$ from the light that is on. Response apparatus R_C is analogous to R_B, except that it requires two hands to manipulate.

The first thing to notice about the reaction times for these conditions is that in each row and column in the table, the fastest reaction time belongs to the one on the main diagonal. For each stimulus apparatus, there is a different response apparatus that produces the fastest times. In the analysis of variance reported by Fitts and Seeger, the effects of stimulus apparatus and response apparatus individually were significant, but in their words:

> The variance that can be attributed to interaction is very much larger than the variance attributable to the primary effects of either stimulus or response sets alone. (p. 204)

	R_A	R_B	R_C
S_A	390	430	580
S_B	450	410	580
S_C	770	580	480

Table 3-2: Mean reaction times (msec) for the nine conditions in Fitts and Seeger (1953).

This experiment also reveals how just labeling conditions compatible and incompatible can miss a good deal of what is going on. Though the conditions on the main diagonal are compatible, and those off the diagonal are incompatible, some of the incompatible times are faster than some of the compatible times. A theory of stimulus-response compatibility should explain these complexities.

Theories of stimulus-response compatibility have been scarce (see Section 3.2), and ones that could predict the results of more than one experiment have been nonexistent. We present here the beginnings of such a theory — the *algorithmic model of stimulus-response compatibility*. We will provide an abstract characterization of the theory, and two different formulations of it. The first formulation, in terms of a simple algorithmic language, is most useful for computing the metric aspects of the theory. It allows quick back-of-the-envelope style calculations in the style of the applied information-processing psychology models of Card, Moran, and Newell (1983).

The second formulation, in terms of goal hierarchies, facilitates the integration of the theory with the general formulation of the chunking theory; both of which can then be implemented within a production-system architecture. The discussion of goal hierarchies is delayed until Chapter 4, where compatibility and practice are integrated into a single framework. In the remainder of this chapter we deal with the abstract characterization of the theory, and its algorithmic formulation. But first, it is worthwhile to review the existing state of compatibility theory.

3.2. Existing Stimulus-Response Compatibility Theory

The current theoretical state does not yield any full theories of compatibility. Instead, there is a piecemeal set of factors that various researchers have proposed as contributing to the phenomena. These factors are described in this section with little comment. Analysis and synthesis will be attempted during the subsequent development of our macrotheory.

The most widely accepted statement about S-R compatibility is that it is a function of the transformations or encodings that must be performed on the stimulus to yield the response. Deininger and Fitts (1955) put it this way:

> The fundamental assumption for the model used in developing the S-R compatibility concept is that all perceptual-motor performance involves one or more steps of information transformation, since the response must always be encoded in a manner different from the stimulus. (p. 318)

In addition, Deininger and Fitts (1955) went on to propose one other factor they felt was important — whether "the pairings of stimulus and response elements agree with strong population stereotypes (p. 320)". This is primarily a matter of transfer of training, either positive or negative, from earlier learning (or from inherited tendencies).

Brebner (1973) took the Deininger and Fitts model one step further, by considering what happens in a multistage transformation between stimulus and response. He proposed that in more compatible situations a single recoding or translation process can be applied to all of the steps. An example would be a multistage numerical computation in which Brebner's hypothesis would imply that it is easier to do a string of three additions than two additions with a subtraction sandwiched between them.

The closest anyone has come to a metric was in the work of Morin & Grant (1955) — though it was still for only one set of task variations. They examined a set of tasks based on eight lights, and eight response keys, in which the mapping of light to key could be changed. On each trial, a pattern of lights was presented, and the subject made the appropriate response. They compared reaction time with the rank correlation of the mapping, and found an effect of the absolute value of the correlation (a quadratic effect), and the sign (a linear effect). Shepard (1961) showed that a partial account for this effect can be obtained by looking at the stimulus and response generalizations (or confusions) and the permutation matrix defining the mapping.

To explain the results of mixed conditions, such as in the Duncan (1977) study described earlier, Smith (1977) proposed a parallel iterative scheme. Each S-R pair had an *association time*, reflecting some unspecified function of the compatibility of that pair. Each iteration took a time proportional to a weighted sum of the association times for all of the pairs in the condition (not just of the pair for the current trial). This theory predicts that the time to do a mixed mapping will be between the times to do the respective pure mappings. It also predicts that the addition of more S-R pairs to the condition will always raise the reaction time for the other pairs (though the effect may be small if the association times for the new pairs are small).

Smith's theory treated each S-R pair as a distinct component in the response selection process. In contrast, Duncan (1977) proposed that: "Responses may be selected, not on the basis of individual S-R associations, but by use of a rule or system of rules". Duncan concluded that there were two factors determining spatial stimulus-response compatibility:

> Spatial CRT [Choice Reaction Time] is influenced by two different properties of the mapping. One is the spatial relationship of individual S-R pairs, this is, in terms of the proposed model, which transformation must be made. The other is the number of different relationships in the whole mapping; that is, the number of transformations from which selection must be made. (p. 60)

Thus, we see that some factors have been proposed, and some attempts have even been made to consider how to combine components of complex situations, but still no metric, to use Welford's term, has been found.

3.3. The Algorithmic Model of Stimulus-Response Compatibility

The *algorithmic model of stimulus-response compatibility* is based on the supposition that people perform reaction-time tasks by executing *algorithms* (or programs) developed by them for the task — what we can call the *algorithmic assumption*. Card, Moran, and Newell (1983) have already made a general proposal of this sort for tasks involving cognitive skill. They have worked this out for one domain; computer text-editing and text-based command language interaction. They showed that models based on the concepts of goals, operators, methods, and selection rules — GOMS models — provide excellent matches to the behavior of human subjects.

The first (algorithmic) formulation of the theory is a GOMS model for compatibility. The second formulation, in terms of goal hierarchies (Chapter 4), goes seriously beyond GOMS because it provides the architectural embedding — exactly what GOMS does not do (and explicitly claims not to do).

Given the algorithmic framework, the path to a compatibility metric is straightforward. The first step is to analyze the task situations to ascertain the algorithms employed in their performance. This could be done either experimentally, by analyzing the behavior of subjects while they perform the task, or through an abstract task analysis similar in nature to the process a programmer goes through in developing an algorithm for a task.

The second step is to perform a *complexity analysis* of the algorithms (Aho, Hopcroft, & Ullman, 1974; Knuth, 1968). For our purposes, this involves assigning cost measures to the primitive steps in the algorithm and determining how many of each type of step would be executed in the process of performing a trial. Given these values, it is straightforward to predict the mean reaction-times for the conditions of the experiment.

As noted, Duncan (1977) took the first step towards a model of this type in his formulation of compatibility in terms of the selection and application of a possibly general transformation rule. What he didn't do was specify the nature of those choices and rules in enough detail for the development of process models of compatibility tasks. It is these process models that yield a metric of stimulus-response compatibility. In addition we think he was too modest in limiting the scope of the theory to spatial stimulus-response compatibility tasks. We believe that it holds generally over all stimulus-compatibility tasks.

Before we can develop algorithms for the stimulus-response compatibility tasks, we must have a language in which to write the algorithms. The language determines the ease with which the algorithms can be expressed, and what the time-consuming primitive operations are. In the following section we describe a simple algorithmic language, called *Artless*, that forms our first formulation of the algorithmic model of compatibility. We will then proceed to develop and analyze algorithms for the conditions in three qualitatively different stimulus-response compatibility experiments.

3.3.1. Artless: An algorithmic reaction-time language

There are six constructs in *Artless: operators, constants, variables, assignments, blocks,* and *branches.* The operators do all of the real work in the system. An operator can be thought of as a parameterized black box that performs some computations, and optionally returns a value. Two typical operators are **GetStimulus**("Line") and **Negate**(Horizontal-Location)[8]. The **Get-Stimulus** operator receives some characterization of what to look for in the stimulus display, and it returns a complete description of the object found. In this instance, the object was specified by the constant "Line", so the operator should return the description of a particular stimulus line. *Artless* is an informal language in that it allows algorithms to be specified that ignore the details of how the concepts "Line" and "complete description of the stimulus object" are represented.

The operator **Negate**, takes a number as parameter, and returns the result of multiplying it by -1. In this case it receives a horizontal location (a number between -1000 and 1000) as the value of a variable and inverts it, performing the *opposite* transformation for Duncan's task. Operators may either succeed or fail. If an operator succeeds, it is guaranteed to have accomplished everything it set out to do. If it fails, it may have been for any number of reasons, such as the lack of needed parameters or because some stimulus situation does not hold. However, the system only knows that the operator failed, not why it failed.

Predicates are a subclass of operators that don't return a value. They are used to test for the truth of some condition. If the predicate succeeds, the condition is true. If it fails, the condition may be false, or it may be that the operator did not know how to test the condition in the current situation. A typical predicate is **One-Light-On?**, which succeeds only if there is only one light that is on in the stimulus display.

The assignment construct is used to give values to variables. For example, the following statement changes the value of the variable Horizontal-Location

---

[8]To highlight the operator, its name is displayed in **bold** face. Variables are displayed in the normal roman font, and constants are quoted.

by negating it.

Horizontal-Location ← **Negate**(Horizontal-Location)

In order to do a sequence of operators, the block construct is used. We shall use the *Pascal* convention for delineating blocks. The block begins with the keyword BEGIN, ends with the keyword END, and has a list of operators between. For example, the following block gets the description of a line displayed in the stimulus environment, gets the horizontal location of the line from the description, and then presses the button at that horizontal location.

```
BEGIN
Stimulus ← Get-Stimulus("Line")
Horizontal-Location ← Get-Value(Stimulus, "Horizontal-Location")
Make-Response("Press-Button", Horizontal-Location)
END
```

Decisions can be made based on the outcome of a predicate (actually, of any operator) by employing a branch. A branch checks for the success of a predicate and does a specific operator or block of operators if the condition is met. Suppose we wanted to add 45° to an angle only if it is a right angle. We could do it by the following algorithm.

```
IF-SUCCEEDED Is-Divisible?(Angle, 90°) THEN
        Angle ← Add(Angle, 45°)
```

Branches also have an optional ELSE clause that allows some other operator or block to be performed if the predicate failed.

General rule-like behavior, as described by Duncan (1977), occurs in this model when the same algorithm is used for the different trials in a condition. The more branches that exist to subalgorithms, the less rule-like the behavior is, and the more the model looks like a bunch of individual stimulus-response associations. For the mixed conditions, we expect to find something in between — perhaps an algorithm that has a single branch to the subalgorithms for the two subconditions.

Given the flexibility of this language, there will not be a unique algorithm for each task. If the language is an accurate reflection of human capabilities, then each of the alternatives represents a strategy that a human subject could use in the performance of the task (see Newell (1973) and Baron (1978) for a discussion of the issues surrounding the availability of multiple strategies). Since reaction-time tasks emphasize speed, we can make the assumption that subjects will tend to use the simpler (faster) algorithms if they can and have had modest practice. We have tried to use this as a constraint on the algorithms we present. Even with this constraint, there may be more than one reasonable algorithm. Since we have no data on the relative frequencies of the alternatives, we make the minimal (Laplacian) *mixing assumption*: assume the algorithms are equally likely (across subjects), and take their mean behavior.

Another form of flexibility at the disposal of subjects, concerns the representation of the tasks' spatial information. Do subjects employ rectangular coordinates, polar coordinates, or something else? We make a second assumption to deal with this uncertainty. The *coordinate-system assumption* says that subjects employ the coordinate system that they are led to by a combination of the instructions, and surface structure of the stimulus and response displays. If the stimulus consists of a circle of lights, subjects will tend to use polar coordinates; if it is a linear display, rectangular coordinates will be appropriate. This assumption is a specialization of the strong psychological assumption that subjects create *problem spaces* for task performance from the surface structure of the task (Hayes & Simon, 1974; Simon & Hayes, 1976).

The one aspect of the model remaining to be specified, is the cost model. We have a very simple model of cost for *Artless* algorithms: each operator takes one unit of time while all other constructs are free of charge. This is the same sort of minimal assumption as the one just described for algorithm frequency. Estimating the amount of real time in milliseconds that each model unit of time takes must wait until we have actually looked at some task algorithms

3.3.2. The analysis of some task algorithms

In this section we present algorithms for three different stimulus-response compatibility experiments — the three experiments that have so far proven tractable. Two of them — Duncan (1977) and Fitts and Seeger (1953) — have already been described. The third experiment (Morin & Forrin, 1962) employed a set of symbolic tasks, in contrast to the spatial tasks of the previous two. There were five conditions (Table 3-3). In conditions I and IV, each trial consisted of the visual presentation of an arabic numeral to which the subject was to respond by saying the number (for example, see "2", say "two"). The conditions differed in the number of alternatives in the task environment (2 and 4, respectively). In conditions II and V, each trial consisted of the visual presentation of a symbol (+, ■, ●, or ▲) to which the subject was to respond by saying a number that had been associated with it (4, 7, 2, and 8 respectively). Again the conditions differed in the number of alternatives that could be presented. Condition III was a mixed condition in which the stimulus environment consisted of two numbers (2 and 8) and two symbols (+ and ■). In Table 3-3, condition III has been split according to whether a number (IIIa) or a symbol (IIIb) appeared on the trial.

Cond.	S-R Pairs		RT	Cond.	S-R Pairs		RT
I	$2-2$ $8-8$		520	II	$+-4$ $\blacksquare-7$		590
IIIa	$2-2$ $8-8$	$+-4$ $\blacksquare-7$	600	IIIb	$+-4$ $\blacksquare-7$	$2-2$ $8-8$	710
IV	$2-2$ $8-8$	$4-4$ $7-7$	490	V	$+-4$ $\blacksquare-7$	$\bullet-2$ $\blacktriangle-8$	720

Table 3-3: Compatibility conditions and RT (msec) from Morin and Forrin (1962).

The reaction times for these conditions divide up into three groups separated by about 100msecs each. Conditions I and IV are the fastest (the "compatible" conditions), at around 500msec. At around 600msec we find conditions II and IIIa, and at around 700msec we find conditions IIIb and V.

In the remainder of this section we present the algorithms for this, and the other two experiments. The times predicted by these algorithms are compared to the data, both within each experiment, and across all three experiments.

3.3.2.1. Duncan (1977)

Figures 3-2, 3-3, and 3-4 show algorithms for the three conditions in Duncan's experiment. For these tasks, we use a rectangular coordinate system for the stimulus and response environments. The origin is at the center of the stimulus display (and the response apparatus), allowing the *opposite* transformation to be performed by negating the horizontal location of the light. We also assume that subjects define the two coordinate spaces so that they just bound the stimulus display and response apparatus, respectively. The minimal horizontal location (-1000) corresponds to the location of the left-most line in the stimulus display, and to the leftmost button in the response apparatus. The same holds true for the maximal value (1000). This assumption allows the analogous locations in the two environments to be directly linked.

The *corresponding* algorithm (Figure 3-2) is quite simple, consisting of a single block of three operations. The first operation generates an internal representation for the line perceived in the stimulus display. The second operation gets the horizontal location of the line from the representation of the stimulus. The final operation presses the button at that horizontal location. Three operations performed, yields a cost for executing this algorithm of 3.

Algorithm *Duncan-Corresponding*:
```
BEGIN
Stimulus ← Get-Stimulus("Line")
Horizontal-Location ← Get-Value(Stimulus, "Horizontal-Location")
Make-Response("Press-Button", Horizontal-Location)
END
```

Figure 3-2: Task algorithm for the *corresponding* condition in Duncan (1977).

The algorithm for the *opposite* condition (Figure 3-3) is the same as the *corresponding* one with the addition of one new operation. The operation (**Negate**) is responsible for finding the opposite location, which it does by negating the horizontal location of the line. Neglecting to perform this operation can lead to what Duncan (1977) referred to as *corresponding errors*; that is, making the corresponding response when the opposite one is appropriate. The opposite algorithm performs four operations, so its cost is simply 4.

Algorithm *Duncan-Opposite*:
```
BEGIN
Stimulus ← Get-Stimulus("Line")
Horizontal-Location ← Get-Value(Stimulus, "Horizontal-Location")
Horizontal-Location ← Negate(Horizontal-Location)
Make-Response("Press-Button", Horizontal-Location)
END
```

Figure 3-3: Task algorithm for the *opposite* condition in Duncan (1977).

The *mixed* algorithm (Figure 3-4) is by far the most complex of the three. A decision is required as to whether the stimulus line is in the middle of the display, or on the fringes. In this particular variant of the mixed condition, the middle two lights are mapped *opposite*, while the outer two are mapped *corresponding*. The model makes identical predictions for the other variant — there is no model of differences in discriminability — so it is only necessary to look at one.

Implicit in Algorithm *Duncan-Mixed-1* is a model of *choice reaction time* — how reaction time varies with the number of alternatives from which the subject can choose. It is the *Positive-Check Model* discussed by Welford (1980). The alternatives are broken up into two classes (if possible), and the first class is checked. If it is correct, the choice has been made; otherwise the second class is also checked. This seemingly redundant test is forced by the nature of the predicates. Failure of a predicate does not necessarily mean that the predicate is

Algorithm *Duncan-Mixed-1*:
```
BEGIN
Stimulus ← Get-Stimulus("Line")
Horizontal-Location ← Get-Value(Stimulus, "Horizontal-Location")
IF-SUCCEEDED In-Middle?(Horizontal-Location) THEN
    BEGIN
    Horizontal-Location ← Negate(Horizontal-Location)
    Make-Response("Press-Button", Horizontal-Location)
    END
  ELSE
    IF-SUCCEEDED Outside-Of-Middle?(Horizontal-Location) THEN
        Make-Response("Press-Button", Horizontal-Location)
END
```

Figure 3-4: Task algorithm for the *mixed* condition in Duncan (1977).

false, so not checking the second alternative can lead to errors if the first predicate is true but fails. The whole process continues in a hierarchical fashion as long as necessary. The positive-check model gives results that agree with Hick's law (Hick, 1952) — choice reaction time is proportional to the logarithm of the number of choices. More will be said on the relationship between the current work and choice reaction time in Chapter 7.

Algorithm *Duncan-Mixed-1* highlights another important aspect of task algorithms. The complexity of the task algorithm is a function of the entire task-environment. Even though any particular task may not be too complex, the combination of all of the tasks in the environment can lead to a complex algorithm. In this task environment, the subject may have to do either the corresponding task or the opposite task on each trial. It is this combination that makes Algorithm *Duncan-Mixed-1* more complex than the two pure algorithms.

The cost of executing Algorithm *Duncan-Mixed-1* is 5 for both corresponding and opposite trials. Though negation of the location is not necessary in the corresponding case, an extra predicate must be tested. However, this is not the whole story, because the order in which the predicates are tested is arbitrary. There is a very similar algorithm (which we can call Algorithm *Duncan-Mixed-2*) in which the order of the two predicates (**In-Middle?** and **Outside-Of-Middle?**) is reversed. For a cost measure, we want to take the mean cost for the two algorithms. The costs for algorithm *Duncan-Mixed-2* are determined by adding the cost of one predicate to the opposite case (yielding 6), and subtracting the same value from the corresponding case (yielding 4). The average costs are thus 4.5 (mean of 4 and 5) for the corresponding trials, and 5.5 (mean of 5 and 6) for the opposite trials.

The algorithmic costs for the four types of trials are plotted against the data in Figure 3-5. The points are well fit by a straight line — determined through a linear regression. The regression gives us both an estimate for the time per algorithm operation, and an analytic means of evaluating how well the data is fit by the model. It yields the following equation for the reaction time in milliseconds.

$$RT = 51 \times Operations + 257, \quad r^2 = 0.999 \tag{3.1}$$

The r^2 value of 0.999 verifies the excellent fit that is apparent in the graph. The equation implies that each operator requires 51 milliseconds for completion. The intercept (257 milliseconds) includes the time required for the subject to do all of the processing that falls outside of the scope of the model, such as low-level perception and motor behavior.

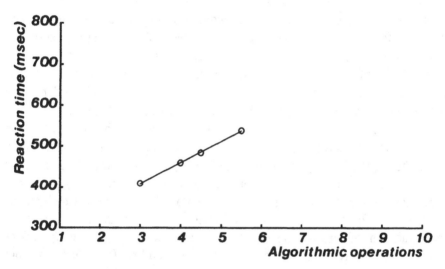

Figure 3-5: Regression of reaction time against algorithmic cost for Duncan (1977).

3.3.2.2. Fitts and Seeger (1953)

For the Fitts and Seeger (1953) experiment we have developed algorithms for the four conditions involving stimulus and response apparatuses A and B[9]. For these tasks a polar coordinate system with origin at the center of the circle of lights is used. Polar coordinates are also used for the response apparatus, however the origin is always reset to be at the current location of the lever.

In condition S_A-R_A the subject must simply push the response lever at the same angle as the light that is on. This is a very compatible situation, with an algorithm (Figure 3-6) analogous to the one for the corresponding condition in

---

[9]There are added complexities in those conditions involving the C apparatuses that have not yet been tackled.

Duncan's task (Figure 3-2). There are three operations that (1) get a description of the light that is on; (2) get the angle of that light with respect to the center; and (3) push the lever at that angle. The cost of executing this algorithm is 3.

Algorithm *Fitts&Seeger-S$_A$-R$_A$*:
    BEGIN
    Stimulus ← **Get-Stimulus**("On-Light")
    Angle ← **Get-Value**(Stimulus, "Angle")
    Make-Response("Push-Lever", Angle)
    END

Figure 3-6: Task algorithm for condition S$_A$-R$_A$ in Fitts and Seeger (1953).

In condition S$_A$-R$_B$, the subject is always presented with one light on, but must make one or two movements, depending on the angle of the light. The algorithm for this task (Figure 3-7) uses a strategy of branching to one of two subalgorithms, depending on whether the angle of the light that is on is a multiple of 90°. If it is, the lever is pushed in that direction; otherwise, the lever is pushed at the 90° angles on either side of the stimulus angle. The order of the two tests (**Is-Divisible?** and **Is-Not-Divisible?**) is arbitrary, so there are two equivalent variations on this algorithm that must be considered when computing the cost. Separate computations are also required for the two cases of divisibility. For right angles, the algorithm in Figure 3-7 predicts a cost of 4. For the symmetric algorithm, the cost is 5 (one additional test is performed). For non-right angles, the corresponding costs are 6 and 5. Fitts and Seeger defined the reaction time to be the time until the subject first moves the lever. To have comparable numbers, the non-right-angle costs reflect only the operations through the first response. Averaging the four numbers (4, 5, 5, 6) together yields a mean cost of 5 for this condition.

For this task, and for most of the following ones, there are other algorithm variations — such as delaying the two initial operations until after the branch is performed — that do not affect the time predicted by the algorithm. These are legitimate strategies that subjects can employ, but since they do not change the predictions, they can be ignored in these computations.

When stimulus apparatus S$_B$ is employed, either one or two lights are on during every trial. When S$_B$ is paired with response apparatus R$_A$, the stimulus pattern is always converted into a single push of the lever. The task algorithm for condition S$_B$-R$_A$ (Figure 3-8) starts in the same fashion as the previous two. It gets the description of an on-light from the stimulus display, and retrieves the angle of the light from the description. This process always yields exactly one on light; if there are two lights on, then one of them is selected arbitrarily.

At this point, the algorithm branches to one of two subalgorithms according to whether one or two lights are on. If there is only one light on, the lever is

Algorithm *Fitts&Seeger-S$_A$-R$_B$*:
```
    BEGIN
    Stimulus ← Get-Stimulus("On-Light")
    Stimulus-Angle ← Get-Value(Stimulus, "Angle")
    IF-SUCCEEDED Is-Divisible?(Stimulus-Angle, 90°) THEN
        Make-Response("Push-Lever", Stimulus-Angle)
      ELSE
        IF-SUCCEEDED Is-Not-Divisible?(Stimulus-Angle, 90°) THEN
            BEGIN
            Response-Angle ← Add(Stimulus-Angle, 45°)
            Make-Response("Push-Lever", Response-Angle)
            Response-Angle ← Add(Stimulus-Angle, −45°)
            Make-Response("Push-Lever", Response-Angle)
            END
    END
```

Figure 3-7:   Task algorithm for condition S$_A$-R$_B$ in Fitts and Seeger (1953).

Algorithm *Fitts&Seeger-S$_B$-R$_A$*:
```
    BEGIN
    Stimulus ← Get-Stimulus("On-Light")
    Angle ← Get-Value(Stimulus, "Angle")
    IF-SUCCEEDED One-Light-On?() THEN
        Make-Response("Push-Lever", Angle)
      ELSE
        IF-SUCCEEDED Many-On-Lights?() THEN
            BEGIN
            Stimulus2 ← Get-Second-Stimulus("On-Light", Angle)
            Angle2 ← Get-Value(Stimulus2, "Angle")
            Angle ← Average(Angle, Angle2)
            Make-Response("Push-Lever", Angle)
            END
    END
```

Figure 3-8:   Task algorithm for condition S$_B$-R$_A$ in Fitts and Seeger (1953).

pushed in the direction of that light. If there is more than one on-light, the second on-light must be found (the on-light not at the angle of the first on-light found), and its angle must be determined. The lever is pushed between the two on-lights (equivalent to averaging the angles). Once again, the order of execution of the predicates (**One-Light-On?** and **Many-Lights-On?**) is arbitrary, so we have two similar algorithms to consider, as well as two paths in each algorithm. The average cost over the four possibilities (4, 5, 7, 8) is 6.

In condition S$_B$-R$_B$, the lever must be pushed in each of the directions in which there is a light on (either one or two). There are two qualitatively different algorithms (Figure 3-9) that subjects may be employing for this condition. The faster of the two alternatives supposes that the subject begins by making the total response for one light, and only then checks to see if there is another light on. Algorithm *Fitts&Seeger-S$_B$-R$_B$-1* requires only the same number of operations before the first push as did the easiest condition (S$_A$-R$_A$), that is, 3. This value holds irrespective of the order in which the predicates are tested, because the first movement has already occurred.

Algorithm *Fitts&Seeger-S$_B$-R$_B$-1*:

```
BEGIN
Stimulus ← Get-Stimulus("On-Light")
Angle ← Get-Value(Stimulus, "Angle")
Response ← Make-Response("Push-Lever", Angle)
IF-SUCCEEDED One-On-Light?() THEN
    BEGIN
    END
    ELSE
    IF-SUCCEEDED Many-On-Lights?() THEN
        BEGIN
        Response-Angle ← Get-Value(Response, "Angle")
        Stimulus ← Get-Second-Stimulus("On-Light", Response-Angle)
        Angle ← Get-Value(Stimulus, "Angle")
        Make-Response("Push-Lever", Angle)
        END
END
```

Algorithm *Fitts&Seeger-S$_B$-R$_B$-2*:

```
BEGIN
IF-SUCCEEDED One-Light-On?() THEN
    BEGIN
    Stimulus ← Get-Stimulus("On-Light")
    Angle ← Get-Value(Stimulus, "Angle")
    Make-Response("Push-Lever", Angle)
    END
ELSE
    IF-SUCCEEDED Many-On-Lights?() THEN
        BEGIN
        Stimulus ← Get-Stimulus("On-Light")
        Angle ← Get-Value(Stimulus, "Angle")
        Response ← Make-Response("Push-Lever", Angle)
        Response-Angle ← Get-Value(Response, "Angle")
        Stimulus ← Get-Second-Stimulus("On-Light", Response-Angle)
        Angle ← Get-Value(Stimulus, "Angle")
        Make-Response("Push-Lever", Angle)
        END
END
```

Figure 3-9: Two task algorithms for condition S$_B$-R$_B$ in Fitts and Seeger (1953).

If instead the subject decides at the very beginning how many lights are on, then Algorithm *Fitts&Seeger-S_B-R_B-2* would summarize his behavior. There are two variations on this algorithm (varying the order of the predicates), and two paths in each variation, yielding four values (4, 4, 5, 5) for an average cost of 4.5.

There is a conflict in what "equally probable" means for this condition. It could mean either that the two major variations are equally likely, with the minor variations equally likely within a major variation. On the other hand, it could mean that all variations are equally likely. The first definition yields an estimate of 3.75, while the second estimate yields 4.2. There is no good justification for averaging these two values together (though averaging them does produce the best fit to the data), so we just take one of them (3.75) and comment that they do not differ by much.

It is important to ask why there are two major variations for this condition while the other three conditions have only one. Examining the algorithms closely bears out the legitimacy of this choice. Condition S_B-R_B is the only one in which a response can legitimately be made both before and after a decision. In Condition S_A-R_A, no decision is required at all. In the two cross-conditions (S_A-R_B and S_B-R_A), a manipulation of the angle may (or may not) be required before the first response is made. The decision therefore must occur before any response is made.

Comparing the simulated costs for the four conditions with the data appearing in Fitts and Seeger (1953) yields the following equation for reaction time (in milliseconds) in terms of the number of operations.

$$RT = 19 \times Operations + 334, \quad r^2 = 0.992 \tag{3.2}$$

Again an excellent fit is achieved (see also Figure 3-10), albeit with different values for the slope and intercept. This topic will be picked up again later.

3.3.2.3. Morin and Forrin (1962)

In the experiment reported by Morin and Forrin (1962), there were five conditions and six data points of interest, but there are only four task algorithms. The first and simplest algorithm (Figure 3-11) is sufficient for both conditions I and IV. The rule-like nature of the algorithms is crucial here because it allows a single algorithm to be used for reading numbers aloud, no matter how many alternatives there may be. There is one qualification on this statement, namely, it assumes that reading numbers aloud is so well practiced that determining the vocal response to a visual numeral can be done in a single operation. If there is a relatively unlearned mapping (as appears in the other conditions of this same experiment), making that connection is difficult.

The algorithm for conditions I and IV is again analogous to the easiest

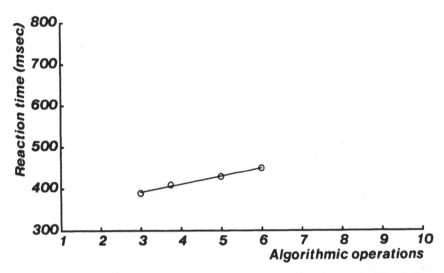

Figure 3-10: Regression of reaction time against algorithmic cost for Fitts & Seeger (1953).

Algorithm *Morin&Forrin-I-IV*:
    BEGIN
    Stimulus ← **Get-Stimulus**()
    Name ← **Get-Value**(Stimulus, "Name")
    Make-Response("Say-Name", Name)
    END

Figure 3-11: Task algorithm for Conditions I and IV in Morin and Forrin (1962).

conditions of the previous two experiments. The subject must (1) get a description of the stimulus, (2) get the name (such as "2") from that description, and (3) say that name. This results in a net cost of 3.

Condition II is like condition I except for the fact that the association between the visual stimulus and the vocal response is not well learned. It is assumed that while the subject assimilated the instructions for this condition, he created operators like **Get-Plus-Number**, that when executed gave him the number that was associated with the symbol +. The subject's main problem, therefore, is to determine which of these operators to use. Using the same positive-check model for choice in this situation as has been used throughout, yields the algorithm in Figure 3-12. In computing the cost of this algorithm, we must average over the amount of time taken for the two symbols. These yield values of 5 for + and 6 for ■, for an average of 5.5.

Condition III is a mixed task in which one of two numbers or one of two symbols will appear. If we assume that included in the description of the

Algorithm *Morin&Forrin-II*:
```
BEGIN
Stimulus ← Get-Stimulus()
Name ← Get-Value(Stimulus, "Name")
IF-SUCCEEDED Is-Plus?(Name) THEN
    Name ← Get-Plus-Number()
  ELSE
    IF-SUCCEEDED Is-Square?(Name) THEN
        Name ← Get-Square-Number()
Make-Response("Say-Name", Name)
END
```

Figure 3-12:   Task algorithm for Condition II in Morin and Forrin (1962).

stimulus is a statement of its class (either symbol or number) as well as its name, then the obvious algorithm for this condition is the one in Figure 3-13. The class decision is first made, and then a symbol decision and mapping are made if necessary. The number subalgorithm is essentially the algorithm for condition I, and the symbol subalgorithm is essentially the same as the one for condition II.

Algorithm *Morin&Forrin-III*:
```
BEGIN
Stimulus ← Get-Stimulus()
Class ← Get-Value(Stimulus, "Class")
Name ← Get-Value(Stimulus, "Name")
IF-SUCCEEDED Is-Number?(Class) THEN
    Make-Response("Say-Name", Name)
  ELSE
    IF-SUCCEEDED Is-Symbol?(Class) THEN
        BEGIN
        IF-SUCCEEDED Is-Plus?(Name) THEN
            Name ← Get-Plus-Number()
          ELSE
            IF-SUCCEEDED Is-Square?(Name) THEN
                Name ← Get-Square-Number()
        Make-Response("Say-Name", Name)
        END
END
```

Figure 3-13:   Task algorithm for Condition III in Morin and Forrin (1962).

For trials in which a number appears (condition IIIa), there are two algorithm variants, determined by the order of the two class tests. The average cost for these two algorithms (5, 6) is 5.5. For the symbolic case (condition IIIb), each of these two variations has two variations determined by the order of the name tests. The mean cost for these four variations (7, 8, 8, 9) is 8.

The final condition, number V, is the four-choice case analogous to condition II. The structure of the algorithm (Figure 3-14) is the same except for the addition of the tests and information for the two extra symbols. The decisions are arranged serially rather than in a logarithmic (hierarchical) fashion because there is no obvious and well learned class distinction between any of the pairs of the four symbols. The average cost for performing this algorithm is the mean of the costs of performing it for each of the four symbols. These costs are 5, 6, 7, and 8, for an average of 6.5.

```
Algorithm Morin&Forrin-V:
    BEGIN
    Stimulus ← Get-Stimulus()
    Name ← Get-Value(Stimulus, "Name")
    IF-SUCCEEDED Is-Plus?(Name) THEN
        Name ← Get-Plus-Number()
      ELSE
        IF-SUCCEEDED Is-Square?(Name) THEN
            Name ← Get-Square-Number()
          ELSE
            IF-SUCCEEDED Is-Circle?(Name) THEN
                Name ← Get-Circle-Number()
              ELSE
                IF-SUCCEEDED Is-Triangle?(Name) THEN
                    Name ← Get-Triangle-Number()
    Make-Response("Say-Name", Name)
    END
```

Figure 3-14: Task algorithm for Condition V in Morin and Forrin (1962).

Comparing the six simulated results with the six data points in Morin and Forrin (1962) yields the curve in Figure 3-15, and the following regression equation for reaction time (in milliseconds) versus number of operations.

$$RT = 45 \times Operations + 367, \quad r^2 = 0.884 \qquad (3.3)$$

Though this a worse fit than the previous two experiments, the model still accounts for over 88% of the variance. If we look more carefully at the results we can come up with an explanation for why this fit is somewhat worse. The simulated cost for condition V is just too small. In the experimental data, condition V takes 10 milliseconds longer than condition IIIb; but in the simulated data, condition IIIb costs 1.5 operations (approximately 67 milliseconds) more than condition V. At present we do not have a solution to this problem, we merely note that if in fact the simulated cost for condition V were raised to be equal to the cost for condition IIIb, the fit improves so that over 98% of the variance is accounted for.

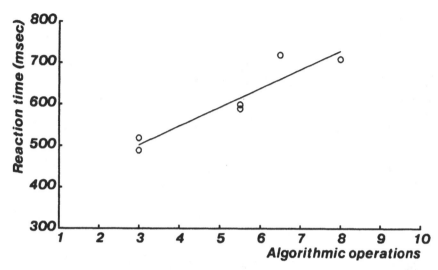

Figure 3-15: Regression of reaction time against algorithmic cost for Morin & Forrin (1962).

3.3.3. Putting the results together

So far the model has produced good fits to the three experiments in-dividually, but to have a predictive theory for new experiments, more is needed. Specifically, we need a set of task-independent parameters. This is fine for the slope parameter (milliseconds per operations), but we cannot expect to find a task-independent intercept. The reason is that the experiments differ in many ways not captured by the theory. For example, in the Morin and Forrin (1962) experiment responses are vocal, while in the other two experiments they are manual. Such differences will affect the intercept, but should leave the slope unchanged.

The following equation is the result of regressing the data for the fourteen conditions against task times. Each of the three experiments has its own inter-cept (specified as the coefficient of a boolean variable which is true only for that experiment), but a single slope parameter is used.

$$RT = 41 \times Operations + 300 \times Duncan$$
$$+ 238 \times Fitts\&Seeger + 389 \times Morin\&Forrin, \quad r^2 = 0.943 \qquad (3.4)$$

Figure 3-16 plots the data points against the simulated reaction times predicted by Equation 3.4. Both the equation and the graph show the linearity of the fit. Examining the graph reveals that the individual experiments still show different slopes, but this effect disappears into the noise.

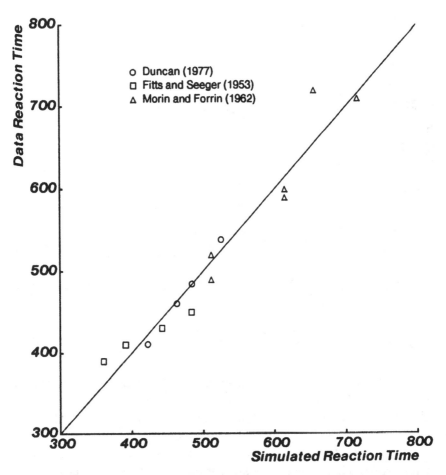

Figure 3-16: Comparison of simulated and true reaction times for the three compatibility experiments. The results are generated from the algorithmic
formulation of the algorithmic model of compatibility.

It is interesting to note that the predicted time per operation of 41msec is
essentially the same as the comparison time derived by Sternberg (1966) for
high-speed scanning of short-term memory. Though that task is not tradi-
tionally classified as a compatibility task, a set of structures like Algorithm
Morin&Forrin-V, but for different numbers of alternatives, would predict exactly those results (modulo questions about terminating versus nonterminating
searches).

Another point of comparison is with the *cognitive cycle time*, which Card,
Moran, and Newell (1983) determined to be between 25 and 170 milliseconds.
It is conceivable that the cognitive cycle can be associated with the execution of
an operation.

3.4. Other Subphenomena and Experiments

There are quite a few stimulus-response compatibility experiments not covered in this chapter. A number of these fall into a recently active subarea that deals with the question of the laterality of spatial stimulus-response mappings. Filbey and Gazzaniga (1969) argue that tasks requiring cross-hemispheric communication — for example, if the stimulus is perceived with one hemisphere, and the response is to be made by the other — will take longer because of the extra time to do the communication.

On the other hand, a number of investigators have argued that it is not cerebral hemisphere that is crucial (as in which hand performs the response), but the absolute spatial relationship between the stimulus and the required response (Simon, Hinrichs, & Craft, 1970; Brebner, Shephard, & Cairney, 1972; Nicoletti, Anzola, Luppino, Rizzolatti, & Umilta, 1982). This is an assumption that is compatible with the model presented here.

Other experiments were not discussed because of their strong interaction with other effects such as preparation (Broadbent & Gregory, 1965), sequential dependencies (Broadbent & Gregory, 1965; Smith, 1977), discriminability (Garvey & Knowles, 1954; Broadbent & Gregory, 1965), interference (Smith, 1977), and the addition of irrelevant but misleading information (Wallace, 1971).

The experiment that seems most in conflict with the model presented here is that of Smith (1977). He performed an experiment much like that of Duncan (1977) but found that performance in the mixed condition was between the levels of performance on the two pure conditions, rather than more difficult than either. There are four factors that could contribute to these seemingly anomalous results. The stimuli in Smith's task were direct finger stimulation, a situation which should make corresponding responses quicker, and opposite responses slower. In addition, Duncan's subjects were within conditions, while Smith's were across conditions. This should increase the interference on all conditions. The net effect of these two factors should be to increase the spread between the corresponding and opposite conditions, an effect that does appear in the data. The other two factors stem from the fact that Smith's mixed condition involved half as many response keys as the pure cases. This should decrease the problem of discriminating which response key to use, and should increase the amount of practice on the mixed responses relative to the pure ones (this is the only one of the four factors that is within the scope of the current model). These two factors should lower the reaction time for the mixed condition relative to the pure conditions. Combining all four factors, we see that the pure conditions are spread further apart — leaving more room for the mixed condition to slip between — and the mixed condition's reaction time is lowered so that it would slip in between.

There is one other classical compatibility experiment not covered — Fitts and Deininger (1954). We have examined these results in some detail, and did some of our earliest simulations for these conditions. However, a full understanding of the strategies employed by subjects in these tasks is still a bit past our grasp, so we have postponed to a later date, the presentation of an account for them.

4 GOAL-STRUCTURED MODELS

In Chapter 2 we reviewed the nature of practice and how the chunking theory of learning has been shown to be an adequate model for the power-law learning curves produced during practice. In Chapter 3 we showed how stimulus-response compatibility tasks could be modeled by algorithms written in a simple procedural language called *Artless*. In this chapter, these two (until now unrelated) efforts are integrated into a single model, based on the concept of *goal hierarchies*. This model, when combined with the production-system architecture designed to execute it (Chapter 5), has the following properties (in the following, *task independence* means that models make no task-specific assumptions; the behavior the models describe of course depends on the particular task being performed):

- The model contains a task-independent performance model for reaction-time tasks, at least for the Seibel and compatibility tasks.
- It contains a task-independent model of learning by chunking, at least for the Seibel and compatibility tasks.
- It reproduces the results of the algorithmic theory of compatibility, yielding results at least as good as those from the algorithmic formulation.
- It generates power-law practice curves for the Seibel task.
- For the compatibility tasks, where the human practice curves tend to be ambiguously power law or exponential, it produces a mixture of power-law and exponential practice curves.

We will begin this chapter with a discussion of goal hierarchies, using the Duncan tasks to bring out the salient points. We then proceed to look at the goal hierarchy for the Seibel task, and an abstract specification of how chunking applies to goal hierarchies. The goal hierarchies for the other compatibility tasks are presented in Chapter 6, following the description of the *Xaps3* architecture in Chapter 5.

At the end of this chapter, we present the beginnings of a mathematical analysis of the chunking theory as it applies to goal hierarchies. This analysis is modeled after, and is an update to, the analysis presented in Newell and Rosenbloom (1981).

4.1. The Basics of Goal Hierarchies

A *goal* is a data structure representing a desired state of affairs. It is not a procedure for bringing about that state; it is only a description of the state. In order to bring about the goal state, there must be a *method* associated with the goal. The method could be a rigid algorithm, or it could be one of the more flexible *weak methods* (Newell, 1969) such as means-ends analysis (Ernst & Newell, 1969) or heuristic search (Nilsson, 1971).

When a goal can be decomposed into a set of simpler goals (Nilsson, 1971), and those goals can be decomposed even further, a goal hierarchy results. In its simplest form, as an AND hierarchy, a goal is successful if all of its subgoals are successful. The structure to be described here, more closely resembles an AND/OR hierarchy, in which some goals succeed only if all of their subgoals succeed, and others succeed if any one of their subgoals succeed.

One strategy for processing a goal hierarchy is to attempt the goals in a *depth-first* fashion, in which the most recently generated (the deepest) goal is always selected as the next goal to process. With a depth-first paradigm, there is always exactly one goal being actively worked on at any point in time. We will refer to this goal as the *active* or *current* goal. When a subgoal becomes the active goal, the parent goal of that subgoal is *suspended* until control is returned to it by completion of the subgoal, at which point it again becomes the current goal. On completion, the subgoal will either have *succeeded* or *failed*.

The model's *control stack* specifies the location in the hierarchy at which control currently resides. It does this by maintaining the path from the root goal of the hierarchy to the current goal. This path consists of the active goal, and all of its suspended ancestors.

In addition to the goal hierarchy, the model with which we work assumes a working memory for the short-term storage of information relevant to the processing that is going on. For each goal, the working memory is logically partitioned into two components — the *initial state* and the *local state*. The initial state consists of the data existing at the time the goal is first activated. The remainder of the working memory — consisting of those pieces of data created during the processing of the goal — make up its local state. Only the local state of a goal can be modified during the processing of that goal; the initial state can be examined, but not modified. The modularity resulting from this scoping rule increases the likelihood that an arbitrary set of goals can be pursued without interfering with each other. This modularity is also important in ensuring correct performance of the chunking mechanism (Section 4.2).

Each piece of information in the working memory is relevant in a particular temporal *processing context*. As long as the goal during which the datum was created is in the control stack, the system is either working on that goal, or on one of its descendents. The datum may be relevant at any point in this processing. However, once the goal disappears from the control stack, it is no longer being pursued. The datum will most likely no longer be relevant. Let us therefore define the context of a datum to be that period of processing during which its creator goal is in the control stack. Once a piece of information becomes *out of context* — its creator is no longer part of the control stack — it usually can safely be deleted from the working memory. The data that cannot be deleted — because they are needed outside of the context in which they were created — are called the *results* of the goal. Their continued presence in the working memory is accomplished by changing their context to be the context of the parent goal.

The goal hierarchy can be related to the compatibility algorithms of the previous chapter by imagining a fine-grained procedural hierarchy superimposed on top of the algorithms. The top node in the hierarchy represents the whole task, the terminal nodes — those that have no subnodes — are the operators, and the intermediate non-terminal nodes represent segments of the task generated by a top-down decomposition of the top-level node. There can be, of course, different goal hierarchies corresponding to different decompositions.

Figure 4-1 shows two different representations of the goal hierarchy for the Duncan *Corresponding* task (Algorithm *Duncan-Corresponding* in Figure 3-2). The top half shows the bare bones of the hierarchy as a tree structure. The nodes are labeled with a unique number representing the goal at that position. The bottom half shows the same structure as it is traversed in a depth-first fashion. In this representation, the tree structure loses its clarity, but the depth-first order in which the goals are processed becomes clear. In addition, the node labels can be expanded out to the full names of the goals.

The bold-faced goals are the terminal goals[10] — those analogous to operators in the algorithms. For this task, the terminal goals are identical to the

---

[10]Though goals are declarative structures describing a state to be achieved, rather than a procedural description of how to achieve the state, the goal names used in this work will be given in an imperative rather than a declarative form. This is to emphasize the relationship between the goal hierarchies described in this chapter, and the algorithms described in Chapter 3.

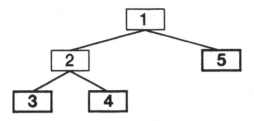

1. Press-Button-Under-Stimulus-Line
 2. Get-Horizontal-Location-Of-Stimulus-Line
  3. **Get-Stimulus-Line**
  4. **Get-Horizontal-Location-Of-Stimulus**
 5. **Press-Button-At-Horizontal-Location**

Figure 4-1: Goal hierarchy for the Duncan (1977) *corresponding* condition.

operators employed in the algorithm. However, some of the other structure in the algorithm does not appear in the goal hierarchy. The explicit parameters of the operators are not shown in this structure. For simplicity, each goal name shown describes exactly what is trying to be accomplished. Thus, it is a composite of the true goal name, and the explicit parameters for the goal instance. In addition to the explicit parameters, a goal can have implicitly defined parameters. Any object in the goal's initial state that is examined during the processing of the goal, is an implicit parameter for the goal.

There are no variables, constants, or assignments shown in this goal structure. These concepts are replaced by the working memory, and the operations that place information in it. This will be left ill-defined for now, to be further specified in Chapter 5 when the working memory is implemented as part of a production system architecture and the operations on the working memory are implemented as productions. Sequential execution, as previously defined by the *block* construct, is performed by a combination of productions and the goal processing of the *Xaps3* architecture (Chapter 5).

Figure 4-2 shows the goal hierarchy for the Duncan *Opposite* task. This is a balanced binary tree in which, once again, the terminal goals in the hierarchy are similar to the operators in the associated algorithm (Algorithm *Duncan-Opposite* in Figure 3-3). However, there is one difference worthy of comment. In the algorithm there is only one horizontal location represented in the system at any one time. When the opposite location is computed, it overwrites the original one. This is impossible in the goal hierarchy, because the stimulus location is part of the initial state of the goal that computes the response location. Therefore, in the hierarchy, both locations will be simultaneously represented. The system must be careful so as to not use the wrong location (producing a corresponding error).

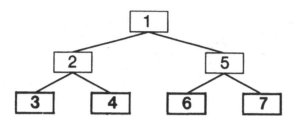

1. Press-Button-Opposite-Stimulus-Line
  2. Get-Horizontal-Location-Of-Stimulus-Line
    3. **Get-Stimulus-Line**
    4. **Get-Horizontal-Location-Of-Stimulus**
  5. Press-Button-Opposite-Horizontal-Location
    6. **Compute-Opposite-Horizontal-Location**
    7. **Press-Button-At-Opposite-Horizontal-Location**

Figure 4-2: Goal hierarchy for the Duncan (1977) *opposite* condition.

This problem is solved by the simple expedient of assigning the two locations to different "variables". The name of the appropriate variable is passed as an explicit (*call-by-name*) parameter to the goal responsible for pressing the button. This is denoted in the structure in Figure 4-2 by the presence of the word "Opposite" in the name of the goal responsible for pressing the button (**Press-Button-At-Opposite-Horizontal-Location**).

Figure 4-3 presents the goal hierarchy for the *mixed* condition in Duncan (1977). It begins, as do the previous two structures, by determining the horizontal location of the line in the stimulus display. A decision is then made as to whether the line is central or distal. Based on the results of this decision, the hierarchy branches to one of two subgoals. The first one (Press-Button-Opposite-Horizontal-Location) is the same as goal number 5 in the *opposite* hierarchy. The other one (**Press-Button-At-Horizontal-Location**) is the same as goal number 5 in the *corresponding* hierarchy.

The only difference of importance between this hierarchy and Algorithm *Duncan-Mixed-1* (Figure 3-4) concerns the structure of predicates and branches. Predicates (such as **Is-Horizontal-Location-In-The-Middle?** in Figure 4-3) are not part of the branch; they are separate goals in the hierarchy, just like all other goals. To make them stand out, the two predicates in the tree structure are starred.

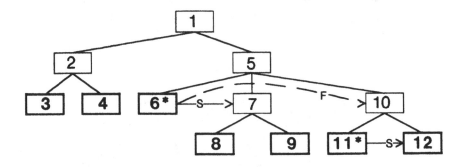

1. Press-Button-At-Or-Opposite-Stimulus-Line
    2. Get-Horizontal-Location-Of-Stimulus-Line
        3. **Get-Stimulus-Line**
        4. **Get-Horizontal-Location-Of-Stimulus**
    5. Press-Button-At-Or-Opposite-Horizontal-Location
        6. **Is-Horizontal-Location-In-The-Middle?**
        IF-SUCCEEDED *Is-Horizontal-Location-In-The-Middle?* THEN
            7. Press-Button-Opposite-Horizontal-Location
                8. **Compute-Opposite-Horizontal-Location**
                9. **Press-Button-At-Opposite-Horizontal-Location**
        IF-FAILED *Is-Horizontal-Location-In-The-Middle?* THEN
            10. Possibly-Press-Button-At-Horizontal-Location
                11. **Is-Horizontal-Location-Outside-Of-Middle?**
                IF-SUCCEEDED *Is-Horizontal-Location-Outside-Of-Middle?* THEN
                    12. **Press-Button-At-Horizontal-Location**

Figure 4-3: Goal hierarchy for the Duncan (1977) *mixed* condition.

Branches simply check the status (*succeeded* or *failed*) of goals that have already completed. The single IF-SUCCEEDED—THEN—ELSE statement appearing in the algorithm is replaced by two single branches (IF-SUCCEEDED—THEN and IF-FAILED—THEN) in analogy to the productions that will implement them. These branches are shown in Figure 4-3 as dashed lines between the predicate and the goal appearing in the THEN clause. The lines are labeled with either an S for *Succeeded*, or an F for *Failed*.

We now have a general task-independent scheme; one that will work for any task for which we can create a goal hierarchy. The scope of this representation is at least as wide as the algorithmic language.

4.2. Chunking on Goal Hierarchies

The excursions through stimulus-response compatibility and goal hierarchies were motivated by the need to generalize the performance and learning models on which the chunking theory of learning is based. Now that we have a task-independent language for performance models, we can return to the original objective of this research project, and describe a task-independent formulation of the chunking theory.

The definition is quite simple, once the mechanism of goal hierarchies is in place. Consider the task-specific goal structure proposed for the Seibel task in Rosenbloom and Newell (1982a) (Figure 4-4). This is a very simple hierarchy in which the main control structure is actually an iteration over a goal (**OnePattern**), rather than a decomposition into subgoals. On each iteration two subgoals were processed. One of them (**OneStimulusPattern**) searched the stimulus display for the next pattern of lights to process (in a left-to-right traversal), returning the pattern as its result. The other subgoal (**OneResponsePattern**) took as parameter a pattern of buttons to press, and its task was to press them. The mapping of stimulus to response was a built-in function of the **OnePattern** goal.

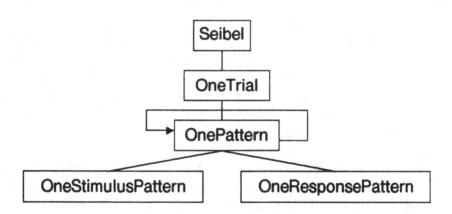

Figure 4-4: The task-specific goal hierarchy for the Seibel (1963) task in Rosenbloom and Newell (1982a).

Though the task decomposition is quite different, and the chunking mechanism used for it was not task-independent, this structure can help in making a key point. The question is how to define chunks with respect to the new general goal scheme. If we look at where the information came from on which chunks were based in the old scheme, it turns out that it all appeared as either the parameters or results of one of these goals. The on-lights appeared as results of the **OneStimulusPattern** goal, and the buttons to be pressed appeared as parameters to the **OneResponsePattern** goal. Chunks were created from successively processed pairs of these parameters and results.

The task-independent formulation of the chunking theory is generated by applying this idea to all of the goals in a hierarchy. Each chunk improves the performance of the system by eliminating the need to fully process a specific instance (a combination of parameter values) of a particular goal. It replaces the normal processing (decomposition into subgoals for non-terminal goals, and direct execution of some code for terminal goals) with a direct connection between the relevant parameter values and results. A goal can (and almost certainly will) have more than one possible chunk. Each combination of parameter values requires its own chunk. Chunking thus implements a store-versus-compute trade-off, a form of goal-based caching of results.

As with the previous version of the chunking theory (see Chapter 2), each chunk consists of three components: *encoding, decoding,* and *connection.* The goal's parameter values form the basis for the encoding component. Given the presence of those values in the working memory, the encoding component generates a new object representing their combination. Encoding is a parallel, goal-independent, data-driven process. Every encoding component executes as soon as appropriate, irrespective of whatever else is happening in the system. The results of encoding components can themselves become parameter values to other goals, leading to a hierarchical encoding process.

The results of the goal form the basis for the decoding component. Given the presence of an encoded result-object in the working memory, the decoding component generates the actual results returned by the goal. Decoding occurs when the results are needed, an obfuscation that will be cleared up when the implementation is discussed in Chapter 5. As with encoding, the set of decoding components forms a hierarchical structure in which complex results are decoded to simpler ones, which are then decoded even further.

The connection component of the chunk generates the encoded result from the encoded parameter. It is the one aspect of the chunk which is goal-dependent. It can only make the connection when the system is working on the goal for which the chunk was formed (and after the encoding component has executed), ensuring that the system's performance remains goal directed.

Chunks are created bottom-up in the goal hierarchy. A chunk can be created for a goal when the following two conditions are met: (1) the goal has just completed successfully, and (2) all of the goal's subgoals were themselves processed by chunks. It is this bottom-up aspect of chunking that leads to hierarchical encoding and decoding networks. However, notice that bottom-up chunking does not imply that all low-level chunks are learned before any high-level chunks are learned, or even that all of the chunks must be learned for a subgoal before any can be learned for its parent goal. The second condition on chunk creation merely states that chunks must exist for the goal's subgoals *in the current situation*. Any other chunks that exist or do not exist for the subgoals are irrelevant.

Given enough practice, all of the situations for all of the goals in the hierarchy will be chunked, and asymptotic behavior will be reached for the task. The amount of time this takes depends on the number of goals, the number of situations for each goal, how frequently the different situations arise, and whether chunks are created whenever they can be.

As a simple example, consider how chunking works for the simple three-goal hierarchy in Figure 4-5. This structure computes the average of two numbers. The top-level goal (Compute-Average-Of-Two-Numbers) takes as parameters the two numbers to be averaged, and returns a single result, which is their mean. The first subgoal (**Compute-Sum-Of-Two-Numbers**) performs the first half of the computation. It takes the two numbers as parameters, and returns their sum as its result. The second subgoal finishes the computation by taking the sum as a parameter, and returning half of it as its result.

1. Compute-Average-Of-Two-Numbers
   2. **Compute-Sum-Of-Two-Numbers**
   3. **Divide-Sum-By-2**

Figure 4-5: A simple three-goal hierarchy for the averaging of two numbers.

Suppose that the first task is to average the numbers 3 and 7. Control would pass from goal number 1 to goal number 2. When goal 2 finishes and returns its result of 10, a chunk of three components is created (bottom left of Figure 4-6). An encoding component is created that encodes the two parameters (3 and 7) into a new symbol (E1). It executes as soon as it is created, because the parameters are in the working memory. A decoding component is created that, when necessary, decodes from a second new symbol (D1) to the result (10). A connection component (the horizontal line with the goal name above it and goal number below it) is created that generates the result symbol (D1) when it detects both the presence of the encoded parameter (E1) and that goal 2 is the active goal. The connection does not execute immediately, because goal 2 is already complete when the chunk is created.

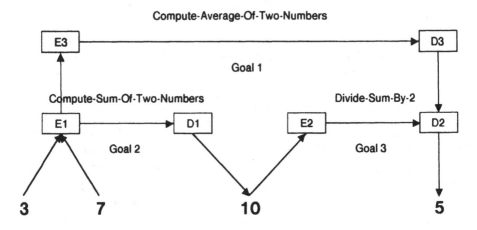

Figure 4-6: Sample chunks created for the hierarchy in Figure 4-5.

Following the termination of goal 2, goal 1 is reactivated, but then is suspended in favor of goal 3 (**Divide-Sum-By-2**). When this goal terminates successfully (returning the number 5), a chunk is created for it (bottom right of Figure 4-6). The encoding component encodes the number 10 into the symbol E2; the decoding component decodes from the symbol D2 to the number 5; and the connection component connects E2 to D2 (in the presence of an active goal 3). In contrast to the chunk for goal 1, this chunk can be used in more than one task situation. It can be used whenever goal 1 generates a sum of 10, whether it does it by adding 3 and 7, 5 and 5, or any other pair of numbers. This is a form of transfer of training.

Following the termination of goal 3, goal 1 is reactivated and terminates successfully (returning the number 5). No chunk is created for goal 1 because its subgoals were not processed by chunks. The task is complete.

Given what was learned during the performance of this task, the next time the same task is performed things will go differently. As soon as the task is restarted (again with 3 and 7), the encoding component from the chunk for goal 2 executes, placing E1 in the working memory. Goal 1 is activated, and then suspended in favor of goal 2. At this point, the connection component for goal 2 executes, generating D1 and successfully completing goal 2. D1 is decoded to the number 10, which is then immediately reencoded to E2 by the encoding component for goal 3. Goal 1 is reactivated, and suspended. Goal 3 is activated, and its connection component executes, generating D2. D2 is returned as the result to goal 1. This time, when goal 1 terminates, a chunk is created (top of Figure 4-6), because both of the subgoals were processed by chunks.

The encoding component for this chunk builds upon the existing encodings by encoding E1 to a new symbol (E3); it does not go straight from goal 1's primitive parameters (3 and 7). This happens (and causes hierarchical encoding) because, for this instance of goal 1, E1 is the implicit parameter, not 3 and 7. Recall from Section 4.1 that the implicit parameters of a goal consist of those pieces of the goal's initial state that are examined during the goal's performance. E1 is generated before goal 1 is activated (so it is part of the goal's initial state) and examined by the connection component for goal 2. On the other hand, neither of the objects representing the numbers 3 and 7 are examined during the processing of goal 1. Therefore, E1 is an implicit parameter (and included in the chunk), while the numbers 3 and 7 are not.

The decoding component is created in a similarly hierarchical fashion. It decodes from a new symbol (D3) to D2. This occurs because D2 (and not "5") is the result of goal 1. It never became necessary to decode D2, so it was passed directly up as the result of both goals 3 and 1. The connection component of this chunk links E3 to D3 in a straightforward manner.

If the same task is performed yet again, the encoding components immediately generate E1, followed by E3. Goal 1 is activated and its connection component executes, generating D3 and completing goal 1. If the result is needed by some part of the system outside of the hierarchy, it will be decoded to D2, and then to "5".

The example that we have just gone through outlines the basics of how the chunking mechanism works. The next step is to look at the more complex situation of the Seibel task. Figure 4-7 shows the goal hierarchy for that task. This structure is based on a recursive divide-and-conquer algorithm in which the stimulus display is broken up into smaller and smaller horizontal segments, until manageable pieces are generated. This is a different method from the iterative algorithm previously employed for this task. For two reasons it is not critical to look at all reasonable algorithms for this task (as it is for compatibility). The first reason is that we are not trying to match the simulations to particular data values; it is the functional form (a power law) of the simulated practice curves that is critical. The second reason is that the Seibel data is single-subject data, for which it is appropriate to consider a single strategy, rather than a statistical mix of strategies.

The recursive algorithm was selected over the iterative algorithm because no goal formulation of the iterative algorithm was found for which a satisfactory set of chunks would be learned. Rather than creating piecemeal chunks for different segments of the display, the iterative algorithms result in chunks that always start at one end of the display, and build up increasingly big chunks from there (always including the one on the end). A hybrid strategy — in which the

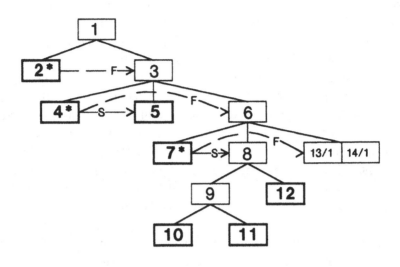

1. Do-Lights-If-Any(Min-X, Max-X)
   2. No-Light-On?(Min-X, Max-X)
   IF-FAILED *No-Light-On?* THEN
      3. Do-Lights(Min-X, Max-X)
         4. No-Light-Off?(Min-X, Max-X)
         IF-SUCCEEDED *No-Light-Off?* THEN
            5. Do-Press-All-Buttons(Min-X, Max-X)
         IF-FAILED *No-Light-Off?* THEN
            6. Do-Off-And-On(Min-X, Max-X)
               7. One-Light-On?(Min-X, Max-X)
               IF-SUCCEEDED *One-Light-On?* THEN
                  8. Press-Button-Under-On-Light(Min-X, Max-X)
                  9. Get-On-Light-X(Min-X, Max-X)
                     10. Get-On-Light-Stimulus(Min-X, Max-X)
                     11. Get-Stimulus-X
                  12. Press-Button-At-X
               IF-FAILED *One-Light-On?* THEN
                  13. Do-Lights-If-Any(Min-X, [Min-X + Max-X]/2)
                  14. Do-Lights-If-Any([Min-X + Max-X]/2, Max-X)

Figure 4-7:   Goal hierarchy for the Seibel (1963) task.

display is decomposed into a few parts, and iteration occurs within the parts —
might be a reasonable alternative. However, the pure recursive algorithm works
adequately, and so has been employed.

In the recursive algorithm in Figure 4-7, there are three types of horizontal
segments that have been defined as manageable. The first type of manageable
segment is one in which no lights are on. Such segments require no explicit

processing, so the goal just returns with success. The opposite of the first type of segment — one in which no lights are off — is also manageable. For such a segment, the system generates a single response specifying that a *press* action must occur in the entire region defined by the segment (using the **Do-Press-All-Buttons** goal). Specifying a single button press is actually a special case of this, in which the region is just large enough to contain the one button. Allowing multi-on-light segments to be manageable implies that sequences of adjacent on-lights can be pressed simultaneously, even before chunking has begun. Such behavior is seen very early in the trial sequence for some subjects. The remaining manageable segments are those that contain exactly one light on. These segments are processed (using the Press-Button-Under-On-Light goal) by finding the location of that light, and generating a button press at that location.

If a generated segment does not meet any of these three criteria, it is unmanageable, and is split into two smaller segments. Figure 4-8 shows the ten lights, their horizontal locations (right below them), and the locations where the display is split. The length of the vertical bar representing the split (and the number above it) corresponds to how early the display is divided at that location (the location of the line is given below it). The first split occurs in the middle (at location 500). The two resulting segments are split at 250 and 750, if needed, and the process continues from there. Note that this strategy produces performance characteristics much like those of the subjects in Rosenbloom and Newell (1982a) — left-to-right processing of groups of adjacent on-lights.

The recursive aspect of the algorithm implies that many different instances of each goal will be simultaneously represented in the system, though at most one can actually be active. In order to keep track of which goal instance is relevant to which segment of the stimulus display, the segment (in terms of its minimum and maximum X values) is an explicit parameter to the goals. Recursion also implies that the system does not start off with a constant built-in goal hierarchy. Instead, it has a generator of goal hierarchies. That chunking works on such a structure is important for any claims about the potential generality of the mechanism (for more on this, see Sections 7.6 and 7.7).

The recursion occurs at goals 13 and 14 in Figure 4-7. They are repetitions of the topmost goal in the hierarchy (Do-Lights-If-Any), but the scope of each is limited to one half of the display currently being processed. The numeric computation to obtain the middle of the segment (involving an addition and a division) is, on the surface, too powerful a computation to appear where it does. However, this is only intended as an approximation to what a human subject would do in such a situation, namely to divide the stimulus display into two (or three) roughly equal parts.

Chunking starts in this structure with the terminal goals (numbers 2, 4, 5, 7, 10, 11, and 12). Take goal 11 (**Get-Stimulus-X**), for example. Successful

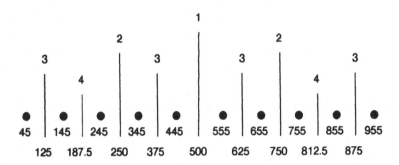

Figure 4-8: The locations of the lights and recursive splits for the simulation of the
Seibel (1963) task.

completion of this goal requires retrieving from the working memory the
representation of a stimulus that has been perceived, and generating a piece of
information representing the horizontal location (X) of that stimulus. The
parameter for this goal is the stimulus — an implicit parameter — and the result
is the location. In the chunk for this situation, the encoding and decoding
components are trivial. They simply recode from the single parameter to a new
symbol, and from a second new symbol to the result. The connection component tests for the presence of an active **Get-Stimulus-X** goal and the encoding
symbol, and produces the decoding symbol.

Goal 10 (**Get-On-Light-Stimulus**) presents a slightly more complicated case
than goal 11. The goal has both explicit and implicit parameters. The explicit
parameters (Min-X and Max-X) define the region of the stimulus display in
which an on-light should be found. The implicit parameter is the actual external representation (in the stimulus display) of the on-light that is found. The
result of this goal is the internal representation of that on-light, as it appears in
the working memory. Just as before, the implicit parameter and the result form
the basis for trivial encoding and decoding components. However, the explicit
parameters are different. They do not exist as separate entities in the working
memory; instead they act as if they were augmentations to the name of the goal.
Therefore, they appear along with the name of the goal, as part of the connection component.

As a final example of the workings of the chunking mechanism, consider
how it creates the kinds of multiple light-button chunks produced by the chunking mechanism in Rosenbloom and Newell (1982a). The locus of these chunks
can be found at the recursive step in the goal hierarchy. The root (and
recursive) goal in the hierarchy (Do-Lights-If-Any) has implicit parameters
which represent on-lights in the stimulus display, and generates results that are
the button presses for those lights. The earliest chunks that can be created for

this goal are those at the bottom of the recursion; that is, goals to process manageable segments of the display. Each of these chunks will represent a single on-light in a region, a region of solid on-lights, or a region with no on-lights. Once the chunks exist for goals 13 and 14 (and their sibling goal 7: the predicate **One-Light-On?**), in a single situation, the parent goal (goal 6: Do-Off-And-On) can be chunked. This yields a new chunk for the combined situation in both segments. This process continues up the hierarchy until goal 1 is chunked for that level of recursion. But goal 1 at that level is just goal 13 or 14 at the next level up. Therefore, gradually (these chunks are acquired one at a time), the level of aggregation of segments covered by chunks increases.

Figure 4-9 shows how the final encoding hierarchy would look if a single task situation — a pattern of 10 lights — were repeated until the root goal at the top level of the recursion has been chunked. The nodes in this hierarchy all represent chunks of the Do-Lights-If-Any goal (numbers 1, 13, and 14). The other goals in the hierarchy also contribute encodings, but they have been left out of this figure so that the hierarchical grouping of the lights is clear. Inside of each node is shown the pattern of lights that it covers. The numbers in the figure specify the horizontal location of the associated split. The left branch from the split represents the contribution from its goal 13, while the right branch is from its goal 14.

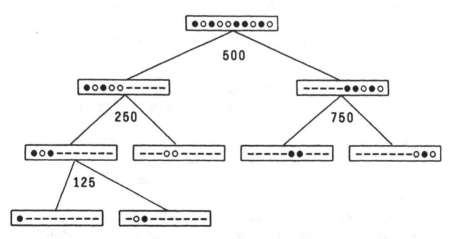

Figure 4-9: The encoding hierarchy for one of the Seibel (1963) task situations. ● is *On,* ○ is *Off,* and – is ignored.

The terminal nodes in the tree represent the manageable segments of the task. One of the terminal patterns (third from the left) requires no explicit processing because it contains no on-lights. Two of the patterns (the left-most, and the second from the right), have no off-lights, and so are processed by goal

Do-Press-All-Buttons. The remaining two manageable patterns contain a single on-light, and one or more off-lights. These are processed by goal Press-Button-Under-On-Light.

Once chunks are acquired for a pair of sibling terminal nodes, it is possible to acquire one for their combination (signified by their parent in the tree), and so on up the tree. If this process were taken to its conclusion, then the tree in Figure 4-9 would represent the hierarchy defined by the chunks' encoding components.

This process always leads to light-button chunks for contiguous light-button pairs. It does not lead to chunks for disjoint patterns such as (only) the two extremal (right and left) light-button pairs. This is not a limitation on the generality of the chunking mechanism. Instead, it is a function of the goal structure employed. A different goal structure (reflecting a different processing strategy) could lead to the creation of such disjoint chunk patterns.

One of the strong task-dependencies present in the Rosenbloom and Newell (1982a) chunking mechanism was that encoding productions had to have a condition added to them that assured that no on-light appeared between the two patterns being chunked together. This was so, even though the information that this condition was necessary appeared nowhere in the task algorithm. In the hierarchy in Figure 4-9 such conditions are generated naturally from the goals for processing segments of the display with no on-lights in them. Once again we see that the task dependencies show up in the goal hierarchy, not in the chunking mechanism.

The following list of points summarizes the key aspects of chunking as it applies to goal hierarchies.

- Each chunk represents a specific goal with a specific set of parameter values. It relates the parameter values to the results of the goal.
- Chunks are created through experience with the goals processed.
- Chunks are created bottom-up in the goal hierarchy.
- A chunk consists of connection, encoding, and decoding components.
- Chunk encoding and decoding are hierarchical, parallel, goal-asynchronous processes that operate on goal parameters and results (respectively).
- Chunk connection is a serial, goal-synchronous process that generates (encoded) results from (encoded) parameters.
- Chunks improve performance by replacing the normal processing of a goal (and its subgoals) with the faster processes of encoding, connection, and decoding.

4.3. A Revised Analysis of the Chunking Curve

Newell and Rosenbloom (1981) derived a functional form for the practice curve predicted by the abstract formulation of the chunking theory. They showed that, though it was not a power law, it could mimic a power law quite well. Now that we have a more precise formulation of chunking — in terms of goal hierarchies — it is important to reformulate this macroscopic analysis in these new terms. In this section we present the beginnings of such an analysis. The analysis should be accurate enough to yield estimates of the family of curves predicted by the model. However, for many aspects of the analysis, we will be satisfied with relatively crude approximations. Specifically, we will feel free to use continuous approximations to discrete forms.

Our aim is to derive an equation relating trial number (N) to the time to perform the task (T). To do this we must characterize the performance and learning aspects of the system. Let us start with performance, and assume that each goal in the hierarchy — whether terminal or non-terminal — requires a constant time γ to process. Then, if there are G goals in the hierarchy, the initial performance time for a depth-first processing of the goal hierarchy is given by the following equation.

$$T = \gamma G \qquad\qquad\qquad (4.1)$$

One way of looking at the effects of chunking on goal hierarchies is that a chunk reduces the effective number of goals in the hierarchy without increasing the amount of computation performed by the remaining goals (modulo the small amount of additional time required for encoding and decoding). Essentially, having a chunk for a goal allows the system to completely bypass the normal processing required for the goal. The goal's subgoals do not need to be processed (or even generated). The chunking process occurs in a bottom-up fashion, so the hierarchy gradually shrinks up to the root node. This process can be described as a change of *height* of the tree. Each goal in the initial hierarchy has a height (Figure 4-10). The lowest terminal nodes are at height 0. Their parents are at height 1, and so on up the tree. The height of the root node is the height of the tree, which we will call H. If we make the simplifying uniformity assumption, that all of the chunks at height h must be created before any can be created at height $h + l$, then the state of learning at any point in time can be characterized by the value of a single parameter — the height to which chunking has progressed (η). At the beginning of performance, η is 0. The value of η increases as chunks are progressively learned at higher and higher levels of the tree. Once all of the chunks have been learned, η has a value of H.

By looking at T as a function of η, and η as a function of N, the differential

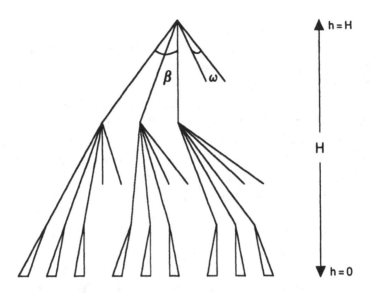

Figure 4-10: The structure of the trees underlying the analytical model of chunking on goal hierarchies.

form of the learning curve can be defined as follows.

$$\frac{dT}{dN} = \frac{dT}{d\eta} \frac{d\eta}{dN} \qquad (4.2)$$

The first factor reflects how changes in η affect performance. It can be computed by expressing G in Equation 4.1 as a function of η. To do this, we need to know the *branching factor* of the tree — the number of subgoals under each goal. The simplest assumption that can be made is that the branching factor is uniform over the entire tree; each goal has the same number of subgoals. We will go one step further, and work with a ragged uniform tree. Each non-terminal goal in the tree is assumed to have β non-terminal subgoals, and ω terminal subgoals (see Figure 4-10). Each terminal goal has, by definition, no subgoals. Let $G_H(h)$ be the number of non-terminal goals at height h and above (in a tree of height H). Initially there are $G_H(0)$ non-terminal goals to be processed. After chunking has progressed to height η, there are only $G_H(\eta)$. The total number of goals at height h and above is the sum of the number of non-terminal goals and the number of terminal goals. Each non-terminal goal has ω terminal subgoals, so there are $\omega G_H(h+1)$ terminal subgoals at height h and above. If we now add the assumption that a chunked goal requires the same amount of time to process as a normal terminal or non-terminal goal (that is, γ), then T can be expressed as the following function of η.

$$T = \gamma[G_H(\eta) + \omega G_H(\eta + 1)] \tag{4.3}$$

If we let $g_H(h)$ be the number of non-terminal nodes at height h, we get the following relationship between G and h.

$$G_H(h) = \sum_{i=h}^{H} g_H(i) = \sum_{i=h}^{H} \beta^{H-i} = \sum_{j=0}^{H-h} \beta^j \tag{4.4}$$

At this point the analysis breaks up into cases, depending on whether β — the number of non-terminal subgoals per goal — is equal to 1 or not equal to 1. When β is 1, $G_H(h)$ is $H-h+1$. Plugging this value into Equation 4.3 yields the following equations for T and $\frac{dT}{d\eta}$.

$$T = \gamma[(1+\omega)(H-\eta) + 1] \tag{4.5}$$

$$\frac{dT}{d\eta} = -\gamma(1+\omega) \tag{4.6}$$

When β is not equal to 1, $G_H(h)$ is a geometric sum having the following closed form.

$$G_H(h) = \frac{1 - \beta^{H-h+1}}{1-\beta} \tag{4.7}$$

Once again we can plug this form into Equation 4.3 to yield T as a function of η.

$$T = \gamma[\frac{1 - \beta^{H-\eta+1}}{1-\beta} + \omega\frac{1-\beta^{H-\eta}}{1-\beta}] \tag{4.8}$$

$$= \frac{\gamma}{1-\beta}[(1+\omega) - (\beta + \omega)\beta^{H-\eta}] \tag{4.9}$$

Computing the differential form of this equation yields the desired value for $\frac{dT}{d\eta}$.

$$\frac{dT}{d\eta} = -\gamma \log(\beta)\frac{\beta+\omega}{\beta-1}\beta^{H-\eta} \tag{4.10}$$

The second factor in Equation 4.2, $\frac{d\eta}{dN}$, is a learning rate. It summarizes how η changes with experience (N). It is convenient to express this factor as the product of two other differentials. The intermediate variable is $C(\eta)$, the total number of chunks needed for all of the non-terminal goals at a height of η and below.

$$\frac{d\eta}{dN} = \frac{d\eta}{dC}\frac{dC}{dN} \tag{4.11}$$

For chunking to have reached a height of η in the tree, $C(\eta)$ chunks would have to have been learned. The first factor in Equation 4.11 thus relates the acquisition of chunks to the increase in η. For each goal in the hierarchy, the total number of chunks it requires is equal to the number of initial states that the goal can have. In reality, each goal can have a different number of initial states. However, such an assumption is intractable, so we will make the simplifying assumption that the number of initial states is constant within a level of the hierarchy (that is, for a fixed height h). This value, called $s(h)$, can vary across levels of the hierarchy.

If we let $c(h)$ be the number of chunks required for all of the goals at height h, we can define $C(\eta)$ and $\frac{dC}{d\eta}$ as follows.

$$C(\eta) = \sum_{h=1}^{\eta} c(h) = \sum_{h=1}^{\eta} s(h)g_H(h) = \sum_{h=1}^{\eta} s(h)\beta^{H-h} \quad (4.12)$$

$$\frac{dC}{d\eta} \approx s(\eta)\beta^{H-\eta} \quad (4.13)$$

The second factor in Equation 4.11, $\frac{dC}{dN}$, is the rate of chunking with respect to trials. As in the earlier derivation, we assume that the chunking rate with respect to time ($\frac{dC}{dt}$) is a constant λ. The time per trial ($\frac{dt}{dN}$) is just T. The second factor is the product of these two.

$$\frac{dC}{dN} = \frac{dC}{dt}\frac{dt}{dN} = \lambda T \quad (4.14)$$

Combining Equations 4.11, 4.13, and 4.14 yields the following equation for $\frac{d\eta}{dN}$ (in terms of $s(\eta)$).

$$\frac{d\eta}{dN} = \frac{\lambda\beta^{\eta-H}}{s(\eta)}T \quad (4.15)$$

We are now in a position to generate the differential form of the learning curve ($\frac{dT}{dN}$). When $\beta = 1$, we combine Equations 4.2, 4.6, and 4.15.

$$\frac{dT}{dN} = -\gamma\lambda(1+\omega)\frac{\beta^{\eta-H}T}{s(\eta)} = -\gamma\lambda(1+\omega)\frac{T}{s(\eta)} \quad (4.16)$$

When $\beta \neq 1$, we combine Equations 4.2, 4.10, and 4.15.

$$\frac{dT}{dN} = -\gamma\lambda \log(\beta)\frac{\beta+\omega}{\beta-1}\frac{T}{s(\eta)} \quad (4.17)$$

Both of these learning equations have the same form (as follows), with only the constant (R) differing.

$$\frac{dT}{dN} = -R\frac{T}{s(\eta)}, \quad \text{or equivalently} \quad (4.18)$$

$$\frac{s(\eta)}{T}dT = -R\,dN \quad (4.19)$$

The family of curves predicted by this equation are inextricably tied to the form of $s(\eta)$. Before proceeding to examine this relationship, it will prove useful to have derived an equation relating η to T. For $\beta = 1$, we can do this by inverting Equation 4.5.

$$\eta = [\frac{1}{1+\omega} + H] - \frac{1}{\gamma(1+\omega)} T \tag{4.20}$$

$$= X - YT \tag{4.21}$$

For $\beta \neq 1$, we must invert Equation 4.9.

$$-\beta^{-\eta} = \frac{(1-\beta)T - \gamma(1+\omega)}{\gamma\beta^H(\beta+\omega)} \tag{4.22}$$

$$\eta = [\log^{-1}(\beta) \log(\gamma\beta^H\frac{\beta+\omega}{\beta-1})]$$

$$- [\log^{-1}(\beta)] \log(T + \gamma\frac{1+\omega}{\beta-1}) \tag{4.23}$$

$$= A - B \log(T + E) \tag{4.24}$$

The form of $s(\eta)$ depends on two factors: (1) the structure of the individual goal hierarchy, and (2) the nature of the task environment. In the following sections we consider the consequences of four different forms for $s(\eta)$ — constant (yielding exponential learning), linear, exponential (yielding power-law learning), and hyper-exponential. These four functions appear to cover the different ways that $s(\eta)$ varies in the current set of goal hierarchies. Unfortunately, these analyses often lead to expressions that cannot be integrated or inverted. When this happens we either try to work with a reasonable approximation, or we terminate the analysis.

4.3.1. The constant case

The function $s(\eta)$ will tend to be constant when three conditions hold. These three conditions are neither necessary or sufficient in their own right, but structures for which they hold will tend to be constant, and those for which they do not hold, will tend not to be. The first condition is that there be no branch statements in the definition of the hierarchy. A branch splits the structure up into two cases, each of which has to handle fewer of the total possibilities. This leads to lower goals in the hierarchy having fewer possible initial states than higher goals.

The second condition that should hold for $s(\eta)$ to be constant is that there be no sharing of learning among tasks in the task environment. If there is transfer of learning — such as using a chunk for one segment of lights in a different trial that shares the same segment — then those goals that are shared, effectively have their number of initial states reduced. In other words, since there are more instances of the goal on which learning can occur, fewer chunks must be learned for each instance. This will make $s(\eta)$ non-constant, because sharing is more likely the smaller the chunk (i.e., the fewer lights specified), and the smaller the chunk, the lower it is in the hierarchy (on average).

The third condition, is that the structure not employ a divide-and-conquer strategy. The hierarchy for the Seibel task (Figure 4-7) does just this by successively dividing the stimulus array into smaller and smaller segments. Each lower level of the recursion has fewer possible initial states.

All three of these conditions hold for the Duncan corresponding and opposite hierarchies (Figures 4-1 and 4-2), and $s(\eta)$ is indeed constant for them (see Chapter 6). When $s(\eta)$ is a constant s, Equation 4.19 takes on the following form.

$$\frac{s}{T} dT = -R\, dN \tag{4.25}$$

Integrating this equation yields the following equation (where Z comes from the integration constant).

$$T = Ze^{-\alpha N}, \quad \text{for } \alpha = \frac{R}{s} \tag{4.26}$$

Learning is thus predicted to be exponential when $s(\eta)$ is constant.

4.3.2. The linear case

The canonical case of a linear increase $(s(\eta) = p + q\eta)$ occurs when a choice is made by a sequence of predicates, each of which removes one possible alternative. The symbolic conditions of the Morin and Forrin (1962) experiment are a good example of where this occurs. Each predicate removes one symbol from consideration, implying that the next predicate has one less possible initial state. Of course there are other ways in which a linear function could show up, but the following analysis is sufficient for all of them.

The learning equation can take one of two different forms when $s(\eta)$ is a linear function. When $\beta = 1$, substituting Equation 4.21 for η in $s(\eta)$ yields:

$$s(\eta) = [p + qX] - qYT \tag{4.27}$$

$$= P - QT \tag{4.28}$$

Now, substituting in for $s(\eta)$ in Equation 4.19 and integrating we get the final result (where Z is the integration constant).

$$[PT^{-1} - Q] \, dT = -R \, dN \qquad (4.29)$$

$$P \log(T) - QT = -RN + Z \qquad (4.30)$$

This equation is a non-invertible mixture of linear and exponential effects. For large T (early in practice), the log term is essentially constant, and this curve is linear. For small T (late in practice), both terms have an effect, with mixed results. Mixed results occur whenever $s(\eta)$ is the sum of two or more functions. In the current instance, there are two terms. The first term is a constant, which on its own yields exponential learning. The second term is proportional to T, which yields linear learning.

When $\beta \neq 1$, Equation 4.24 must be substituted into the linear equation for $s(\eta)$.

$$s(\eta) = [p + qA] - qB \log(T + E) \qquad (4.31)$$

Once again $s(\eta)$ is the sum of two terms, one of which is constant. When the second (log) term of $s(\eta)$ is included in Equation 4.19, it requires the integration of an expression of the form $\log(T + E)/T$. When $T \gg E$, this becomes $\log(T)/T$, which integrates to $\log^2(T)/2$. If this term were the only one involved, then learning would be exponential in the square-root of N. When $E \gg T$, we have $\log(E)T^{-1}$, which integrates to $-\log(E)T^{-2}/2$. If this term were the only one involved, then learning would be a function of $N^{-0.5}$, a special case of the power law (a square root).

From Equations 4.23 and 4.24 we see that E has the value $\gamma \frac{1+\omega}{\beta-1}$. When β is real close to 1 (i.e., $1 + \varepsilon$), then E is likely to be very large, and much greater than T. When β is not real close to 1, the ratio $\frac{1+\omega}{\beta-1}$ is itself likely to be close to 1, and $T \gg E$ when $T \gg \gamma$ is true. But γ is the time to perform one goal, so the condition holds early in practice, when performance is not near asymptote.

4.3.3. The exponential case

When the number of possible initial states grows exponentially with height, learning is power law. The most obvious situation in which $s(\eta)$ is exponential occurs when a hierarchy implements a binary search. In a binary search, each predicate eliminates half of the possibilities, rather than only one. Therefore, the number of possible initial states (that is, number of alternatives to be considered) doubles each time the height increases by 1. In general, $s(\eta)$ is given by the following equation (for arbitrary constants D and α).

$$s(\eta) = De^{\alpha \eta} \tag{4.32}$$

The exponential case breaks down into the same two subcases as did the linear case ($\beta = 1$ and $\beta \neq 1$). When $\beta = 1$, we need to combine Equations 4.19, 4.21, and 4.32.

$$[De^{\alpha X}]\frac{e^{-\alpha YT}}{T}\ dT = -R\ dN \tag{4.33}$$

This equation is not integrable.

For the second case ($\beta \neq 1$), we get $s(\eta)$ by combining Equations 4.24, and 4.32.

$$s(\eta) = De^{\alpha[A - B\log(T+E)]} \tag{4.34}$$

$$= [De^{\alpha A}](T + E)^{-\alpha B} \tag{4.35}$$

When this equation is substituted into Equation 4.19, it requires the integration of an expression of the form $(T+E)^{-x}/T$. This is integrable under the same circumstances which made the linear case integrable. If $T \gg E$, then the expression becomes $T^{-(x+1)}$, which integrates to $-T^{-x}/x$. If the equation is inverted, it becomes a power law in $N+Z$ (Z comes from the integration constant). The power is $-1/x = -1/(\alpha B)$, or $-\log(\beta)/\alpha$ (see Equations 4.23 and 4.24). Just as with the linear case, when $E \gg T$, we get a constant (E^{-x}) over T, yielding learning as a special case of the power law ($N^{-0.5}$).

So we see that power-law practice curves can be generated by the chunking theory when $s(\eta)$ increases exponentially with η, and β is not identically equal to 1.

4.3.4. The hyper-exponential case

The number of possible initial states increases hyper-exponentially with the height of the hierarchy when the number of parameters increases exponentially. The divide-and-conquer aspect of the Seibel hierarchy has this character. The number of lights (the parameters) doubles for each step up the recursion, yielding exponential growth in number of parameters. But the number of states (complete specifications of the segment of lights) is exponential in the number of parameters, so the number of states increases hyper-exponentially.

$$s(\eta) = Be^{\alpha e^{\delta \eta}} \tag{4.36}$$

Unfortunately, for neither value of η — either a linear or logarithmic function of T — does this provide an expression that is integrable when substituted into Equation 4.19. For the linear case, we must integrate an expression of the following form.

$$\int \frac{e^{ae^{\delta T}}}{T} \, dT \tag{4.37}$$

For the logarithmic case, the following form is found.

$$\int \frac{e^{aT^{\delta}}}{T} \, dT \tag{4.38}$$

5 THE XAPS3 ARCHITECTURE

The *Xaps3* production-system architecture was designed to be used in the modeling of goal hierarchies and chunking. It is a new architecture, but it builds upon the work done in the development of the *Xaps2* architecture. In their presentation of *Xaps2*, Rosenbloom and Newell (1982a) began by discussing a set of *constraints* that must be met by any architecture within which the chunking theory of learning is implemented. We don't claim that these constraints are known to be necessary — the arguments are not that tight. But this permits (and encourages) attempts to show how the constraints can be circumvented.

The same constraints still hold — as they must if they are really constraints — for the design of the *Xaps3* architecture. These constraints, as presented and justified in Rosenbloom and Newell (1982a), are five-fold.

- *The parallel constraint*: The model must contain some form of parallel processing — it cannot have a control structure that is totally serial.
- *The bottleneck constraint*: The parallel capability of the control structure must be restricted so that a bottleneck exists. This can be a serial bottleneck, or more generally, some form of resource or capacity limitation.
- *The encoding constraint*: The bottleneck occurs after the process of chunk encoding has completed.
- *The decoding constraint*: The bottleneck occurs before the final process of chunk decoding has begun.
- *The cognitive-parallelism constraint*: The locus of parallelism cannot be constrained to just the sensory and motor portions of the system. Parallelism is required in all aspects of the system's performance, specifically including purely cognitive behavior.

Xaps2 is one architecture that fits within these constraints, but by no means the only one. More recently, two new constraints have been formulated from the consequences of the chunking theory. These new constraints rule out *Xaps2*, and have led to the design of the *Xaps3* architecture. Though it is a direct descendent of *Xaps2*, the constraints have forced a number of significant changes in the *Xaps3* design.

The first new constraint is the *crypto-information constraint*. Crypto-information — "hidden" information — is information that the architecture accesses while making decisions, but that is not accessible to "programs" running within the architecture. In the *Xaps2* architecture, activation is a form of crypto-information. It is used by the architecture to, among other purposes, decide which of multiple instantiations of a production should execute on a cycle. It is crypto-information because knowledge about activation values cannot be represented in the productions executed within the architecture. Another example of crypto-information is the information about working-memory recency used for conflict resolution in the *Ops* languages (Forgy, 1979).

The constraint states that any system that learns through experience cannot contain crypto-information if it wants to guarantee correct learning. Take the use of activation in *Xaps2* as an example. Suppose there is an object A that has an activation of 0.5, and an object B with an activation 0.3. Suppose also that there is a production that matches both A and B, generating two instantiations. When this situation first occurs, the instantiation that matches A will execute because of its greater activation. From this experience, the system learns what action to perform under these circumstances, that is, the action associated with the A instantiation. At some later point both A and B may again both be represented, but this time with the activations reversed. Even though the action associated with B is now the correct one, its previous experience tells the system to do the action associated with A, because the information about relative levels of activation could not be represented in the record of the previous experience. Not only would the previous information be incorrect, but there would in fact be no way to ever learn the correct information.

It is important to note that this constraint does not rule out all activation-based production-system architectures. If either the activation is not used as a basis for an architectural decision, or sufficient knowledge about activation levels is representable within productions, then activation is not a problem, because it is no longer a form of crypto-information.

Though activation was a focal point of the *Xaps2* design, to meet the demands of this constraint, *Xaps3* has been designed to work without it. It is thus a more traditional, purely symbolic, production-system architecture.

The second new constraint is the *goal-architecturality constraint*. The representation and processing of goals must be defined in the architecture itself;

it cannot be left up to the discretion of productions[11]. The reason can be traced to the chunking mechanism's need to understand how goals are represented and processed. This requirement implies that goals must be understood by the architecture, because the chunking mechanism is itself an architectural mechanism.

One way for the architecture to understand the processing of goals, is for the algorithm to be defined within the architecture itself. The obvious alternative — production-defined processing of goals — requires the chunking mechanism to be able to abstract the algorithm and representation from the productions, and tune itself to whatever scheme is being used. This requires considerably more intelligence than we are willing to ascribe to the chunking mechanism, or for that matter, to any mechanism built into the architecture. For a system to exhibit truly adaptive behavior it must be able to apply its full knowledge and learning capabilities to any task requiring intelligence. This is feasible at the program level but not at the architectural level.

In response to the goal-architecturality constraint, the goal processing that occurred at the level of productions in *Xaps2* has been moved down into the architecture of *Xaps3*.

Xaps3 is one architecture sitting within the design space delimited by the seven constraints just outlined. Once again, there is no claim of uniqueness being made for this architecture; but some specific architecture is required in order to allow us to implement the chunking theory and simulate its behavior. There are three reasons why we want an implementation over and above the mathematical analyses in Chapter 4. An implementation (1) helps us debug the design, (2) gives us a working mechanism, and (3) gives us exact solutions for the tasks faced by the system.

In the remainder of this chapter we describe the details of the *Xaps3* architecture (version 0.7[12]). It is like *Xaps2* in the structure of working-memory objects, and in allowing parallelism at the level of production execution, but differs in its lack of activation, and in that goal processing and chunking are built in at the architectural level[13].

Though this information is divided into sections on the working memory,

---

[11] Anderson (1982b) has previously made a similar argument for the placement of goal processing in the architecture of the *Act** production system (Anderson, 1983).

[12] The Seibel (1963) simulations were done in version 0.6, which is identical in effect to version 0.7 for that hierarchy.

[13] See Anderson (1983) and Sauers and Farrell (1982) for other attempts at integrating the processing of goals into the architecture of a production system.

production memory, cycle of execution, processing of goals, and chunking mechanism, there is a strong interaction between all of these components that will show up as cross-references (and unfortunately some forward references) between them.

5.1. Working Memory

With respect to symbols, the working memory in *Xaps3* is nearly identical to the one in *Xaps2*. It consists of an unordered set of *objects*, representing all of the types of information required in an information processing system (except for the types of information represented in productions): goals, patterns of stimuli and responses, intermediate computations, and so forth. As was true in *Xaps2*, each object is a token — in the sense of the classical type-token distinction. It is uniquely specified by a general *type* and a unique *identifier*. A type can be held in common by any number of objects. For example, there is a **Goal** type used for all objects representing goals[14]. This type is even more global than in *Xaps2* where the type of a goal object is its name, rather than a single common symbol. Some of the other types used in simulating the goal hierarchies in Chapters 4 and 6, include: **Angle, Horizontal-Location, Stimulus, Response,** and **Name**.

The definition of the identifier remains unchanged from *Xaps2*, it is a unique symbol for the object, allowing multiple objects of the same type to be simultaneously in working memory. A new identifier is generated dynamically by the architecture whenever a new object is created. A typical object representing a goal looks like:

(Goal Object127**)**

Like objects in *Xaps2*, *Xaps3* objects also have an optional set of *attributes*. However, unlike *Xaps2* objects, each attribute has only one value. In *Xaps2*, attributes had one or more values competing for the spot as the *dominant* value via their relative levels of activation. Without activation (removed because of the crypto-information constraint), multiple values lose their purpose and so are not used. A successfully completed instance of a **Press-Button-At-Horizontal-Location** goal (as used in the hierarchies for the Duncan (1977) conditions in Chapter 4), looks like the following example.

---

[14]The notation for objects has been slightly modified for clarity of presentation. Some of the names have been expanded or modified. In addition, types have been made **bold**, identifiers are in the normal roman font, attributes are in SMALL CAPITALS, and values are *italicized*

> (**Goal** Object127 [NAME *Press-Button-At-Horizontal-Location*]
> [STATUS *Succeeded*] [RESULT-TYPE *Response*])

The interpretation of two of the attributes (NAME and STATUS) should be obvious. They denote that this goal is an instance of the **Press-Button-At-Horizontal-Location** goal that has completed successfully. The third attribute (RESULT-TYPE) specifies the type of object to be returned as the result of this goal (see Section 5.4 for the details).

Working memory objects undergo a lifetime that starts when they enter working memory, either from outside the system or as the result of firing productions (Section 5.3.3). They reside in working memory for a while, during which time they may be examined and modified by productions. They finish their life by being flushed from working memory when they become out of context (see Section 4.1).

During this lifetime two types of auxiliary tags are kept for each object. The first one marks the identifier of the goal that was active — there being at most one — when the object was created. This tag is used for determining the object's status as being either part of the local or initial state of the current goal. The second tag marks the identifier of the goal active when the object was last examined by a production. This tag, in combination with the first one, allows the chunking mechanism to determine the implicit parameters of goals. When the goal object is augmented by these tags, it looks like the following example.

> (**Goal** Object127 |Object124 Object123|
> [NAME *Press-Button-At-Horizontal-Location*]
> [STATUS *Succeeded*] [RESULT-TYPE *Response*])

The first tag (Object124) is the *created-by* tag, and the second (Object123) is the *examined-by* tag. If there was no goal active at the time, then the special symbol <None> is used.

5.2. Production Memory

There is a single homogeneous production memory in *Xaps3*. The productions in it are similar to the productions in *Xaps2* and to those in the *Ops* languages. They have three parts: a name, a list of one or more conditions, and a list of one or more actions. Here is an example production taken from the implementation of the Seibel task (Figure 4-7)[15].

---

[15]As with the format of working-memory objects, the format of this production has been slightly altered to increase the clarity of presentation.

```
(DefProd SubGoal/Do-Lights/Do-Press-All-Buttons
  ((Goal <Exists> [NAME Do-Lights] [STATUS Active]
           [MINIMUM-HORIZONTAL-LOCATION  = Min-Hor-Loc]
           [MAXIMUM-HORIZONTAL-LOCATION  = Max-Hor-Loc])
   (Goal {<Local> <Exists>} [NAME No-Light-Off?]
           [STATUS Succeeded]))
  →
  ((Goal <New-Object> [Name Do-Press-All-Buttons]
           [STATUS Want] [RESULT-TYPE Response]
           [MINIMUM-HORIZONTAL-LOCATION  = Min-Hor-Loc]
           [MAXIMUM-HORIZONTAL-LOCATION  = Max-Hor-Loc])))
```

The name is purely for the convenience of the programmer, it doesn't affect the processing of the system in any way. The conditions (before the arrow), which specify patterns to be matched against the objects in working memory, and the actions (after the arrow) — specifying alterations to working memory — are discussed in the following two sections.

5.2.1. Production conditions

Each condition is a pattern to be matched against the objects in working memory. A condition pattern contains a *type* field (specifying the *type* of the object to be matched), an *identifier* field (containing several different types of information), and an optional set of patterns for attributes.

Condition patterns are primarily built from *constants*, and *variables*. Constants are signified by the presence of the appropriate symbol in the pattern, and only match objects that contain that symbol in that role. Some example constants in production **SubGoal/Do-Lights/Do-Press-All-Buttons** are **Goal**, MINIMUM-HORIZONTAL-LOCATION, and *Succeeded*. Variables are signified by a symbol (the name of the variable) preceded by an equal sign. They match anything appearing in their role in an object. An example is = *Min-Hor-Loc* in the sample production. All instances of the same variable within a production must be bound to the same value in order for the match to succeed. Constants can be used if the desired symbol is known when the production is created. Variables must be used when the desired symbol is not known until match time.

In order to restrict the scope of search performed by conditions, the restriction has been imposed that types and attributes must be known at match time. In *Xaps2*, this restriction was satisfied by forcing types and attributes to be specified by constants. In *Xaps3*, this has been loosened up, without changing the nature of the search. Types and attributes can be specified either by a constant, or by a variable that is bound to the value of an attribute in some other condition of the production. Forcing these variables to be bound elsewhere by a value match, ensures that search is not required during the identifier and attribute matches[16].

Identifiers are never specified by constants because they are dynamically created. The identifiers in production `SubGoal/Do-Lights/Do-Press-All-Buttons` are specified by the special symbol `<Exists>`. Such a condition succeeds if there is any object in working memory that matches the condition. If there is more than one such object, the choice is conceptually arbitrary (actually, the first object found is used). Only one instantiation is generated. As we have seen, the standard production-system mechanism of selecting from multiple instantiations based on criteria such as recency of the matched objects, violates the crypto-information constraint. Selecting one arbitrarily avoids this problem by not letting the system ever count on which alternative is selected. Performance models that work correctly under this assumption will not be made incorrect by the addition of chunking.

If the identifier is specified as a variable, the condition still acts like an exists condition, but the identifier can be retrieved. This allows the object to be modified by the actions of the production.

The opposite of an exists condition is a not-exists condition — commonly called a negated condition. When the symbol `<Not-Exists>` appears in the identifier field, it signifies that the match succeeds only if there is no object in working memory that matches the remainder of the condition pattern. Any variables used in a negated condition must also occur in a value match for some positive condition. This works because the only reason for having a variable in a negated condition is to compare its value with that bound in some other condition. The other two functions of variables — passing parameters to the production's actions, and leaving something unspecified — are meaningless in this context. The only thing that you might want to leave unspecified — the value of an attribute — can be simply ignored by not including the attribute in the condition.

The second condition in the sample production contains the symbol `<Local>`, as well as `<Exists>`, in the identifier field (they are conjoined syntactically by curly-brackets). When this symbol is added to an identifier pattern of any type — constant, variable, exists, and not-exists — it signifies that the condition should only be matched against those objects in working memory that are local to the active goal. This information — provided by the objects' *created-by* tags — is a means by which the productions that work on a goal can

---

[16] As an efficiency measure, the additional constraint is imposed that the condition containing the value match must come before the condition specifying the identifier or attribute match.

determine which objects are part of their local context. For example, the second condition in the sample production is testing whether there is a **No-Light-Off?** goal that has succeeded. If the condition were not marked as being local, then this production could fire as a result of a totally irrelevant test at some earlier point in the structure.

The remainder of the condition specifies a pattern that must be met by the attribute-value pairs of working-memory objects. As already discussed, attributes are specified by either constants or elsewhere-bound variables. The values in attribute-value pairs are specified as either constants, variables, functions of constants and variables, or the negation of any of the previous.

Negation of values is performed by preceding the value with the character "~", as in ~ = *Angle*. This example says that whatever symbol has been bound to the variable = *Angle*, cannot appear as the current value. When variables are used within a negation, they must have been bound elsewhere to a value.

There are some built-in predicates, such as *Greater Than* and *Less Than* (⟨GT⟩ and ⟨LT⟩), that can be used to test something other than exact equality (or inequality) of values. For example, the following condition can be used to look for an angle greater than whatever value is bound to the variable = *Old-Angle*.

(Angle ⟨Exists⟩ [VALUE *(⟨GT⟩ = Old-Angle)*])

Combination tests can be employed through the use of a *Pattern And* (⟨PAND⟩). For example, the following condition looks for an angle greater than 90, but not equal to 180.

(Angle ⟨Exists⟩ [VALUE *{⟨PAND⟩(⟨GT⟩ 90) ~180}*])

The results of arbitrary *Lisp* computations can be used in conditions by enclosing them in an ⟨Eval⟩. Part of the computation of the **Is-Angle-Divisible-By-90?** test in the goal structure for the Fitts and Seeger (1953) S_A-R_B condition (see Figure 6-8) is accomplished by an attribute-value test of the form:

[ZERO *(⟨Eval⟩ (remainder = dividend = divisor))*]

The dividend is the angle of the light, and the divisor is 90. This pattern is compared to an attribute-value pair (in a working-memory object) that has the number 0 as its value.

Each attribute-value pair in a condition must successfully match against a corresponding pair — a pair with the same attribute — in the object being matched, unless the value is negated. In that case, absence of a corresponding pair is sufficient to cause the match to succeed.

If it is desired to copy all of the attribute-value pairs from one object to another, an attribute-value-list (AVL) variable can be employed. An AVL variable looks syntactically like any other variable, it is distinguished only by its location; it comes after the type and identifier patterns. It can appear by itself, as in

> (**Angle** <Exists> = *Attribute-Value-List*)

or it can be intermingled with attribute-value patterns, as in

> (**Goal** <Exists> [NAME *Do-Press-All-Buttons*] = *Goal-Attributes*) .

AVL variables cannot be used for testing the equality of two sets of attribute-value pairs; they can only be used to pass the information to the production's actions. A typical use is to create a new object just like some old one, but with some added information.

5.2.2. Production actions

There is only one kind of action in *Xaps3* — modify working memory. As in *Xaps2*, the interface to the outside world is through working memory, rather than through production actions. Actions can create new objects in working memory and, under certain circumstances, modify existing objects. The act of creating a new object — signified by the symbol <New-Object> appearing in the identifier field of the action — can be seen in production SubGoal/Do-Lights/Do-Press-All-Buttons. When the action is executed, the identifier is replaced by a newly generated symbol, and the variables — both regular and AVL — are instantiated with their values computed during the match. As with conditions, there is an escape mechanism — using <Eval> — that allows execution of an arbitrary *Lisp* function. The result of the function is used as if it were a constant at that location in the action.

In order to modify an existing object, its identifier must be known at the time the action is performed. This is accomplished by passing it as a parameter from a condition with a variable identifier. There is one important restriction placed on this process; only objects local to the current goal can be modified. This fulfills the restriction discussed in Section 4.1 that only the local state of a goal can be modified.

There are no production actions that lead to the deletion of values or objects from working memory. A value can be removed only by superceding it by another value. As discussed in Section 4.1, objects go away when they are no longer part of the current context[17]. No explicit mechanism for deletion has

---

[17] This mechanism bears a relationship to the *dampening* mechanism in the *Act* architecture (Anderson, 1976).

proved necessary, so none have been included.

5.3. The Cycle of Execution

Xaps3 follows the traditional *recognize-act* cycle of production system architectures, with a few twists thrown in by the need to process goals. The recognition phase begins with the *match*, and finishes up with *conflict resolution*. The *cycle number* — the simulated time — is incremented after the recognition phase, whether any productions are executed or not. During the act phase, productions are executed. These three topics (match, conflict resolution, and production execution) form the subject matter for this section.

5.3.1. The match

The match phase is quite simple. All of the productions in the system are matched against working memory in parallel (conceptually), to yield a set of legal instantiations — at most one per production. Each instantiation consists of a production name and a set of variable bindings for that production that yield a successful match. There is no limitation on the number of instantiations that can be based on a single working memory element. The *Xaps3* match is thus more like the one in the *Ops* architectures (Forgy, 1979) than the one in the *Act** architecture (Anderson, 1983).

5.3.2. Conflict resolution

The set of instantiations generated during the match phase are passed in their entirety to the conflict resolution phase[18], where they are winnowed down to the set to be executed on the current cycle. This is accomplished via a pair of conflict-resolution rules.

The first rule is *goal-context refraction*. It states that a production instantiation can fire only once within any particular goal context. It is a form of the standard *Ops* refractory inhibition rule (Forgy, 1979) that differs only in how the inhibition on firing is released. With the standard rule, the inhibition is released whenever one of the working-memory objects on which the instantiation is predicated has been modified. With goal-context refraction, inhibition

---

[18]For purposes of efficiency, these two phases are actually intermingled. However, this does not change the behavior of the system at the level at which we are interested.

is released whenever the system leaves the context in which the instantiation fired. If the instantiation could not legally fire before the context was established, and it could fire both during and after the context was established, then the instantiation must be based, at least in part, on a result generated during the context and returned when the context was left. Therefore, the instantiation should be free to fire again after the context, to reestablish the still relevant information.

The second rule — the *parameter-passing bottleneck* — states that only one parameter-passing instantiation can execute on a cycle (conceptually selected arbitrarily). This rule first appeared in a slightly different form as an assumption in the *Hpsa77* architecture (Newell, 1980a). It will be justified in Section 5.5.

5.3.3. Production execution

All of the instantiations that make it through the conflict resolution phase are fired (conceptually) in parallel. Firing a production instantiation consists of: (1) overwriting the *examined-by* tags of the working-memory objects matched by the instantiation, with the identifier of the active goal; (2) replacing all variables in the actions by the values determined during the match phase; (3) evaluating any <Eval> forms; and (4) performing the actions. This can result in the addition of new objects to working memory and the modification of existing local objects. If conflicting values are simultaneously asserted, the winner is selected arbitrarily. This does not violate the crypto-information constraint because the architecture is using *no* information in making the decision. If the performance system works correctly, even when it can't depend on the outcome of the decision, then the learned information will not lead to incorrect performance.

The performance of production actions does not result in interaction with the outside world. All such interaction is accomplished through working memory. Stimuli appear directly in working memory (with type **Stimulus**), and responses are made based on the objects of type **Response** appearing there.

5.4. Goal Processing

In Chapter 4 we described the processing of goals at an abstract level. In this section we make that processing concrete by describing how it is implemented within the *Xaps3* architecture. The first connection to make with the abstract model of goal processing is the straightforward one of mapping the working memory used in the goal hierarchies, into the working memory of *Xaps3*. The production-system working memory easily fulfills the requirements of goal-based processing.

The goals themselves, unlike chunks, are just data structures in working memory. A typical *Xaps3* goal goes through four phases in its life. The current phase of a goal is represented explicitly at all times by the value associated with the STATUS attribute of the working-memory object representing the goal.

In the first stage of its life, the goal is *desired*. Creating a desire for a goal is like setting up a request that at some point, but not necessarily right then, the goal should be processed. Such a desire is established when a production creates a new object of type **Goal**. Leaving the expression of desires under the control of productions is what allows goals to be processed by the architecture, while still leaving the structure of the hierarchy under program (that is, production) control.

Each new goal object must have a NAME attribute, a STATUS attribute with a value of *Want*, and a RESULT-TYPE attribute. In addition, it may have any number of other attributes, specifying explicit parameters to the goal. The action in production SubGoal/Do-Lights/Do-Press-All-Buttons, creates a desire for the **Do-Press-All-Buttons** goal, with two explicit parameters.

> (Goal <New-Object> [**Name** *Do-Press-All-Buttons*]
>   [STATUS *Want*] [RESULT-TYPE *Response*]
>   [MINIMUM-HORIZONTAL-LOCATION = *Min-Hor-Loc*]
>   [MAXIMUM-HORIZONTAL-LOCATION = *Max-Hor-Loc*])

The value of the RESULT-TYPE attribute specifies the type of the results that are to be returned on successful completion of the goal. All local objects of that type (**Response** in this case) are considered to be results of the goal. That results must be marked explicitly, is a consequence of two other aspects of the architecture. The first follows from the the fact that all out-of-context objects are flushed from the system. If the results of a goal were not treated specially, they would be flushed along with the goal's other local objects. The second reason is that the results must be known explicitly to the chunking mechanism so that they can be included in a chunk for the goal.

There are other means of accomplishing the same end, including: (1) having productions that explicitly mark each result via the addition of a RESULT attribute; (2) marking the temporary rather than the result objects; (3) and having a single type for all results in the system. The scheme used here is simple, adequate, and interacts well with the chunking mechanism.

The second stage in the life of a goal is for it to become *active*. While the expression of goal desires is under program (production) control, goal activation is controlled directly by the architecture. At most one goal is active at any point in time. The architecture attempts to activate a new goal whenever the system is at a loss as to how to continue with the current goal. This occurs when there is an empty conflict set; that is, there is no production instantiation that can legally fire on the current cycle. When this happens, the system looks in working memory to determine if there are any subgoals of the current goal that are desired. A goal is, by definition, a subgoal of the goal active when it was created (as determined by the *created-by* tag). If such a subgoal is found, it is made the active goal, and the parent goal is *suspended* by replacing its STATUS with the identifier of the newly activated subgoal. If more than one desired subgoal is found, one is arbitrarily selected (actually, the last one found is used).

Suspension is the third phase in the life of a goal (it occurs only for non-terminal goals). Replacing the STATUS of the parent goal with the subgoal's identifier accomplishes two things: it halts work on the goal, because the productions that process goals all check for a STATUS of *Active*; and it maintains the control stack for the goal hierarchy. A suspended goal remains suspended until its active subgoal terminates, at which time it returns to being active. If a goal has more than one subgoal, it oscillates between the active and suspended states.

If no progress can be made on the active goal, and there are no desired subgoals, then the system has no idea how to continue making progress, so it terminates the active goal with a STATUS of *Failed*. Following termination, the goal is in its fourth and final phase of life. In addition to a failure termination, goals can be terminated with a STATUS of *Succeeded*. There are no uniform criteria for determining when an arbitrary goal has completed successfully, so it has been left to productions to assert that this has happened. This is done via the creation of an object of type **Succeeded**. When the architecture detects the presence of such an object in working memory, it terminates the current goal, and reactivates its parent.

At goal termination time, a number of activities occur in addition to the obvious one of changing the active goal. The first two activities occur only on the successful termination of a goal. As discussed in the following section, the first step is the possible creation of a chunk. The second step is to return the results of the terminating goal to its parent goal. This is accomplished by altering the *created-by* tags of the objects of that type, so that it looks as if they were created by the parent goal.

The third step is to delete all of the objects from working memory created during the goal to be terminated. This removes all objects that would be out of context in the new goal, thus allowing the system to get along without an explicit delete action. This implies that any information created by a goal that is going to be needed later on must be returned as a result of the goal. The change in the *created-by* tag of the results assures that they do remain available.

The fourth, and final, step is to enable result decoding if it is appropriate (see Section 5.5.1).

5.5. Chunking

As we saw in Section 4.2, chunking improves performance by enabling the system to use its experience with previous instances of a goal to avoid expanding the goal tree below it. In this section we detail how this has been implemented within the *Xaps3* architecture — yielding a working, task-independent, production-system practice mechanism. We begin by describing how chunks are used, proceed to how they are acquired, and finish up with how they are represented.

5.5.1. The use of chunks

The key to the behavior of a chunk lies in its connection component. When a goal is proposed in a situation for which a chunk has already been created, the connection component of that chunk substitutes for the normal processing of the goal. This is accomplished in *Xaps3* by hooking the connection to the *desired* state of the goal. The connection is a production containing a condition testing for the existence of a desired goal and a condition testing for the encoding of the goal's parameters. It has two actions; one marks the goal as having succeeded, and the other asserts the goal's encoded result. If there is a desired goal in working memory in a situation for which a connection production exists, the connection will be eligible to fire. Whether (and when) it does fire depends on conflict resolution. Connection productions are subject to the *parameter-passing bottleneck* conflict-resolution rule, because they pass the identifier of the desired goal as a parameter to the action that marks the goal as having succeeded. Therefore, only one goal can be connected at a time — part of the *bottleneck constraint* — and only one connection can execute for any particular goal instance (removing a source of possible error).

If the connection does fire, it removes the need to activate and expand the goal, because the goal's results will be generated directly by the connection (and decoding), and the goal will be marked as having succeeded. If instead, no connection production is available for the current situation of a desired goal, then eventually the production system will reach an impasse — no productions eligible to fire — and the goal will be activated and expanded. Therefore, we have just the behavior required of chunks — they replace goal activation and expansion, if they exist.

This behavior is, of course, predicated on the workings of the encoding and decoding components of the chunk. The encoding component of a chunk must execute before the associated connection can. In fact, it should execute even before the parent goal is activated, because the subgoal's encoded symbol must be part of the parent goal's initial state. Recall that encodings are built up hierarchically. If the parent goal shares all of the parameters of one of its subgoals, then the encoding of the parent goal's parameters is partly based on the encoding generated for the subgoal. This behavior occurs in *Xaps3* because the encoding components are implemented as goal-free productions that do not pass parameters. They fire (concurrently with whatever else is happening in the system) whenever their parameters are in working memory (subject to conflict resolution). If the parameters exist before the parent goal becomes active, as they must if they are parameters to it, then the encoded symbol becomes part of the parent goal's initial state.

The decoding component must decode an encoded result when it will be needed. It does not need to decode every result of every goal, only those that are needed. There are two cases. In the first case, the results of a goal are to be used by a sibling goal; for example, when one goal is to retrieve a representation of the stimulus, followed immediately by its sibling, which retrieves the horizontal location from that representation (as in the structure for the Duncan (1977) *corresponding* condition in Figure 4-1). Under these circumstances, the results of the first goal should be decoded immediately.

In the second case, the results of a subgoal are not used by the parent goal. Instead, they are just relayed up as results of the parent. The goal structure for the Seibel (1963) task contains a good example of this. When goals 13 and 14 (both are instances of Do-Lights-If-Any) terminate, their results are responses (button presses) to be made. These results are not used by each other, or by the other sibling (One-Light-On?). They are simply passed up again as results of their parent goal (Do-Off-And-On). This process continues on up the hierarchy, and over the levels of recursion. If these results were to be decoded each time they were returned, they would have to be re-encoded before they could be passed up to the next level. There would be repetitive and wasteful multiple cycles of decoding and re-encoding.

One solution to this dual requirement is to only decode a result if the parent goal to which it is being returned has a different RESULT-TYPE than the subgoal that is returning the result. If the types are the same, the parent will just return the encoded result as part of its own results. If they are different, the parent must want the result for some local purpose, so it is decoded immediately. Once decoding is enabled for a type, it proceeds in a parallel fashion, with each decoding production executing as soon as it can, irrespective of whatever else is happening in the system.

This scheme is implemented in the architecture, and is adequate for the current hierarchies, but it ultimately has limits. Specifically, the scheme is inadequate for recursive algorithms in which goals need to process the results of their subgoals before passing them up to their parent goals. However, it should be possible to get around this limitation by allowing production-requested decoding, as well as architecture-requested decoding.

5.5.2. The acquisition of chunks

A complete specification of the chunk acquisition process must include the details of when chunks can be acquired, and from what information they are built. A chunk can be acquired when three conditions are met. The first condition is that some goal must have just completed. The system can't create a chunk for a goal that terminated at some point in the distant past, because the information on which the chunk must be based is no longer available. Chunks also are not created prior to completion (on partial results). Chunks are simple to create in part because they summarize all of the effects of a goal. If chunks were created part way through the processing of a goal — for partial results of the goal — then a sophisticated analysis might be required in order to determine which parameters affect which results, and how. This is not really a limitation on what can be chunked, because any isolatable portion of the performance can be made into a goal.

The second condition is that the goal must have completed successfully. Part of the essence of goal failure is that the system does not know why the goal failed. This means that the system does not know which parameter values have lead to the failure; thus, it can't create a chunk that correctly summarizes the situation. Chunking is success-driven learning, as opposed to failure-driven learning (see for example, Winston, 1975).

The third, and final, condition for chunk creation is that all of the working-memory modifications occurring since the goal was first activated must be attributable to that goal, rather than to one of its subgoals. This condition is implemented by assuring that no productions were fired while any of the goal's subgoals were active. All of the subgoals must either be processed by a chunk, or fail immediately after activation — failure of a subgoal, particularly of predicates, does not necessarily imply failure of the parent goal. This restriction is imposed for three reasons. One of the reasons is that, without the restriction, it is possible for a subgoal to overwrite the information required to determine the parent goal's parameters. This could occur when a subgoal examines a piece of the parent goal's initial state after the parent goal does. The second reason has to do with the treatment of negated conditions, which will be discussed shortly. The third reason for employing this condition is that it forces chunking to proceed bottom-up in the hierarchy.

To summarize, a chunk is created after the system has decided to successfully terminate a goal, but before anything is done about it (such as marking the goal as succeeded, returning the results, and flushing the local objects from working memory). At that point the goal is still active, and all of its information is still available. Most of the information on which the chunk is based can be found in working memory (except, see below).

The first piece of information needed for the creation of a chunk is the name (and identifier) of the goal that is being chunked. This information is found by retrieving the object representing the active goal. The goal's explicit parameters are also available as attribute-value pairs on the goal object. Given the goal's identifier, its implicit parameters are found by retrieving all of the objects in working memory that were part of the goal's initial state — that is, their *created-by* tag contains an identifier different from that of the active goal — and were examined by a production during the processing of the active goal. This last type of information is contained in the objects' *examined-by* tags. The goal's results are equally easy to find. The system simply retrieves all of the goal's local objects that have a type equal to the goal's RESULT-TYPE. Because the parameter and result information is determined from the constant objects in working memory, chunks themselves are not parameterized, producing the table look-up nature of chunking. Each chunk represents a specific situation for a specific goal.

Generating chunks from the constant objects in working memory would not work if the architecture allowed production conditions which specify that every legal instantiation be fired (as in the *Ops* languages). Given such a mechanism, the system would create chunks that enumerate the set of objects matched by the condition. Now, suppose that the goal is processed again, in a situation in which the same set of objects is in working memory, plus some additional ones. The chunk will do the right thing for the objects it recognizes (marking the goal as successfully completed), but it will ignore the new ones, generating errors of omission.

The one complication to the clean picture of chunk acquisition so far presented, concerns the use of negated conditions during the processing of a goal. When a negated condition successfully matches working memory, there is no working-memory object that can be marked as having been examined.

Therefore, some of the information required for chunk creation cannot be represented in working-memory. The current solution for this problem is not elegant, but it works. A temporary auxiliary memory is maintained, into which is placed each non-local negated condition occurring on productions that fire during the processing of the goal (local negated conditions can be ignored because they do not test the initial state). This memory is reinitialized whenever the goal that is eligible to be chunked changes. Before the conditions are placed in this memory, their variables are instantiated with the values bound to them by the other conditions in their production.

This negated-condition memory yields the second reason for only chunking goals for which nothing had been done in subgoals. Once a subgoal starts being processed, the negated-condition memory must be initialized for it. When the subgoal terminates, returning control to the parent goal, any conditions previously placed in the memory will be lost. This problem could be solved by maintaining a stack of such memories, but the solution already discussed was preferred because of its more bounded memory requirements. It is also a point in its favor that it reinforces the need to do chunking in a bottom-up fashion.

5.5.3. The representation of chunks

As in the Rosenbloom and Newell (1982a) implementation, each chunk consists of three productions — one for each component. In the following discussion of these productions, we will use a set of example chunks selected from a 268 trial simulation of the Seibel (1963) task, using the goal structure in Figure 4-7 (for more on this simulation, see Chapter 6).

Figure 5-1 shows the connection production for the first chunk learned for the **Press-Button-At-X** goal; it was learned on the first trial of the sequence. Several pieces of information are coded into the production name: the type of the production (connect, encode, or decode), the trial on which the chunk was created, the name of the goal for which the chunk was created, and a unique number. This information is for the benefit of the analyst, not the system.

```
(DefProd Connect-Trial1-PressButtonAtX-176
    ((Goal {<Local> =Goal177} [NAME Press-Button-At-X]
           [STATUS Want] [RESULT-TYPE Response])
     (X <Exists> [x 555]))
    →
    ((Response <New-Object> [x 555] [NAME Button-Press]
           [SPACE Fingers])
     (Goal =Goal177 [STATUS Succeeded]))))
```

Figure 5-1: A simple connection production for the **Press-Button-At-X** goal in the Seibel (1963) task.

In processing this goal, the system must find the working-memory object representing a horizontal location (specified as a value of *x* between 0 and 1000), and create a response consisting of a button press at that location. This connection production does all of this for an *x* value of 555 (just right of the display's center). As an efficiency measure, encoding and decoding productions are not created when there would be only one object encoded or one object produced by decoding (respectively). Instead, the object is placed directly into the connection production. Chunks can therefore consist of one (connection), two (connection and either encoding or decoding), or three (connection, encoding, and decoding) productions.

The conditions and actions in this production are straightforward. The first condition determines if there is a local, desired instance of the goal. It has a variable identifier so that the second action can mark the goal as having been successfully completed (by modifying its STATUS). The second condition contains the information that would otherwise be in an encoding production. It determines the existence of the appropriate value for the goal's one implicit parameter.

The first action generates the response — a button press at a horizontal location of 555 in the region defined by the locations of the fingers. The second action has already been mentioned; it changes the goal's status from *Want* to *Succeeded*, signifying successful completion.

Figure 5-2 shows our second example — a two-production chunk created on trial 43 for the Do-Off-And-On goal. This is the parent goal of the recursive, divide-and-conquer aspect of the algorithm. From the **Goal** condition in the connection production, we find that this chunk covers the region from 0 to 250 — the left-most three lights in the display. This pattern is built from two primitive patterns that separately describe the regions from 0 to 125 and from 125 to 250. This chunk is not built until after chunks have already been created for the two sub-regions. The implicit parameters for this goal are **Stimulus** patterns describing these two regions, and the results are the appropriate button presses (of type **Response**).

The pattern detected by this chunk can be determined by examining the three **Stimulus** conditions in the connection production. The first two take care of the region from 125 to 250. There are two lights in this region, at 145 and 245. The ⟨Exists⟩ condition tests that the first light (at 145) is on. The ⟨Not-Exists⟩ condition makes sure that no other light in the region is on; that is, that there is no light on in the region that is not at 145. Therefore these two conditions test for a pattern in which the light is on at 145 and off at 245.

This same pattern could have been tested by a number of alternative sets of conditions. For example, there could be two ⟨Exists⟩ conditions. The first one would be like the one already used — it would test that the light at 145 is

```
(DefProd Connect-T43-DoOffAndOn-6464
    ((Goal {<Local> =Goal6465} [NAME DoOffAndOn]
           [STATUS Want] [RESULT-TYPE Response]
           [MAX-X 250] [MIN-X 0])
     (Stimulus <Exists> [SPACE Lights] [NAME Light] [STATE On]
           [X 145] [Y 150] [DELTA-X 70] [DELTA-Y 300])
     (Stimulus <Not-Exists> [SPACE Lights] [NAME Light]
           [STATE On] [X {<PAND><(GT> 125)(<LT> 250) ~145}])
     (Stimulus <Not-Exists> [SPACE Lights] [NAME Light]
           [STATE Off] [X {<PAND><(GT> 0)(<LT> 125)}]))
    →
    ((Response <New-Object> [NAME DoOffAndOn6462])
     (Goal =Goal6465 [STATUS Succeeded])))

(DefProd Decode-T43-DoOffAndOn-6463
    ((Decode {<Local> <Exists>} [TYPE Response])
     (Response <Exists> [NAME DoOffAndOn6462]))
    →
    ((Response <New-Object> [NAME Press-Button] [X 145]
           [SPACE Fingers])
     (Response <New-Object> [NAME Press-Button] [X 62]
           [DELTA-X 125] [SPACE Fingers])))
```

Figure 5-2: An early two-production chunk for the Do-Off-And-On goal in the Seibel (1963) task.

on. The second one would test that the light at 245 is off. The system created the chunk as it did because of the structure of the goal hierarchy. Recall that any region in which there is more than one light, and in which there is only one light on, is processed by the Press-Button-Under-On-Light goal. In order to reach this goal in the hierarchy, the **One-Light-On?** predicate must have been tested and succeeded. The predicate works by testing for the existence of one on light, and the absence of any other on lights. Therefore, the chunk reflects this structure. The alternative structure would have been built if this kind of region were processed by dividing it in half, and testing explicitly for the existence of a light that is off (in addition to making sure that there is exactly one light in the region).

This example points out how important the goal hierarchy is in determining what chunks are created. Different subjects with different hierarchies will create different chunks. Even a single subject may create non-transferable chunks if he alters his goal structure between trials. For example, the subject may divide a region into two sub-regions on some trials, and into three sub-regions on other trials.

The remaining **Stimulus** condition in production **Connect-T43-DoOffAndOn-6464** assures that all of the lights in the region from 0 to 125 are on; that is, that there is no light off in the region. In this case there is only one light (at 45), and it is on. The region is processed by the

Do-Press-All-Buttons goal — press all of the buttons in a region — because the **No-Light-On?** predicate fails, and the **No-Light-Off?** predicate succeeds.

Before proceeding to the actions of this connection production, a comment is required as to why there is no encoding production for this chunk. One would appear to be called for because three aspects of the initial state are being tested. However, only one of these conditions is a positive (`<Exists>`) condition. It turns out that negated conditions cannot be safely included in an encoding production. We can show this by contradiction; assume that negated conditions are included in an encoding production. Then the production may fire early in processing before all of the relevant objects have been produced. Later, some objects may be added to working memory that invalidate the negated condition, but the object generated by the encoding would remain in working memory. Therefore, a wrong chunk could be used. This does not happen generally for positive conditions because once an object has been encoded, it will be part of the initial state of the subsequent goals, and thus cannot be changed or deleted (but see the discussion on errors in Chapter 7). When the object is deleted (because its context is no longer valid) the encoding in which it participates will also be deleted. To avoid the errors that can occur when negated conditions are included in the encoding productions, all negated conditions are placed in the connection production, and encoding productions are only created when there is more than one positive condition.

The actions of this connection production are considerably simpler than its conditions. They merely mark the goal as having succeeded, and generate an object representing a non-primitive response pattern. The latter object is of type **Response** because it is formed from two objects of that type. It can thus be returned as a result of the goal (without being decoded) in place of its component patterns. The NAME of the pattern is a newly generated symbol (*DoOffAndOn6462*) that is only recognized by the decoding production for this chunk.

The decoding production keys off of the non-primitive response pattern, and off of an object of type **Decode**. As discussed earlier, the architecture determines when decoding should occur. When this determination has been made, it places a **Decode** object in working memory, with the type of the object to be decoded specified by the TYPE attribute (*Response* in this case).

The two actions of the decoding production specify the two primitive responses to be made by the system. The first one enables a button press at location 145. The second one says to press all of the buttons in a region centered at 62, and of size 125. This presses all of the buttons in the region 0 to 125 (modulo truncation errors), of which there is only one.

The final example of a chunk can be seen in Figure 5-3. This is a three-production chunk created on trial 70 for the Do-Off-And-On goal in the region

0 to 500. It makes use of the previous chunk for the 0 to 250 region, while adding information about the 250 to 500 region. There are two lights in the 250 to 500 region (at 345 and 445). The first one is on and the second is off. It should be clear that this region can be processed just like the 125 to 250 region, in which there was also one light on and one off. This adds one positive (<Exists>) condition to test for the light that is on, and one negated condition (<Not-Exists>) to test that there are no other lights on in the region.

```
(DefProd Connect-T70-DoOffAndOn-9271
    ((Goal {<Local> =Goal9272} [NAME DoOffAndOn]
            [STATUS Want] [RESULT-TYPE Response]
            [MAX-X 500] [MIN-X 0])
     (Stimulus <Exists> [NAME DoOffAndOn9267])
     (Stimulus <Not-Exists> [SPACE Lights] [NAME Light]
            [STATE Off] [x {<PAND>(<GT>0)(<LT>125)}])
     (Stimulus <Not-Exists> [SPACE Lights] [NAME Light]
            [STATE On] [x {<PAND>(<GT>125)(<LT>250) ~145}])
     (Stimulus <Not-Exists> [SPACE Lights] [NAME Light]
            [STATE On] [x {<PAND>(<GT>250)(<LT>500) ~345}]))
     →
    ((Response <New-Object> [Name DoOffAndOn9269])
     (Goal =Goal9272 [Status Succeeded])))

(DefProd Encode-T70-DoOffAndOn-9268
    ((Stimulus <Exists> [SPACE Lights] [NAME Light] [STATE On]
            [x 145] [y 150] [DELTA-X 70] [DELTA-Y 300])
     (Stimulus <Exists> [SPACE Lights] [NAME Light] [STATE On]
            [x 345] [y 490] [DELTA-X 70] [DELTA-Y 300]))
     →
    ((Stimulus <New-Object> [NAME DoOffAndOn9267])))

(DefProd Decode-T70-DoOffAndOn-9270
    ((Decode {<Local> <Exists>} [TYPE Response])
     (Response <Exists> [NAME DoOffAndOn9269]))
     →
    ((Response <New-Object> [NAME DoOffAndOn6462])
     (Response <New-Object> [SPACE Fingers] [NAME Press-Button]
            [x 345])))
```

Figure 5-3: A three-production chunk for the Do-Off-And-On goal in the Seibel (1963) task.

As usual, the negated condition is added to the connection production. However, an encoding production is now required because there are two positive conditions. The encoding production simply detects the presence of the two positive conditions and generates a new object representing their combination. This object has a unique NAME (*DoOffAndOn9267*) to distinguish it from the other objects in the system. Higher level chunks can be defined hierarchically by using this object in their encoding, rather than the primitive objects.

The encoding production fires as soon as its conditions are fulfilled — asynchronous with respect to goal processing — depositing the new object into working memory. The connection production then tests for the presence of such an object, rather than testing the two positive conditions. When the connection production executes, it asserts a chunked result object. This object is decoded into a primitive object for a button press at location 345 and another chunked result. Checking the NAME of this result, we see that it is the result symbol generated by the previous chunk. It can therefore be decoded by that chunk's decoding production, yielding two levels of a decoding hierarchy.

6 SIMULATION RESULTS

The four experiments discussed so far (Seibel, 1963; Duncan, 1977; Fitts & Seeger, 1953; Morin & Forrin, 1962) have been simulated within the *Xaps3* architecture. This has meant devising and implementing a goal hierarchy for each condition of each task. The architecture, plus the productions for one hierarchy, forms the performance program for a condition. Each performance program is executed for a sequence of trials, yielding a simulated practice curve for the condition. These simulations, and the hierarchies that generate them, are the topic of this chapter.

We will break this discussion up into three sections. In the first section we present the simulations for the Seibel task. This serves to bring the earlier work on the chunking theory (Newell & Rosenbloom, 1981; Rosenbloom & Newell, 1982a; Rosenbloom & Newell, 1982b) up to date. In the next section we show that the compatibility results are preserved in the transformation from algorithms to goal hierarchies and productions. This involves the presentation and discussion of the goal hierarchies for the remaining conditions, and the abstraction of compatibility results from the practice curves. In the final section we discuss the practice curves generated by the compatibility tasks.

6.1. Update on the Seibel (1963) Task

Two different sequences of trials were simulated for the Seibel task. The first sequence is the same as the one used in Rosenbloom and Newell (1982a). The simulation completed 268 trials before it terminated because of lack of memory. A total of 682 productions were learned. On the second sequence of trials — from a newly generated random permutation of the 1023 possibilities — 259 trials were completed before termination. For this sequence, 652 productions were learned.

Figure 6-1 shows the first sequence as fit by a simple power law. Each point in the figure represents the mean value over five data points (except for the last one, which only includes three)[19]. This curve shows a familiar pattern. It is linear over most of the range, but there is a deviation early in practice. There is also an apparent discontinuity in performance between trials 100 and 200. However, this is an artifact of the trial sequence; a string of atypically easy trials was reached.

For comparison purposes, the first 268 trials of subject 3's data (Rosenbloom & Newell, 1982a) for this same sequence of trials is reproduced in Figure 6-2. It shows much the same pattern as does the simulation, including the presence of the same discontinuity in performance. It differs primarily in being more shallow, lacking the initial deviation, and having more variation.

The initial deviation in the simulated curve (Figure 6-1) can be straightened out in the usual fashion by going to a general power law (Figure 6-3). For this curve, the asymptote parameter (A) has no effect. It is E, the correction for previous practice, that straightens out the curve. At first glance, it is nonsensical to talk about previous practice for such a simulation, but a plausible interpretation is possible. In fact, there are two independent explanations — either or both may be responsible.

The first possibility is that the level at which the terminal goals are defined is too high (complex). If the "true" terminals are more primitive, then chunking starts at a lower level in the hierarchy. During the bottom-up chunking that would occur, the system would eventually reach the lowest level in the current hierarchy. All of the practice prior to that point is effectively previous practice for the current simulation.

The other source of previous practice, is the goal hierarchy itself. At the beginning of the simulation, this structure is already known perfectly. There must be a process of *method acquisition* by which the subject goes from the written (or oral) instructions to an internal goal hierarchy. Though method acquisition does not fall within the domain of what we have here defined as "practice", in Chapter 7 we will propose a scheme whereby chunking may lead to a mechanism for method acquisition.

In addition to showing that the simulation produces practice curves that plot as straight lines on log-log paper, we need to show that this is a better fit than would be achieved by employing an exponential model. Figure 6-4 shows the data as fit by a general exponential function on semi-log paper. The general

---

[19]This data appear noisier than that in Figure 2-3 showing the human data from Seibel (1963). This is accounted for by each point in Figure 2-3 being the mean of 1023 data points, rather than the 5 data points of this figure.

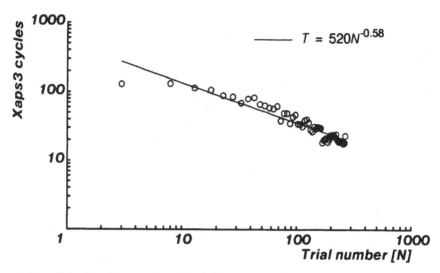

Figure 6-1: Simple power law fit to 268 simulated trials of the Seibel (1963) task.

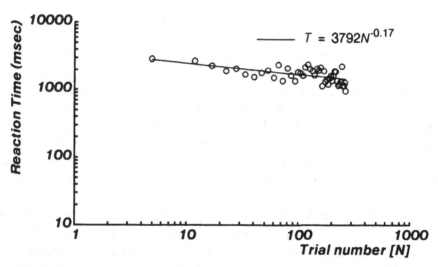

Figure 6-2: Simple power law fit to the 227 non-error trials in the first 268 trials of the Seibel (1963) task for subject 3 in Rosenbloom and Newell (1982a).

exponential has an asymptote parameter, but E is not necessary because exponentials are translation invariant.

This curve shows a high degree of linearity as well. This is not too surprising, because a power-law with a large E parameter (in comparison to the total length of the curve) looks somewhat like an exponential. For example, Figure 6-5 shows a true general power law, with the same parameters as those fit to the

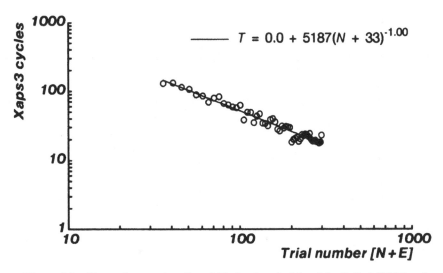

Figure 6-3:   General power law fit to 268 simulated trials of the Seibel (1963) task.

simulated data. It too looks much like an exponential when plotted on semi-log paper (after being fit by an exponential with asymptote). However the deviations are now clear, because of the lack of noise in this artificial data. Comparing this curve with the exponential fit to the simulated data shows that the same deviations are apparent in the simulation. The data starts out above the line, then shifts below it at around trial 50, then back above it at around trial 150. The curves differ in two ways. The first way — the anomalously low points between trials 165 and 200 — has already been discussed with respect to the simple power-law fit to the data. The second difference occurs at the very last point on the curves, where the pure power-law dips below the regression line, while the simulated data goes up. This can be chalked up to noise in the trial sequence.

Table 6-1 shows a slightly different analysis of the same problem. Included in this table are the exponential, simple power-law, and general power-law fits to the unaggregated data for both trial sequences. The left-hand column contains the fits to the human data, and the right-hand column contains the fits to the simulated data. The curves listed here may differ slightly from those in the previous figures, because of the difference in aggregation. The main columns of interest are the ones containing the r^2 values — the proportion of the data's variance accounted for by the fit.

We see essentially the same pattern for the simulated data from both trial sequences. The simple power law is comparable to the exponential, while the general power law is better than either. The simple power law is a two parameter fit, while the exponential has three, so the power law should be

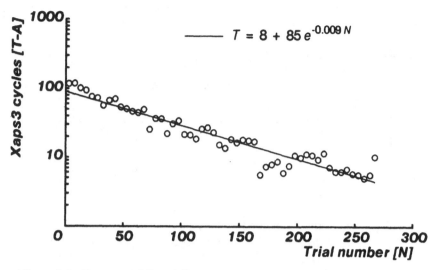

Figure 6-4: Exponential fit to 268 simulated trials of the Seibel (1963) task.

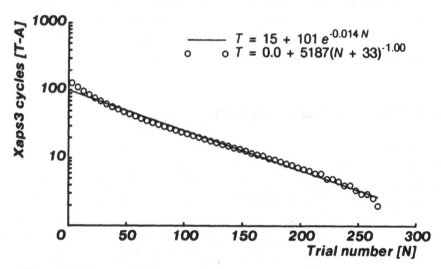

Figure 6-5: Exponential fit to power law with a large E parameter.

favored as an explanation. The general power law has four parameters, though only three are actually needed for these fits (the asymptote is a different kind of parameter at 0, because it is constrained by the analysis program to be greater than or equal to 0). The human data shows the same ambiguity between the exponential and simple power-law forms. However, it is surprising that the general power-law does not significantly improve on the simpler two forms. This same data set yields a power-law curve when the full 408-trial sequence is

Trial Seq.	Human Data			Simulated Data	
	Equation	r^2		Equation	r^2
1	$T = 383 + 1718\, e^{-0.00251\, N}$	0.138		$T = 8 + 85\, e^{-0.009\, N}$	0.753
	$T = 3384 N^{-0.16}$	0.135		$T = 462 N^{-0.56}$	0.751
	$T = 18 + 3679(N + 3)^{-0.17}$	0.136		$T = 0 + 4773(N + 33)^{-0.99}$	0.811
2				$T = 4 + 88\, e^{-0.008\, N}$	0.733
				$T = 473 N^{-0.56}$	0.746
				$T = 0 + 4161(N + 29)^{-0.97}$	0.807

Table 6-1: Exponential, simple power-law, and general power-law fits to human and simulated data from two trial sequences (only one sequence for the human) for the Seibel (1963) task.

used.

In conclusion, it appears that the simulation does produce power-law practice curves, but the evidence is not very strong. Longer simulated curves would be the best way to strengthen this conclusion, but the system in which the simulations were run was not capable of this.

6.2. The Compatibility Hierarchies

This section covers much of the same ground as was already covered in Chapter 3. Its purpose is to show what the goal hierarchies look like for the remaining tasks, to compare them with the analogous algorithms, and to show that the compatibility results are maintained across the shift in representation. In order to avoid needless reiteration of the same material, we will focus on the differences between the hierarchies and algorithms. In addition, we will abandon the practice of presenting both representations for each goal hierarchy. Only the depth-first goal structure (with full goal names) will be given.

There is a fair degree of latitude available when selecting which results to use in comparing the simulations with the data. We can choose simulated results from any point in the practice curves, or we can even use averaged values over sections of the curves. The same holds true for the experimental data for those instances in which practice curves are given — the Duncan (1977) conditions, and two of the Fitts and Seeger (1953) conditions[20].

Our answer is to define a default assumption: use the first data point from both the simulated and experimental curves (for Fitts and Seeger we use the non-practice data). For the cases in which this does not produce optimal results, we also look at an alternate, more optimal, assumption.

6.2.1. Duncan (1977)

The goal hierarchies for the Duncan (1977) conditions have already been presented and discussed in Chapter 4. The simulated times for the *corresponding* and *opposite* hierarchies are 15 and 21 cycles, respectively. Two versions of the mixed hierarchy (Figure 4-3) were simulated, corresponding to Algorithms *Duncan-Mixed-1* (Figure 3-4) and *Duncan-Mixed-2*. The results from these two simulations were averaged, to yield net values for the mixed condition. For mixed corresponding trials, the two algorithms required 25 and 20 respectively, for an average of 22.5 cycles. For mixed opposite algorithms, the two numbers were 26 and 31, for an average of 28.5 cycles.

The results for both the default and alternate assumptions are shown in Figure 6-6. The alternate assumption for the experimental data is the same one that was made in Chapter 3 — use the data from the sixth experimental run. For the simulated data, the default assumption (first trial data) is used in both comparisons. The figure, and the following equations, reveal that the simulation models the data quite well. The fit is better when the more practiced human data is used, but both fits are good. If we accept the alternate assumption, then the regression equation provides an estimate of the time per production-system cycle of 9.6 milliseconds.

Default: $RT = 18.0 \times Cycles + 176, \quad r^2 = 0.959$ (6.1)

Alternate: $RT = 9.6 \times Cycles + 266, \quad r^2 = 0.994$ (6.2)

This value is a factor of 5 smaller than the estimate of time per operation in Chapter 3; or, in other words, there are five production-cycles per operation.

---

[20] The Fitts and Seeger (1953) practice curves are from a different experiment (reported in the same article) using a subset of the conditions.

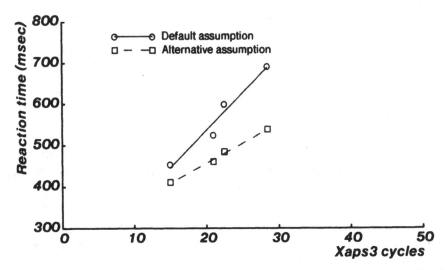

Figure 6-6: Regression of reaction time against simulated cost for Duncan (1977). Simulations generated by the *Xaps3* implementation of the goal-hierarchy formulation of the algorithmic model of compatibility.

6.2.2. Fitts and Seeger (1953)

Figure 6-7 contains the goal hierarchy for the S_A-R_A condition from Fitts and Seeger (1953). No comment is necessary, as it is essentially identical to Algorithm *Fitts&Seeger-S$_A$-R$_A$* in Figure 3-6. The cost to execute this hierarchy is 15 cycles.

    1. Push-Lever-Towards-On-Light-Stimulus
      2. Get-Angle-Of-On-Light-Stimulus
        3. Get-On-Light-Stimulus
        4. Get-Angle-Of-Stimulus
      5. Push-Lever-At-Angle

Figure 6-7: Goal structure for condition S_A-R_A in Fitts and Seeger (1953).

The goal hierarchy for condition S_A-R_B, is shown in Figure 6-8. This structure is also very similar to its algorithm (Figure 3-7). The only significant alteration consists of splitting the IF-SUCCEEDED—THEN—ELSE branch into separate tests for success and failure. The one additional complication in the algorithm — the successive assignment of two values to a single variable (Response-Angle) — is handled by the goal processing in *Xaps3*. The first response angle is generated by goal number 12 (**Compute-Response-Angle**) — it generates a new angle by adding 45 (its explicit parameter) to the existing angle — and used in goal number 13 (**Push-Lever-At-Response-Angle**). When goal 11 (Push-Lever-At-Angle-Plus-45) completes, the response angle becomes out of context, and is deleted. This leaves the system in a fresh state for the second generation and use of a response angle.

    1. Push-Lever-Orthogonal-To-On-Light-Stimulus
      2. Get-Angle-Of-On-Light-Stimulus
        3. Get-On-Light-Stimulus
        4. Get-Angle-Of-Stimulus
      5. Push-Lever-At-Orthogonal-Components-Of-Angle
        6. Is-Angle-Divisible-By-90?
        IF-SUCCEEDED *Is-Angle-Divisible-By-90?* THEN
          7. Push-Lever-At-Angle
        IF-FAILED *Is-Angle-Divisible-By-90?* THEN
          8. Possibly-Push-Lever-At-2-Orthogonal-Angles
            9. Is-Angle-Not-Divisible-By-90?
            IF-SUCCEEDED *Is-Angle-Not-Divisible-By-90?* THEN
              10. Push-Lever-At-2-Orthogonal-Angles
                11. Push-Lever-At-Angle-Plus-45
                12. Compute-Response-Angle
                13. Push-Lever-At-Response-Angle
                14. Push-Lever-At-Angle-Minus-45
                15. Compute-Response-Angle
                16. Push-Lever-At-Response-Angle

Figure 6-8: Goal structure for condition S_A-R_B in Fitts and Seeger (1953).

Two simulations — one for each ordering of the predicates — were run. Each simulation provided two kinds of data points: trials for which the stimulus angle was a multiple of 90°, and trials for which it wasn't. The simulated times were 20 and 25 (mean of 22.5) for multiples of 90°, and 33 and 28 (mean of 30.5) for non-multiples. Just as with the computation of the algorithm's cost, these values are averaged to yield the final cost of 26.5 production cycles. We should expect to find considerable noise in the results for this condition, because the two kinds of trials differ by 8 cycles — about 77 milliseconds, if we use the time per cycle from the Duncan simulations.

The hierarchy for condition S_B-R_A can be found in Figure 6-9. The one non-obvious operation in this structure is the retrieval of the second on-light stimulus from the display. This is accomplished by looking for an on-light that is not at the angle already found.

There are two variations on this hierarchy, and two types of trials in each — one or two lights on. When one light is on, the two versions cost 20 and 25 (mean of 22.5). With two lights on, they cost 45 and 40 cycles (mean of 42.5).

1. Push-Lever-At-Or-Between-On-Light-Stimuli
   2. Get-Angle-Of-On-Light-Stimulus
      3. **Get-On-Light-Stimulus**
      4. **Get-Angle-Of-Stimulus**
   5. Push-Lever-At-Or-Between-Angles
      6. **One-On-Light?**
      IF-SUCCEEDED *One-On-Light?* THEN
         7. **Push-Lever-At-Angle**
      IF-FAILED *One-On-Light?* THEN
         8. Possibly-Push-Lever-Between-Angles
         9. **Many-On-Lights?**
         IF-SUCCEEDED *Many-On-Lights?* THEN
            10. Push-Lever-Between-Angles
            11. Get-Angle-Between-Angles
               12. Get-Angle-Of-Second-On-Light-Stimulus
                  13. **Get-Second-On-Light-Stimulus**
                  14. **Get-Angle-Of-Stimulus**
               15. **Compute-Mean-Angle**
            16. **Push-Lever-At-Mean-Angle**

Figure 6-9: Goal structure for condition S_B-R_A in Fitts and Seeger (1953).

The overall mean is 32.5, but we should expect to see even more variation in this condition than in condition S_A-R_B.

Figures 6-10 and 6-11 show the hierarchies corresponding to the two algorithms for condition S_B-R_B. The first hierarchy takes a constant time of 17 cycles, irrespective of the order of the predicates, and whether there is one or two lights on. This happens because the first response is generated before either predicate is tested. The system doesn't worry about those details until it has responded to one light. The second hierarchy, like the second algorithm, does predict different values as a function of predicate ordering and number of lights. For one light on, the two variations generate times of 20 and 25 cycles (mean of 22.5). When two lights are on, the times are 27 and 22 (mean of 24.5). The net result is 23.5 cycles. Averaging the values for the two qualitatively different algorithms, yields an average time for the condition of 20.25.

Figure 6-12 and Equation 6.3 summarize the results for the four conditions of this experiment. The fit is so good for the default assumption that no alternate assumption is necessary. However, the time per cycle (3.4) is still off by a factor of 3 from the time predicted from the Duncan simulations.

Default: $RT = 3.4 \times Cycles + 340,$ $r^2 = 0.999$ (6.3)

1. Push-Lever-Towards-1-Or-2-On-Light-Stimuli (#1)
  2. Push-Lever-Towards-On-Light-Stimulus
    3. Get-Angle-Of-On-Light-Stimulus
      4. Get-On-Light-Stimulus
      5. Get-Angle-Of-Stimulus
    6. Push-Lever-At-Angle
  7. Done-Or-Second-On-Light
    8. One-On-Light?
   IF-FAILED *One-On-Light?* THEN
      9. Possibly-Push-Lever-Towards-Second-On-Light-Stimulus
      10. Many-On-Lights?
     IF-SUCCEEDED *Many-On-Lights?* THEN
        11. Push-Lever-Towards-Second-On-Light-Stimulus
        12. Get-Angle-Of-Stimulus-Not-At-Response-Angle
          13. Get-Angle-Of-Response
          14. Get-Angle-Of-Second-On-Light-Stimulus
            15. Get-Second-On-Light-Stimulus
            16. Get-Angle-Of-Stimulus
        17. Push-Lever-At-Angle

Figure 6-10: Goal structure 1 for condition S_B-R_B in Fitts and Seeger (1953).

6.2.3. Morin and Forrin (1962)

The goal hierarchies for the Morin and Forrin (1962) conditions are all very closely modeled after their algorithms. The only discrepancies again involve the splitting of the branch statements. Figure 6-13 shows the hierarchy that is used for both conditions I and IV — read one out of a set of either 2 or 4 numbers — corresponding to Algorithm *Morin&Forrin-I-IV* in Figure 3-11. It is identical to the algorithm (with the addition of two higher-level goals). Goal 2 (**Get-Stimulus-Object**), retrieves a representation of the stimulus object (a number). Goal 4 (**Get-Stimulus-Name**) gets the name of the number (such as, "two") from the stimulus object. Goal 5 (**Say-Name**) generates a response consisting of a vocalization of the name. The hierarchy requires 14 cycles to execute.

Figure 6-14 shows the hierarchy for condition II — say the number associated with either a plus or a square. As in Algorithm *Morin&Forrin-II* (Figure 3-12), the hierarchy begins by retrieving the stimulus object (**Get-Stimulus-Object**) and its name (**Get-Stimulus-Name**). A sequence of tests are then performed (**Is-Plus?** and **Is-Square?**) until the system figures out which stimulus it has seen. It then retrieves the number associated with the symbol, using either **Get-Plus-Number** or **Get-Square-Number**. The association is stored in a production — the only form of long-term memory in the system — that is

1. Push-Lever-Towards-1-Or-2-On-Light-Stimuli (#2)
   2. **One-On-Light?**
   IF-SUCCEEDED *One-On-Light?* THEN
      3. Push-Lever-Towards-On-Light-Stimulus
         4. Get-Angle-Of-On-Light-Stimulus
            5. **Get-On-Light-Stimulus**
            6. **Get-Angle-Of-Stimulus**
         7. **Push-Lever-At-Angle**
   IF-FAILED *One-On-Light?* THEN
      8. Possibly-Push-Lever-Towards-2-On-Light-Stimuli
         9. **Many-On-Lights?**
         IF-SUCCEEDED *Many-On-Lights?* THEN
            10. Push-Lever-Towards-2-On-Light-Stimuli
               11. Push-Lever-Towards-On-Light-Stimulus
                  12. Get-Angle-Of-On-Light-Stimulus
                     13. **Get-On-Light-Stimulus**
                     14. **Get-Angle-Of-Stimulus**
                  15. **Push-Lever-At-Angle**
               16. Push-Lever-Towards-Second-On-Light-Stimulus
                  17. Get-Angle-Of-Stimulus-Not-At-Response-Angle
                     18. **Get-Angle-Of-Response**
                     19. Get-Angle-Of-Second-On-Light-Stimulus
                        20. **Get-Second-On-Light-Stimulus**
                        21. **Get-Angle-Of-Stimulus**
                  22. **Push-Lever-At-Angle**

Figure 6-11: Goal structure 2 for condition S_B-R_B in Fitts and Seeger (1953).

accessible during the processing of the goal. Once the name of the associated number is retrieved, it can be vocalized (Say-Number). The hierarchy differs from the algorithm only in its need to store this name in a different "variable" from the one containing the name of the stimulus.

The mean time for executing this hierarchy is the average over the two stimuli, automatically taking into account the possible orderings of the predicates. The times are 26 cycles for a plus, and 32 cycles for a square, for a mean value of 29 cycles for this condition.

The goal hierarchy for Condition III (Figure 6-15 — say one of two numbers, or the number associated with one of two symbols) is essentially the combination of the structures for conditions I and II, with an additional choice to be made. The first thing to do is to get the representation of the stimulus (Get-Stimulus-Object). From this representation, the stimulus' class is determined (Get-Stimulus-Class) — either *symbol* or *number*. The decision is then made as to whether to branch to the goal to handle numbers, or to the one to handle symbols. The goal to handle numbers (Say-Stimulus-Name) is the same as goal number 3 in the structure for Condition I. Likewise, the goal to handle

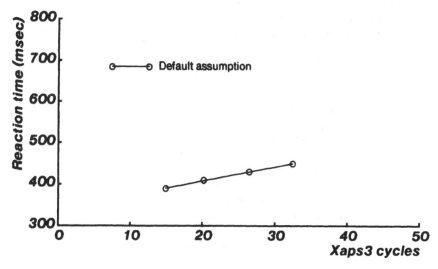

Figure 6-12: Regression of reaction time against simulated cost for Fitts and Seeger (1953). Simulations generated by the *Xaps3* implementation of the goal-hierarchy formulation of the algorithmic model of compatibility.

   1. Read-Number-Say-Number
     2. **Get-Stimulus-Object**
     3. Say-Stimulus-Name
       4. **Get-Stimulus-Name**
       5. **Say-Name**

Figure 6-13: Goal structure for conditions I & IV in Morin and Forrin (1962).

the two symbols (Say-Number-From-Plus-Or-Square-Stimulus) is the same as goal number 3 in the structure for Condition II.

Two versions of this structure were run, corresponding to the two orderings of the **Is-Symbol?** and **Is-Number?** predicates. For the symbolic case, the results were then averaged over the times for the two symbols (plus and square). For numbers (condition IIIa), the two versions took 25 and 30 cycles (mean of 27.5). The plus required 42 and 37 cycles (mean of 39.5), while the square required 48 and 43 cycles (mean of 45.5). Therefore, the total symbolic average (condition IIIb) is 42.5.

Figure 6-16 shows the last goal hierarchy, the one for Condition V — say the number associated with one of four symbols. It is an extended version of the hierarchy for Condition II, where the chain of predicates has been extended to handle the two additional symbols (circle and triangle). The mean time to perform this task is the average over the times for the four alternative stimuli

1. Read-Plus-Or-Square-Say-Number
   2. **Get-Stimulus-Object**
   3. Say-Number-From-Plus-Or-Square-Stimulus
      4. **Get-Stimulus-Name**
      5. Say-Number-From-Plus-Or-Square-Name
         6. Get-Number-From-Plus-Or-Square-Name
            7. **Is-Plus?**
            IF-SUCCEEDED *Is-Plus?* THEN
               8. **Get-Plus-Number**
            IF-FAILED *Is-Plus?* THEN
               9. Possibly-Get-Square-Number
                  10. **Is-Square?**
                  IF-SUCCEEDED *Is-Square?* THEN
                     11. **Get-Square-Number**
   12. **Say-Number**

Figure 6-14:   Goal structure for condition II in Morin and Forrin (1962).

1. Read-Plus-Square-Or-Number-Say-Number
   2. **Get-Stimulus-Object**
   3. Say-Number-From-Plus-Square-Or-Number-Stimulus
      4. **Get-Stimulus-Class**
      5. Say-Number-From-Plus-Square-Or-Number-Class
         6. **Is-Number?**
         IF-SUCCEEDED *Is-Number?* THEN
            7. Say-Stimulus-Name
               8. **Get-Stimulus-Name**
               9. **Say-Name**
         IF-FAILED *Is-Number?* THEN
            10. Possibly-Say-Number-From-Plus-Or-Square-Stimulus
               11. **Is-Symbol?**
               IF-SUCCEEDED *Is-Symbol?* THEN
                  12. Say-Number-From-Plus-Or-Square-Stimulus
                     13. **Get-Stimulus-Name**
                     14. Say-Number-From-Plus-Or-Square-Name
                        15. Get-Number-From-Plus-Or-Square-Name
                           16. **Is-Plus?**
                           IF-SUCCEEDED *Is-Plus?* THEN
                              17. **Get-Plus-Number**
                           IF-FAILED *Is-Plus?* THEN
                              18. Possibly-Get-Square-Number
                                 19. **Is-Square?**
                                 IF-SUCCEEDED *Is-Square?* THEN
                                    20. **Get-Square-Number**
   21. **Say-Number**

Figure 6-15:   Goal structure for condition III in Morin and Forrin (1962).

(26, 32, 38, 44) — an average of 35 cycles.

1. Read-Plus-Square-Circle-Or-Triangle-Say-Number
    2. **Get-Stimulus-Object**
    3. Say-Number-From-Plus-Square-Circle-Or-Triangle-Stimulus
        4. **Get-Stimulus-Name**
        5. Say-Number-From-Plus-Square-Circle-Or-Triangle-Name
            6. Get-Number-From-Plus-Square-Circle-Or-Triangle-Name
            7. **Is-Circle?**
            IF-SUCCEEDED *Is-Circle?* THEN
                8. **Get-Circle-Number**
            IF-FAILED *Is-Circle?* THEN
                9. Get-Number-From-Plus-Square-Or-Triangle-Name
                10. **Is-Triangle?**
                IF-SUCCEEDED *Is-Triangle?* THEN
                    11. **Get-Triangle-Number**
                IF-FAILED *Is-Triangle?* THEN
                    12. Get-Number-From-Plus-Or-Square-Name
                    13. **Is-Plus?**
                    IF-SUCCEEDED *Is-Plus?* THEN
                        14. **Get-Plus-Number**
                    IF-FAILED *Is-Plus?* THEN
                        15. Possibly-Get-Square-Number
                        16. **Is-Square?**
                        IF-SUCCEEDED *Is-Square?* THEN
                            17. **Get-Square-Number**
    18. **Say-Number**

Figure 6-16: Goal structure for condition V in Morin and Forrin (1962).

Figure 6-17 and Equation 6.4 summarize the results for the Morin and Forrin (1962) experiment. The slope of the default equation lies between those found for the previous two experiments. This fit suffers from the same problem as did the algorithmic formulation of the model for these tasks. No alternate assumption was used for this experiment.

$$\text{Default:} \quad RT = 7.9 \times Cycles + 391, \quad r^2 = 0.900 \tag{6.4}$$

6.2.4. Putting the results together

Just as with the algorithmic version of the model, the fourteen conditions from the three different experiments can be lumped together into a single regression equation, with one slope parameter (milliseconds per cycle), and three intercept parameters (one for each experiment). The following two equations represent the results of this analysis for the default and alternate assump-

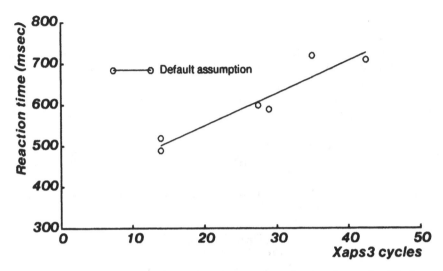

Figure 6-17: Regression of reaction time against simulated cost for Morin and Forrin (1962). Simulations generated by the *Xaps3* implementation of the goal-hierarchy formulation of the algorithmic model of compatibility.

tions.

Default: $RT = 8.1 \times Cycles + 392 \times Duncan + 230 \times Fitts\&Seeger$
$+ 387 \times Morin\&Forrin, \quad r^2 = 0.886$ \hfill (6.5)

Alternate: $RT = 7.2 \times Cycles + 317 \times Duncan + 250 \times Fitts\&Seeger$
$+ 410 \times Morin\&Forrin, \quad r^2 = 0.946$ \hfill (6.6)

The alternate equation is nearly identical to the one derived for the algorithmic formulation of the model (Equation 3.4). Figure 6-18 plots simulated reaction-time versus true reaction-time for the alternate assumption. It too is quite close to the analogous curve for the algorithmic formulation (Figure 3-16).

In conclusion, it appears that nothing has been lost in shifting from algorithms to goal hierarchies (except the ease in hand-computing the predicted reaction-times), and we have gained the ability to apply chunking to these tasks.

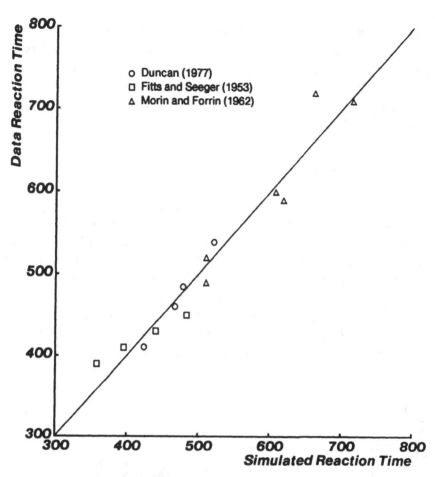

Figure 6-18: Comparison of simulated and experimental reaction times for the three compatibility experiments. Simulations generated by the *Xaps3* implementation of the goal-hierarchy formulation of the algorithmic model of compatibility.

6.3. Compatibility and Practice

One of the positive aspects of modeling two independent phenomena within the same system is that a third, and unpredictable, phenomenon emerges — the interaction between the planned two. It is usually possible to develop independent models for different sets of phenomena, and combine them into a big-switch type system that uses each model individually when appropriate. It is only when the interactions between the phenomena are also adequately modeled that we can have some confidence that we have a synthesis rather than a pastiche.

In this section we look at the interactions between stimulus-response compatibility and practice for the three compatibility experiments. For each of the fourteen conditions we have generated simulated practice curves for random sequences of trials. These curves are evaluated by (1) determining whether they are reasonable practice curves; and (2) comparing them with the human practice curves where available.

6.3.1. Duncan (1977)

Figure 6-19 shows the practice curves generated by Duncan's subjects for the four different kinds of trials. This figure shows the mean data for experimental runs 2 through 6, at 144 trials per run per subject (averaged over eight subjects for the pure cases, and 16 subjects for the mixed case). There is one ambiguity in how this information should be plotted. The mixed condition contained 144 trials per run, just as did the pure conditions. However, that means that each type of mixed trial received half as much practice as did the corresponding pure trial. For these curves, this manipulation has only a minor effect, so they have just been kept as they were presented by Duncan (1977).

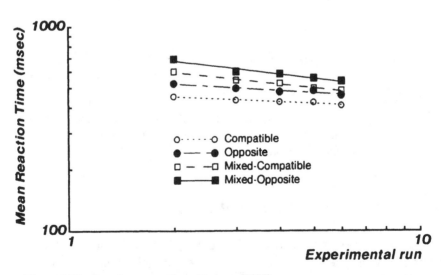

Figure 6-19: Practice curves from Duncan (1977).

The curves present a neat pattern, with straight-line fits (power laws), and the four conditions maintaining their relative standing over the entire practice sequence. Some convergence is apparent, at least between the mixed and the pure cases. The left half of Table 6-2 shows the fits to exponential, simple power-law and general power-law functions for these curves. These equations confirm that the data is well fit by a power law, though exponentials cannot be ruled out. In all cases, the general power-law fit better than the exponential (even though only three out of the four general power-law parameters were non-zero in three of the cases), but in two of the cases, the exponential fit better than the simple power-law.

Cond.	Human Data Equation	r^2	Simulated Data Equation	r^2
Pure Corr.	$T = 348 + 131\, e^{-0.117\,N}$ $T = 480 N^{-0.08}$ $T = 38 + 451(N + 0.3)^{-0.10}$	0.952 0.961 0.960	$T = 1.6 + 19.2\, e^{-0.185\,N}$ $T = 30.8 N^{-0.85}$	0.868 0.748
Pure Opp.	$T = 387 + 174\, e^{-0.137\,N}$ $T = 563 N^{-0.11}$ $T = 40 + 523(N + 0.0)^{-0.12}$	0.884 0.912 0.912	$T = 0.0 + 23.0\, e^{-0.129\,N}$ $T = 76.4 N^{1.22}$	0.748 0.696
Mixed Corr.	$T = 457 + 315\, e^{-0.404\,N}$ $T = 681 N^{-0.19}$ $T = 317 + 390(N + 0.0)^{-0.47}$	0.989 0.988 0.990	$T = 0.0 + 20.4\, e^{-0.110\,N}$ $T = 57.6 N^{1.06}$ $T = 0.0 + 80.1(N + 0.6)^{-1.16}$	0.609 0.699 0.699
Mixed Opp.	$T = 517 + 432\, e^{-0.488\,N}$ $T = 788 N^{-0.22}$ $T = 473 + 437(N + 0.0)^{-1.04}$	0.977 0.955 0.979	$T = 0.0 + 42.4\, e^{-0.117\,N}$ $T = 176.6 N^{1.24}$	0.924 0.837

Table 6-2: Exponential, simple power law, and general power law fits to the human and simulated data for the Duncan (1977) conditions.

In all of the 15 fits presented in Newell and Rosenbloom (1981), there are only three conditions that come close to the ambiguity of these fits. The first condition is from Neisser, Novick, and Lazar (1963). They had subjects search for a single target in a display. The values of r^2 were 0.938, 0.944, and 0.951 for the exponential, simple power-law, and general power-law. The other two conditions were from an experiment by Card, English, and Burr (1978). Their subjects had to move a cursor on a video terminal to a location marked by a target, using either a mouse, or stepping keys. The results for these two conditions were (0.335, 0.335, 0.340) and (0.452, 0.398, 0.729). It is interesting that these three conditions were the simplest perceptual-motor tasks included in the Newell and Rosenbloom (1981) work. They are quite analogous in complexity to the Duncan task.

Another aspect of the Duncan curves worth noting is that the exponents of the simple power-law fits are ordered according to difficulty. The more difficult the task, the steeper the curve. There is a relatively large jump between the pure and mixed curves, corresponding to the convergence that can be perceived in the plot. In addition, there are small amounts of convergence between the pair of mixed curves and between the two pure curves.

Figure 6-20 shows the simulated practice curves for the Duncan conditions. The two pure conditions were each run for one random sequence of 25 trials. The mixed condition was run for two random sequences of 25 trials, one for each of the two hierarchy variations. The mixed corresponding data from the two simulations was combined into a single curve. Likewise, the mixed opposite data was combined into a single curve. The trial numbers were kept as generated, so this figure is analogous to the human one in how the mixed conditions are plotted.

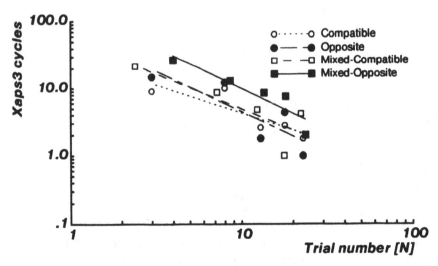

Figure 6-20: Simulated practice curves for the Duncan (1977) conditions. The mixed curves are averaged over the two hierarchy variations.

These curves are messier because of the reduced amount of aggregation done (five trials per data point[21]) as compared to the human curves (1152 trials

---

[21]The final data points for the two mixed curves do not have exactly five points, because the random sequences did not guarantee equal numbers of the two types of trials.

per point). The functional fits for these curves can be found in the right half of Table 6-2. General power-law fits are not presented for three of the conditions because they could not be generated. The procedure used to generate optimal general power-law fits blows up when the data takes a sharp drop at the high-practice end of the curve. This effectively implies a negative asymptote, which is not allowed by the data-fit procedure. The only option left open is for the procedure to assume that the falling portion is the "true" curve, while the remainder of the curve is flattened out by a huge E parameter (previous practice on the task). This assumption leads the procedure to exceed the precision of the machine on which the analyses were done, yielding divisions by zero.

A falling tail in a log-log plot can also be indicative of an exponential curve. As the fits in Table 6-2 show, three of the curves are better fit by an exponential than by a simple power-law, though one parameter is lost in going to the simple power-law. There are three reasons why this is not totally unexpected. The first two have already been discussed in the context of the Seibel task: (1) there may be effective previous practice caused by defining the terminal goals at too high a level; and (2) there is previous practice in the learning of the goal hierarchy.

The third reason comes from the revised chunking equation presented in Chapter 4. The chunking equation predicts exponential learning when $s(\eta)$ — the number of possible initial states for a goal as a function of the height of the goal in the hierarchy — is a constant. For the corresponding and opposite hierarchies (Figures 4-1 and 4-2), every goal has exactly four possible initial states, irrespective of the height of the goal in the hierarchy. The state can involve one of four lights, or one of four locations, but there is always four — one for each light-button pair. Thus, for these hierarchies we in fact get $s(\eta) = 4$ and hence we would expect exponential learning.

For the mixed hierarchy (Figure 4-3), the goals through the first predicate (numbers 1 to 6) all have four initial states, while those after the predicate (numbers 7 to 12) have two. The effect of the predicate in this hierarchy is to split up the set of initial states, and pass half of them to each subalgorithm — yielding exponential growth in $s(\eta)$ for this portion of the hierarchy (and power-law practice). We should expect to see a mixture of power law and exponential effects in the mixed hierarchy. What we do find, is that one of the mixed curves (the corresponding one) is a power law, and the other curve (the opposite one) is an exponential.

As to the ordering of the simple power-law exponents, we don't see the total ordering that was found in the human data — the mixed-corresponding slope is shallower than that of the pure-opposite curve. However, all of the key one-dimensional relationships still hold: (1) the pure-corresponding is less than the pure-opposite; (2) the mixed-corresponding is less than the mixed-opposite; (3) the pure-corresponding is less than the mixed-corresponding; and (4) the pure-opposite is less than the mixed opposite.

When the simulated exponents are compared to the human exponents, it is apparent that the simulated ones are consistently larger. We conjecture that this is tied up with the exponential flavor of the simulations, but do not currently have an explanation for this effect.

6.3.2. Fitts and Seeger (1953)

Fitts and Seeger (1953) provide practice curves for the conditions in which the A response apparatus — a lever that can be pushed in one of eight directions — is employed. The curves for conditions S_A-R_A and S_B-R_A can be seen in Figure 6-21. This data is aggregated across 48 trials per session and 5 subjects, so that 240 trials are represented per data point.

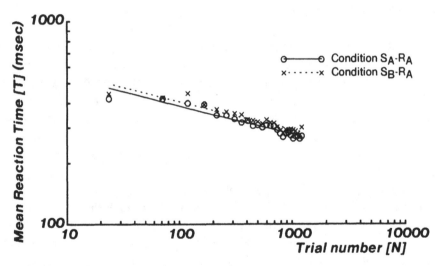

Figure 6-21: Practice curves for conditions S_A-R_A and S_B-R_A from Fitts and Seeger (1953).

The functional fits for these curves can be found in the left half of Table 6-3. They show the same pattern evidenced by the Duncan (1977) data. There is no strong trend when the exponential is compared with the simple power-law, but the general power-law is consistently better than the exponential. The optimal general power-law fits employ small asymptotes and moderately large E parameters for previous practice (notice the flattening evident in the initial segment of both curves).

Figure 6-22 shows the results of simulated practice on these same two con-

Cond.	Human Data Equation	r^2	Simulated Data Equation	r^2
S_A-R_A	$T = 242 + 169\, e^{-0.00165\,N}$ $T = 749 N^{-0.14}$ $T = 57 + 1506(N + 126)^{-0.28}$	0.928 0.918 0.961	$T = 0.0 + 12.6\, e^{-0.0472\,N}$ $T = 43.6 N^{-0.82}$ $T = 0.0 + 1254.3(N + 12.7)^{-1.63}$	0.611 0.606 0.630
S_A-R_B			$T = 0.0 + 23.3\, e^{-0.0368\,N}$ $T = 59.6 N^{-0.63}$ $T = 0.0 + 3942.3(N + 20.6)^{-1.61}$	0.709 0.679 0.739
S_B-R_A	$T = 245 + 178\, e^{-0.00138\,N}$ $T = 780 N^{-0.14}$ $T = 22 + 1326(N + 106)^{-0.23}$	0.886 0.905 0.945	$T = 0.0 + 29.4\, e^{-0.0339\,N}$ $T = 67.5 N^{-0.57}$	0.824 0.760
S_B-R_B			$T = 0.0 + 12.9\, e^{-0.0303\,N}$ $T = 34.3 N^{-0.59}$ $T = 0.0 + 34.3(N + 0.0)^{-0.59}$	0.663 0.816 0.816

Table 6-3: Exponential, simple power law, and general power law fits to the human and simulated data for the Fitts and Seeger (1953) conditions.

ditions. The simulated practice curves for the other two conditions are in Figure 6-23. These curves contain fifty trials each, aggregated by five trials per data point. The equations for these four curves can be found in the right half of Table 6-3. Again we see a mix of effects. For two of the curves (S_A-R_A and S_A-R_B), the fit improves as it proceeds from simple-power law, to exponential, and general power-law. For one of the curves (S_B-R_A), the results were more strongly exponential, and a general power-law could not be fit. The remaining curve (S_B-R_B) is a power law.

Interpreting these results is complex. Based on the arguments presented during the discussion of the Duncan (1977) data, we would expect the one condition without branches (S_A-R_A) to be the most exponential (when comparing the relative r^2 values). The equations show that it is the steepest, but not the most exponential. However, the graphs tell a different story. Ignoring the anomalous data point at around trial 23 (caused by the aggregation of an unusually high percentage of tasks that were already at asymptote), the curve for the S_A-R_A condition does show the exponential character predicted. When the data is fit without this one point, the r^2 values were (0.892, 0.758, can't do) for exponential, simple power-law, and general power-law.

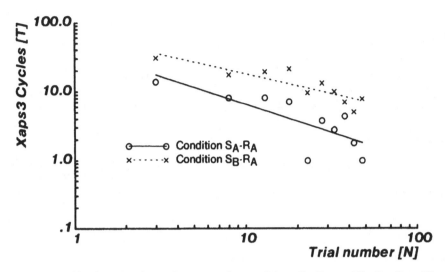

Figure 6-22: Simulated practice curves for conditions $S_A\text{-}R_A$ and $S_B\text{-}R_A$ from Fitts and Seeger (1953). The latter curve is the average over two hierarchy variations.

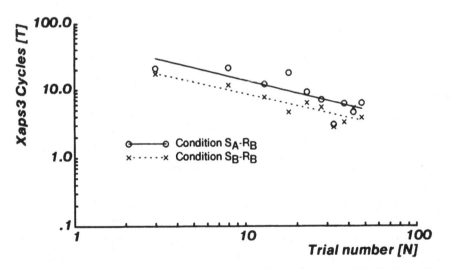

Figure 6-23: Simulated practice curves for conditions $S_A\text{-}R_B$ and $S_B\text{-}R_B$ from Fitts and Seeger (1953). The curves are the averages over two and three hierarchy variations, respectively.

The other three conditions all contain branches, and so can be expected to be more power-law than condition $S_A\text{-}R_A$. They also have another factor in their favor. They all allow some form of transfer of training. For example, in condition S_A-R_B, the **Push-Lever-At-Response-Angle** goal is used to push the lever at $+45°$ and $-45°$. The angle at $+45°$ for a stimulus light at $45°$ is the same as the angle at $-45°$ for a stimulus light at $135°$.

As discussed in Chapter 4, transfer of training effectively reduces the number of initial states that each instance of a goal must chunk. Since this is mainly occurring low in the hierarchy, it provides a second means by which $s(h)$ decreases as h decreases. Condition S_B-R_B should be, and is, the most power-law of these three conditions. It allows transfer of training on both the perceptual and motor portions of the hierarchy. Condition S_B-R_A allows transfer of training only on the perceptual portion of the hierarchy, and condition S_A-R_B allows it only on the motor portion.

6.3.3. Morin and Forrin (1962)

Morin and Forrin (1962) did not provide any practice data, so we can go straight to the simulated practice curves. The curves can be seen in Figures 6-24, 6-25, and 6-26. Each curve contains 50 trials — except for conditions IIIa and IIIb, which contain 54 and 46 points respectively — aggregated by 5 trials per data point. The equations are in Table 6-4.

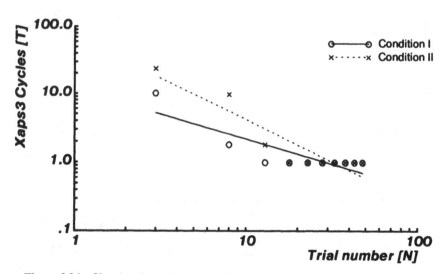

Figure 6-24: Simulated practice curves for Conditions I and II in Morin and Forrin (1962).

These curves are the most complex so far. Four of them are power laws (I,

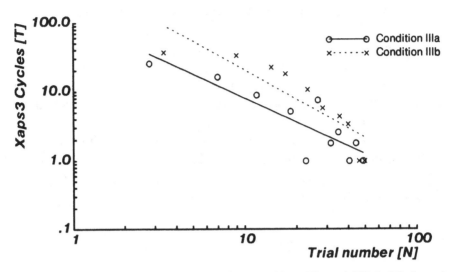

Figure 6-25: Simulated practice curves for Conditions IIIa and IIIb in Morin and Forrin (1962). The curves are averaged over the two hierarchy variations.

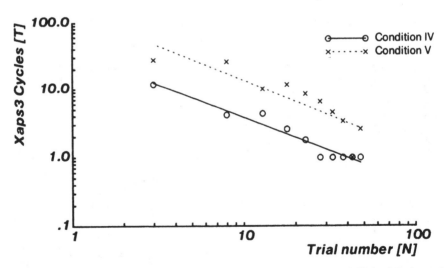

Figure 6-26: Simulated practice curves for Conditions IV and V in Morin and Forrin (1962).

Cond.	Simulated Data Equation	r^2
I	$T = 0.9 + 1.1\,e^{-0.0681\,N}$ $T = 11.7N^{-0.73}$ $T = 0.9 + 20.4(N + 0.0)^{-1.56}$	0.459 0.729 0.788
II	$T = 0.9 + 5.6\,e^{-0.111\,N}$ $T = 70.9N^{-1.22}$ $T = 0.8 + 176.2(N + 0.0)^{-1.93}$	0.635 0.850 0.863
IIIa	$T = 0.0 + 19.9\,e^{-0.0647\,N}$ $T = 116.0N^{-1.15}$ $T = 0.0 + 1232.5(N + 6.0)^{-1.75}$	0.727 0.761 0.777
IIIb	$T = 0.0 + 67.1\,e^{-0.0822\,N}$ $T = 520.8N^{-1.40}$	0.972 0.780
IV	$T = 0.9 + 10.2\,e^{-0.116\,N}$ $T = 37.0N^{-0.98}$ $T = 0.0 + 56.8(N + 1.2)^{-1.09}$	0.869 0.942 0.944
V	$T = 0.0 + 34.6\,e^{-0.0640\,N}$ $T = 152.1N^{-1.04}$	0.883 0.770

Table 6-4: Exponential, simple power law, and general power law fits to the simulated data for the Morin and Forrin (1962) conditions.

II, IIIa, and IV), while two conditions (IIIb and V) show exponential character. We have so far been unable to properly explain why these results (both the equations and the graphs) are as they are. Further investigation is needed.

7 DISCUSSION

In this chapter we pick up a number of topics that have been glossed over in the previous chapters. Specifically, we look at seven topics: (1) considerations in the choice of a set of primitive algorithmic operators; (2) the rate of learning; (3) errors; (4) other reaction-time phenomena; (5) the relation of chunking to previous research on learning mechanisms; (6) the application of chunking to more complex tasks; and (7) the emergence of complicated forms of learning from the integration of chunking and problem-space search.

7.1. On Choosing a Set of Model Operators

The set of operators employed in the *Artless* language determines the range of tasks that can be modeled with the language. We have a set that have proved adequate for the set of experiments we have worked with, but several caveats are in order. The first warning is that the set of operators employed here is not all-encompassing in terms of breadth of coverage. Other experimental situations may require additional operators, but as long as they are defined analogously to the ones here, the results should extrapolate to them.

The second caveat has to do with the level of abstraction of the operators. It is perfectly possible to come up with a set of operators that are simpler than the ones used here, out of which these more complex ones can be built. It is also theoretically possible to start with a set of more complex ones than is provided here — for example, modeled after some of the non-terminal nodes in the goal hierarchies. The level chosen says something about the level of detail to which the model can be built, but as long as the operators chosen do not differ radically among themselves in terms of execution time, the metric aspects of the results should not be radically changed. Card, Moran, and Newell (1983) have investigated this issue in the context of manuscript editing. They found that changing the level of analysis affected the accuracy with which the exact sequence of operators could be predicted — the finer the grain of analysis, the poorer the predictions — but that the total time predictions were all about equally accurate.

The third, and final, caveat is that it is not important which aspects of the *Artless* operators are fixed and which are parameterized. Fewer parameters means more operators (and vice-versa), but again the metric aspects of the model are not altered. In the algorithmic formulation of the theory we have used parameters as much as possible because they simplify the description.

7.2. The Rate of Learning

In the chunking model of Rosenbloom and Newell (1982a), learning was demonstrably too fast. We speculated that this could have been caused by one (or both) of two factors: (1) there are more chunks to be learned than are captured by the model; and (2) chunks are not learned at every opportunity. At the time it was unclear how to use the first factor to yield a better model, so we experimented with the second factor. Considerably better practice curves were obtained by creating chunks probabilistically. When the opportunity to create a chunk arose, the probability was 0.02 that a chunk would be created.

In the current model, an exogenous learning rate parameter has not proven necessary, because the first factor has come into play. Because the task analyses are more detailed, there are many more chunks to be learned in the current model. All of the chunks learned by the Rosenbloom and Newell (1982a) model are accounted for by just 1 of the 12 goals in the hierarchy for the Seibel Task (Figure 4-7) (not counting the recursive goals at 13 and 14). Additional chunks are required for the 11 other goals in the structure.

When chunks are acquired at every opportunity, the model does constrain the maximum rate of learning. However, the minimum rate of learning is left unconstrained. As with the previous model, it is possible to add an exogenous rate parameter to slow the learning down to any arbitrary degree. Whether this is either necessary or desirable is still an open issue.

A related open question exists about how to account for learning in even simpler situations, such as *simple reaction-time* experiments — situations in which there is only one stimulus and one response. It has been suggested that learning in such situations is more gradual and long term than would be predicted by the chunking theory. However, we are not currently aware of any evidence to support this claim.

7.3. Errors

Up until this point, we have focused on one basic response measure — reaction time. Reaction time is clearly important, and we have had a lot to say about it, but there is another important response measure that we have ignored — errors. It has been assumed that the system is capable of error-free performance and learning. Errors are important both for a psychological model and an AI program. In psychology, no model of a phenomenon is truly complete unless it predicts subjects' errors as well as their reaction times. In addition, errors can be used to get at the fine-grain structure of performance, yielding information on which design decisions can be based (see for example Van Lehn, 1981). In AI, any sufficiently complex program will operate heuristically, with no guarantee of correctness. Errors will occur. A robust system must be able to perform under these conditions, and recover when an error is made.

Though we do not yet have a complete theory of errors, there are a number of issues that can be covered. We start out with a discussion of the human error data for the four tasks covered in this research. There are some results available both on the frequency and the kinds of errors that people make. Following this discussion, we examine the kinds of errors the model can currently make. We then look at what other sources of error there could be, and finish up by considering how the system could be made to recover from errors.

7.3.1. Human error data

In the Seibel (1963) results, an error occurred when subjects either pressed extra keys or did not press all of the appropriate keys within 100 msec of the first key that was pressed. This information was presented in terms of plots of error percentage (by 1023-trial block) versus practice, with no commentary. The percent oscillates in the region of 5 to 15 percent, with no strong practice effects apparent (by eye), except possibly very early in practice.

Table 7-1 shows the error percentages for the conditions in the Duncan (1977) experiment. Except for the *Pure-Opposite* condition, error rate increases with mean reaction-time. Duncan did not provide an explanation for why the error rate is so high for the pure-opposite condition (and we do not have one to add).

Duncan also broke down the errors into four classes. *Corresponding* errors occur when the corresponding button is pressed in a situation in which the opposite one should have been pressed. *Opposite* errors occur when the opposite button is pressed in a situation in which the corresponding button should have been pressed. *Adjacent* errors occur when either the incorrect finger on the

	Corresponding	Opposite
Pure	2.0	3.3
Mixed	2.4	2.5

Table 7-1: Error percentages from Duncan (1977).

correct hand is used, or when a response is made that is appropriate to the incorrect stimulus on the correct side of the display. The fourth class of errors (termed *Other*) is a catch-all for the remaining (very few) errors.

Corresponding and Opposite errors would appear to involve the choice of a wrong algorithm (or sub-algorithm). Adjacent errors would appear to mainly involve problems in discrimination. Duncan (1977) concluded that

> under Pure mappings the dominant type of error is Adjacent, though there is some tendency when the S-R pair is Opposite to make a Corresponding response. Under Mixed mappings Adjacent errors decrease in frequency, and Corresponding and Opposite errors become dominant. (p. 57)

Table 7-2 shows the error percentages for the nine conditions in the Fitts and Seeger (1953) experiment. Fitts and Seeger concluded that "These error data agree in general with the time data in respect to the rankings assigned to the different S-R ensembles. (p. 205)".

Fitts and Seeger (1953) also presented data on the interaction between practice and error percentage for the conditions using response apparatus R_A. If there is any trend in these numbers, it is that error rate tended to *increase* with practice, and become more uniform across conditions.

Instead of presenting error data, Morin and Forrin (1962) presented *information transmitted*, an information-theoretic measure that combines both the number of alternative responses and the error rate. We have not tried to unconfound this data.

	R_A	R_B	R_C
S_A	4.4	7.5	11.6
S_B	6.6	3.4	17.8
S_C	16.3	18.8	8.4

Table 7-2: Error percentages from Fitts and Seeger (1953).

7.3.2. Errors in the current model

A complete explanation of human errors must predict both the frequency and kinds of errors made. On frequencies, we are a long way from explaining their absolute values. However, an explanation of their relative values seems within reach. Any mechanism that generates errors in proportion to reaction time would do a fair job of predicting the relative error frequencies. In the current system, this amounts to an assumption that the number of errors is proportional to the number of goals processed — a reasonable assumption for a number of different types of errors.

The system is currently capable of four classes of errors, of which it has exhibited two. The first class is the creation of overspecific chunks. This is an error in learning that can stretch out the amount of learning required but cannot lead to errors in performance. Overspecific chunks can be of two types. The first type, and the only type that the system has been observed to make, occurs when irrelevant objects are tested in the encoding component of the chunk. This happens when an encoding production executes that is irrelevant to the processing of the active goal. Any portions of the goal's initial state examined by the encoding production are included in the encoding component of the chunk for the active goal. The result is a chunk that is applicable in fewer situations than it should be. This is a very infrequent kind of error, but it has been observed.

The other way in which overspecific chunks can be created is if objects can contain superfluous but varying information. Because the encoding component tests for the existence of an exactly identical object, superfluous information in the object can lead to chunks that cannot be used everywhere that they are applicable. This has not been a problem for the current tasks. If it were, the chunking procedure could be altered to keep track of the examined portions of working memory on an attribute-by-attribute basis rather than on an object-by-object basis.

The second class of error the system is capable of making can lead to performance errors. Consider what can happen if an existing object in working memory is modified. If an encoding production has already fired based on the unmodified object, the result of that encoding remains in working memory, even though it may no longer be valid. This in turn can lead to the incorrect use of a connection production, and an error in behavior. The large majority of this type of error is already ruled out by two choices made in the design of the architecture: (1) the architectural restriction disallowing the modification of objects that are part of the initial state of the active goal; and (2) the location of negated conditions in the connection production rather than the encoding production.

The only way this error can occur requires the following sequence of four actions: (1) a local object is created; (2) an encoding production executes based on it; (3) the object is modified; and (4) one of the descendents of the active goal has a chunk based on the encoding. This conjunction of events has not been observed in the simulations run so far.

The third class of possible errors results from incorrect goal hierarchies. Currently, this happens simply because the system was incorrectly programmed. The cause of these errors is therefore external, but the performance errors engendered are themselves internal to the system. In the long run, when the system is building its own hierarchies (Section 7.7), these errors will be internally generated.

Programming mistakes is actually a huge domain of possible errors. All we can afford to do is list a sampling of the kinds of errors that could be made. One common type of human error — using the wrong object of the right type — shows up a lot in the human performance of the compatibility tasks. For example, a Corresponding error in the Duncan (1977) task could be caused by such a mistake. These errors are avoided in the correct goal hierarchies by using working memory objects of different types for the stimulus and response locations, and passing the name of the type as an explicit parameter to the goals that need to use it. If a single type were used, or if the wrong parameter were given, these errors would be made.

Most programming errors lead to goals that fail. If it is a predicate that failed, then the system may be lead down a primrose path. However, for most goals, a failure will ripple up the hierarchy leading to total task failure. If a human subject suffered total task failure, they would probably just start over, and the only evidence of a problem would be an abnormally long reaction time (see below on recovery from errors).

The last possibility to be discussed happens when the wrong goal is pursued. This could happen because of a failed predicate, or it could just be a sign of a wrong link in the hierarchy. In either case, one of several things could happen. The goal could fail, putting us in the previous case. Alternatively, if the goal were just superfluous, and it succeeded, then the correct response would be made, but the reaction time would be lengthened. If the wrong goal is executed in the place of another correct goal, then some other goal further down the line might fail because of its dependence on the results of the goal that did not execute. The final possibility is that the wrong goal may succeed, yielding a result resembling the result of the correct goal. This incorrect result may be successfully used in the remainder of the hierarchy, resulting in an incorrect response. This is another way that Corresponding and Opposite errors could come about.

The fourth class of errors happens when a goal succeeds, but generates an incorrect response (such as by the mechanism just described). When this happens, a chunk will be created, ensuring incorrect performance on all future similar instances of the goal. Both this class of errors and the previous one were not allowed to occur in the final simulations. They don't become intrinsically important until the system is developing its own hierarchies, and maintaining what it has learned over more than one simulation run.

7.3.3. Other sources of error

The previous section described the kinds of errors that could occur within the model. However, there are two important sources of errors that are outside of that scope. Looking downwards from the model, we see the architecture. The implementation of the architecture is not intended to be a model of how the architecture might be implemented in people. Errors — such as the failure to find an applicable production when it does exist, or the failure to execute a successfully matched production — can occur at this level. There could be errors in the processing of productions, in the processing of goals, and in the creation of chunks.

The final locus of error is conceptually sideways from the model — in the perceptual and motor systems. The model boundaries are defined by the abstract representation of stimuli and responses that it employs. Beyond these bounds, errors of discrimination and action can occur. These types of failures can lead to the Adjacency errors observed by Duncan (1977).

7.3.4. Recovery from error

There are two types of errors that the system may have to recover from — errors of performance and errors of learning. Performance errors are the easiest to recover from. One simple method is to abort the current performance, and start over from scratch. This probably is not a good approach for complex time-consuming problems, but for quick reaction-time tasks it seems adequate.

Card, Moran and Newell (1983) describe a more sophisticated approach that can be used in problem solving situations in which an error amounts to going off the path to the solution. They propose that once the system makes an error, it can recover by first performing a search for the correct path. Once it has been found again, the performance picks up where it left off.

If incorrect chunks have been learned, there are again several possible resolutions. The solution used in the *Act* system (Anderson, 1982a) is to assign strengths to competing productions (connection productions in this case), and select probabilistically among the alternatives, according to these strengths. Correct performance leads to strengthening, and incorrect performance leads to weakening. A related but more problem-solving oriented approach is to treat the selection of the alternatives (either alternative chunks, or a chunk versus the regular method for the goal) as a problem to be solved in a problem space constructed for this purpose.

A third alternative is to completely flush the goal for which the incorrect chunk was learned, and replace it with a fresh goal. This is simple to do, but may require the relearning of some correct chunks for the new goal.

7.4. Other Reaction-Time Phenomena

Practice and stimulus-response compatibility are two phenomena that occur in reaction-time tasks. For a complete model, we will need to include a number of other related phenomena. For some of these — including the speed-accuracy trade-off, sequential dependencies, interference, discrimination, and RT distributions — the current system does not seem to provide an explanation. For others — including transfer of training, plateaus and reversals in learning curves, preparation, and choice behavior — we have some idea as to what is happening. In this section we look at those topics for which we have the beginning of an explanation that fits within the current model.

7.4.1. Transfer of training

Transfer of training (see Ellis (1965) for a review of the important concepts) occurs when something that is learned in one context is usable in another. In the current system, there are two ways in which the learning of a chunk can transfer to a similar situation. In the most pervasive form of transfer, the encoding or decoding symbol for a chunk is used as part of the encoding or decoding component of a later chunk. This form of transfer is what leads to the hierarchical nature of encoding and decoding.

The first form of transfer makes it easier to create a chunk, but it does not cut down on the number of chunks that must be created. This latter form of transfer occurs only when the connection component can be shared. A single connection can be used for any instance of its goal for which the same parameter values exist. This is true even if the goal is used in some other position in the hierarchy, or in a totally different hierarchy. As long as it is the same goal, with the same parameter values, the chunk will be usable. This form of transfer — transfer of "identical elements" (Thorndike, 1913) — is rarer, but produces real savings when it does occur.

7.4.2. Plateaus and reversals in learning curves

One phenomenon that often shows up in learning curves is that of *plateaus* (see for example, Kao, 1937). A plateau is a region of a practice curve in which no improvement is apparently occurring. The *reversal* is a similar phenomenon, in which the time may temporarily increase with practice. Given a pure power-law model of practice, plateaus and reversals are not expected. Performance should improve uniformly over the entire length of practice.

Both of these phenomena can occur in the simulations. Plateaus are caused by one of two mechanisms. If the subject is repetitively practicing a set of tasks, then a plateau occurs whenever a set of similarly difficult (and/or practiced) tasks are performed in sequence. A more interesting source of plateaus stems from the structure of the goal hierarchies. Consider the first structure for Condition S_B-R_B in the Fitts and Seeger (1953) experiment (Figure 6-10). The time to perform the task is only counted up until the first movement is made (at goal number 6), but to complete the task, the subject must do considerably more work (goals 7 through 17). A plateau begins when a chunk is created for goal number 2 (Push-Lever-Towards-On-Light-Stimulus). The performance can't improve further until the root node can be chunked, but that must wait until a chunk is created for its other subgoal (number 7: Done-Or-Second-On-Light). This portion of the hierarchy is more complex, and takes longer to learn. The plateau ends after a chunk is finally created for goal number 7. Such plateaus do occur in the simulations of this condition for sequences of trials of one particular kind (a specific pair of lights on). When all eight kinds of trials are averaged together (as in Figure 6-23) the effect disappears.

Just as with plateaus, reversals can be caused by the ordering of the trial sequence. In addition, there are two, more mechanistic, ways in which reversals can appear. One way occurs when an encoding production is created. The production may fire at the very beginning of performance, increasing the cycle number on which the first response is generated. The other way can occur when the architecture must make an arbitrary decision as to the order in which to process several goals. A typical example is the order in which the two lights are processed in the Fitts and Seeger (1953) S_B-R_B condition. Suppose one of the lights is highly chunked, while the other is not. Then, how long the trial takes depends on which light is processed first — an arbitrary decision. This causes a reversal when the chunked light is processed first on one trial, and the un-chunked one is processed first on a succeeding trial.

7.4.3. Preparation

Preparation — how performance is improved when the subject has free time just before the trial — is perhaps the phenomenon that most easily drops out of the current model. Reaction times are measured from the time the stimulus is presented, until the time the response is made. Any processing that the subject can shift to before the stimulus appears, will decrease his reaction time. When placed in the task situation, the subject can immediately process as much of the goal hierarchy for which he has the knowledge and time.

7.4.4. Reaction time under uncertainty

As uncertainty increases, so does reaction time. The classical means of measuring uncertainty is in terms of the information-theoretic concept of *information*. The more uncertain the subject is as to what is required of him next, the more information there is conveyed by the next stimulus. The Hick-Hyman law (Hick, 1952; Hyman, 1953) states that reaction time (T) is linearly related to information (H).

$$T = A + BH \tag{7.1}$$

There have been many experimental studies that have investigated the relationship of uncertainty to reaction time. These have manipulated the uncertainty (information) by varying: 1) the number of equally likely alternatives (Merkel, 1885; Hick, 1952; Crossman, 1953; Hyman, 1953); 2) the probabilities of individual alternatives (Crossman, 1953; Hyman, 1953); 3) the probability of the sequential appearance of a pair of alternatives (Hyman, 1953); 4) the stimulus foreperiod (Drazin, 1961); 5) the discriminability of the stimuli (Crossman, 1955); and 6) individual stimulus and response probabilities (Laberge & Tweedy, 1964; Hawkins & Hosking, 1969; Hawkins, Thomas, & Drury, 1970).

Except in highly compatible (Leonard, 1959) or practiced (Seibel, 1963) tasks, the Hick-Hyman law holds over all of these manipulations. Many models have been proposed to explain this phenomenon (Smith (1968) contains a good introduction to the different classes of models). However, it is not our intent to survey them. What we want to do is look briefly at how uncertainty interacts with our current model. For now, we focus only on the dominant case — a choice between alternatives with equal probabilities.

There are two aspects of the current system that affect its performance in choice situations. The first aspect is the explicit model of choice employed in the task models — the positive-check model (Welford, 1980). This model has already been discussed in Chapter 3. Briefly, the alternatives are broken up into two classes (if possible), and the first class is checked. If it is correct, the choice has been made; otherwise the second class is also checked. This produces logarithmic choice curves if the alternatives can always be split in half — as is done in discriminating numbers from symbols in Condition III of Morin and Forrin (1962) — and linear choice curves when each alternative must be tested individually, as in Condition V of that same experiment. There are also other experimental situations similar to the choice experiments that do produce such linear choice curves — the short-term memory scanning experiments (Sternberg, 1966).

The second, more subtle influence on the system's choice behavior is a function of the power law of practice. Consider the following example experiment. Assume that there are two conditions: 1) *two* alternatives, and 2) *four* alternatives. According to the information-theoretic model of the simple choice task, reaction time should increase according to the logarithm of the number of choices (k) (Hyman, 1953)[22]:

$$T = A + B \log(k) \tag{7.2}$$

Now consider what happens when subjects practice this task. Suppose the subjects are run for 1000 trials in each of these two conditions. Each alternative in condition 1 receives 500 trials of practice, while each alternative in condition

---

[22]See Hick (1952) for a slightly different formulation.

2 receives only 250 trials of practice. Subjects will therefore be faster in the condition with the smaller number of alternatives, merely because of a higher level of practice on the individual choices.

Therefore, practice must produce curves that increase with the number of choices. However, the predicted curve for $T(k)$ turns out to be a power law, rather than the logarithm. To derive this result, we start with the equation for the simple power-law (Equation 2.1), and assume that there are k alternatives. In N trials, each of the k alternatives receives $\frac{N}{k}$ trials of practice. The learning curve is therefore given by the following equation.

$$T = B\left(\frac{N}{k}\right)^{-\alpha} \tag{7.3}$$

$$= [BN^{-\alpha}]k^{\alpha} \tag{7.4}$$

For a given amount of practice (ie., keeping N constant), reaction time can be seen to increase as a power law in the number of choices. Taking the logarithm of both sides of this equation highlights the difference between the power-law and log formulations of the choice equation. The critical difference turns out to be the log transform of T that occurs in the power-law formulation:

$$\log(T) = \log(BN^{-\alpha}) + \alpha \log(k) \tag{7.5}$$

$$= A' + B' \log(k) \tag{7.6}$$

From this analysis, we can conclude that practice must have a power-law effect on choice behavior. How big this effect is, can be evaluated by comparing power-law and logarithmic fits to some choice curves. Table 7-3 shows this comparison for the four subjects in experiment I (equal probability) in Hyman (1953). For all four subjects, the power law fits better than the logarithm, though the differences are not large. The results support the notion that differential practice is an important component in the choice curve.

One implication of the relationship between practice and choice is that practice exacerbates the effects of choice early in practice (helping to bring about the differences in reaction time), and reduces them later in practice, as the reaction time approaches 0 (or asymptote) for all of the conditions. We do not currently have a good set of data on which to test this hypothesis, but there is at least one experiment (Mowbray & Rhoades, 1959) that produced curves of this type.

The power-law equation for choice (Equation 7.4) has one more consequence of interest. It predicts that the choice curve should have a power equal to the negative of the power of the practice curve. If the practice effect were the dominant influence on the choice curve, we would expect to find this relation-

Subj.	Equation	r^2	Subj.	Equation	r^2
FK	$T = 153 + 231 \log_2(N)$ $T = 174N^{0.55}$	0.963 0.969	FP	$T = 176 + 223 \log_2(N)$ $T = 231N^{0.66}$	0.961 0.981
GC	$T = 222 + 150 \log_2(N)$ $T = 250N^{0.50}$	0.983 0.987	LS	$T = 183 + 220 \log_2(N)$ $T = 241N^{0.63}$	0.961 0.991

Table 7-3: Simple power-law and logarithmic (base 2) fits to the four subjects' choice curves in Experiment I (equal probabilities) in Hyman (1953).

ship in the data. So far, we have seen no evidence supporting this prediction, and some that disconfirms it (Hale, 1968; Hellyer, 1963).

7.5. Relation to Previous Work on Learning Mechanisms

The current formulation of the chunking theory of learning provides an interesting point of contact between three previously disparate concepts: (1) classical chunking (Section 2.2), (2) production composition (Lewis, 1978; Neves & Anderson, 1981; Anderson, 1982a) (Section 7.5.1), and (3) table look-up (memo functions (Michie, 1968) and signature tables (Samuel, 1967)) (Section 7.5.2). Though these mechanisms were proposed in quite different contexts, and bear little obvious relationship to each other, the current formulation of the chunking theory of learning has strong ties to all three. It (1) explains how classical chunks can be created and used; (2) results in productions similar to those generated by goal-directed production composition (Sauers & Farrell, 1982; Anderson, 1983); and (3) caches the results of computations, as in a table look-up scheme. The chunking theory differs from these three mechanisms in a number of ways, but at the same time it occupies a common ground between them. This leads us to propose that all four mechanisms are different manifestations of a single underlying store-versus-compute idea. We feel that the chunking theory has a lot going for it, but it is probably too early to know what formulation will work out to be the correct one in the long run for a general practice mechanism.

7.5.1. Production composition

Production composition (Lewis, 1978; Neves & Anderson, 1981; Anderson, 1982a) is a learning scheme whereby new productions are created through the combination of old ones. Given a pair of productions that executes successively, their composition is created from their conditions and actions (Figure 7-1). The condition side of the new production consists of all of the conditions of the first production (C_1, C_2, and C_3), plus those conditions from the second production that do not match actions of the first production (C_5). The conditions of the second production that match actions of the first production (C_4 matches A_4) are not included in the composition (removing the serial dependency between the two productions). All of the actions from both productions are combined in the action side of the new production (A_4 and A_6).

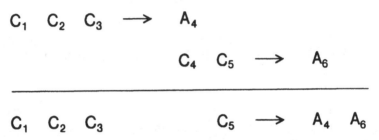

Figure 7-1: An example of production composition.

The resulting composition is a single production that accomplishes the combined effects of the older pair of productions. As learning continues, composed productions can themselves be composed, until there is a single production for an entire task.

In some recent work with the *Grapes* system (Sauers & Farrell, 1982; Anderson, Farrell, & Sauers, 1982), production composition was integrated with goal-based processing. In *Grapes*, specific goals are designated by the programmer to be ones for which composition will occur. When such a goal completes successfully, all of the productions that executed during that time are composed together, yielding a single production that accomplishes the goal.

Because the main effects of chunking and goal-based composition are the same — short-circuiting of a goal — it is probably too early to know which mechanism will work out to be the correct one for a general practice mechanism. However, there are a number of differences between them worth noting. We will focus on the three most important: (1) the knowledge required by the learning procedure; (2) the generality of what is learned; and (3) the hierarchical nature of what is learned.

7.5.1.1. Knowledge-source differences

With chunking, all of the information required for learning can be found in working memory (modulo negated conditions). With production composition, the information comes from production memory (and possibly working memory). Being able to ignore the structure of productions has two advantages. The first advantage is that the chunking mechanism can be much simpler. This is both because working memory is much simpler than production memory — productions contain conditions, actions, variables, function calls, negations, and other structures and information — and because, with composition, the complex process of matching conditions of later productions to actions of previous productions is required, in order that conditions which test intermediate products are not included in the composition. Chunking accomplishes this by only including objects that are part of the goal's initial state.

The second advantage of the chunking strategy, of learning from working memory, is that chunking is applicable to any goal, no matter what its internal implementation is. As long as the processing of the goal leaves marks on the working memory objects that it examines, chunking can work.

7.5.1.2. Generalization differences

The products of chunking are always constant productions (except for the identifiers of objects) that apply only for the situation in which they were created (though, as already discussed, the determination of implicit parameters performs an abstraction function). With production composition, the variables existing in the productions to be composed are retained in the new production. The newly learned material is thus more general than that learned by chunking. The chunking mechanism definitely has more of a table look-up flavor. Section 7.5.2 contains a more thorough discussion of chunking as table look-up, and Section 7.7 discusses how a chunking mechanism could possibly learn parameterized information.

7.5.1.3. Hierarchical differences

Both mechanisms learn hierarchically in that they learn for goals in a hierarchy. They differ in how it is decided on which goals to learn, and in whether the learned material is itself hierarchical.

Chunking occurs bottom-up in the goal hierarchy. Production composition — in *Grapes* at least — works in isolation on any single goal in the hierarchy. For this to work, subgoals are kept as actions in the new productions. The composition approach is more flexible, but the chunking approach has two compensating advantages. The first advantage is that, with chunking, the encoding and decoding components can be themselves hierarchical, based on the encoding and decoding components of the previously chunked subgoals. Productions produced by composition tend to accumulate huge numbers of conditions and actions because they are flat structures.

The second advantage is again simplicity. When information is learned about a goal at an arbitrary position in the hierarchy, its execution is intermingled with the execution of its subgoals. Knowing which information belongs in which context requires a complete historical trace of the changes made to working memory, and the goals that made the changes.

7.5.2. Table look-up

We have seen that if it is looked at one way, chunking resembles production composition. Looked at another way, it resembles a table look-up scheme, in which a table of input parameters versus results is gradually learned for each goal in the system (see Section 7.7 for a discussion of how the limitations of a table look-up scheme can be overcome). As such, it has two important predecessors — *memo functions* (Michie, 1968; Marsh, 1970) and *signature tables* (Samuel, 1967).

7.5.2.1. Memo functions

A memo function[23] is a function with an auxiliary table added. Whenever the function is evaluated, the table is first checked to see if there is a result stored with the current set of parameter values. If so, it is retrieved as the value of the function. Otherwise, the function is computed and the arguments and result are stored in the table. Memo functions have been used to increase the efficiency of mathematical functions (Michie, 1968; Marsh, 1970), and of tree searches (Marsh, 1970).

Chunking can be looked at as generating memo functions for goals. But these are hierarchical memo functions, and ones in which the arguments need not be specified explicitly. Chunking also provides a cleaner implementation of the ideas behind memo functions, because the table is not simply an add-on to a different processing structure. It is implemented by the same "stuff" (productions) as is used to represent the other types of processing in the system.

---

[23]Memo functions themselves are derived from the earlier work by Samuel (1959) on creating a rote memory for the values of board positions in the game of checkers.

7.5.2.2. Signature tables

Signature tables were developed as a means of implementing non-linearities in an evaluation function for checkers (Samuel, 1967). The evaluation function is represented as a hierarchical mosaic of signature tables. Each signature table had between 2 and 4 parameters, each of which had between 3 and 15 possible values. The parameters to the lowest-level tables were measures computed on the checker board. For each combination of parameter values, a number was stored in the table, representing how good that combination was. There were 9 of these tables arranged in a three-level hierarchy. The values generated by lower tables were fed into higher tables. The final value of the evaluation function was the number generated by the root (top) table.

Signature tables capture the table look-up and hierarchical aspects of chunking — though only for encoding. There is no decoding because signature tables are not a model of action; they act simply as a classifier of board positions. Another difference between chunking and signature tables is that information is stored in the latter, not as a direct function of experience, but as correlations over a number of experiences.

7.6. Chunking in More Complex Tasks

All of the tasks to which we have so far applied the chunking theory, have been quite simple in nature. This naturally brings up the issue of whether (and how) the model will scale up for more complex AI tasks. We see no reason why the model should not scale up, but a number of issues will have to be addressed in the process. Among the issues that will arise are the following.

- The use of large, generative goal structures. This issue has already been addressed on a small scale with the hierarchy for the Seibel task (Figure 4-7).
- The adequacy of the representational scheme for performance algorithms. How much will the goal hierarchy mechanism need to be extended to handle more complex tasks?
- How to deal with actions that must remain sequenced. The current specification of the chunking mechanism does nothing to preserve the order of sequential actions; in fact, it tries to destroy the order by making the actions concurrent. This is clearly inadequate for tasks such as typing, in which ordering must be preserved.
- How to handle very large numbers of chunks. This is a practical memory-management problem that occurs when a huge memory of chunks may need to be stored and accessed on a limited capacity

device.

7.7. Chunking, Learning, and Problem-Space Search

In this work we have shown how chunking can provide a model of practice for tasks that can already be accomplished. Performance is sped up, but not qualitatively changed. It is interesting to ask whether chunking can be used to implement any of the other more complex forms of learning — such as method acquisition, concept formation, generalization, learning by being told, and expectation-driven learning. Chunking does not directly accomplish any of these forms of learning, and on first glance, the table look-up nature of chunking would seem to preclude its use in such sophisticated ways. However, we would like to at least raise the possibility that the scope of chunking may extend much further.

Method acquisition is the prototypical case of "hard" learning. Given an arbitrary task, how does the system first construct a method (goal structure) for it? The answer may lie in the integration of chunking with problem-space search. The *problem space hypothesis* (Newell, 1980b; Laird & Newell, 1983a; Laird & Newell, 1983b) states that intelligent agents are always performing in a problem space. At any instant, the agent will have a *goal* which it is attempting to fulfill. Associated with that goal is a *problem space* in which the goal can be pursued. The problem space consists of a set of *states*, a *problem* (initial and desired states), a set of *operators* that move the agent between states, and *search control* information which assists in guiding the agent efficiently from the initial to the desired state.

One way to look at the goal structures used in the current model, is as degenerate problem spaces. The goals are certainly there as needed. The current state can be identified with the contents of working memory, with the set of possible states being defined as all possible working memories. The initial state for a goal is its initial state in the production system. The desired state is defined by the production that tests for goal success. The operators are the subgoals — an operator is simply a goal that the system knows how to accomplish. The search control consists of those productions that specify which subgoals to do when. The one thing missing is the ability to search — the essence of working in a problem space.

Adding a search capability to the current system could be the first step towards method acquisition. It would allow the system to perform tasks that it does not already "know" how to do. The second step must be to show how chunking could lead from an inefficient search, to the development of an efficient goal-structured method.

This may go as follows. Suppose the system is at some state for which it does not know how to make further progress towards the desired state. What should it do? It should create a subgoal in which it can figure out which operator to do next. This subgoal could be pursued in any number of ways. One of the simplest is to ask someone else what to do next (leading to learning by being told). Another possibility is that the problem space for the problematic goal can be simulated, and a look-ahead search performed. If a path is found to the desired goal, the first operator on that path is returned as the result of the search. This is of course the paradigm case for a game-tree search, in which the goal is to win the game, but choosing the next move (operator) may be problematic. Game playing programs effectively go into a choose-operator subgoal in which they simulate future paths in the game tree. They evaluate the alternatives, and return information allowing the selection of an operator in the top-level problem space.

Given such an augmentation to the current system, it would require only a small conceptual leap to imagine how chunking could be applied to these choose-operator subgoals. The resulting chunk would test those aspects of the situation that were examined during the evaluation of the operators, and yield the next operator (subgoal) to pursue. This is a search control chunk for the problem space — part of the backbone of the goal hierarchy.

One limitation of the current chunking mechanism that such a method-acquisition scheme could alleviate, is the inability of chunks to implement parameterized operators. Chunking always creates a totally specified piece of knowledge.   As currently formulated, it cannot create the kinds of parameterized operators used as terminal nodes in the goal hierarchies (though it can achieve a form of separation of parameters[24]).   On the other hand, problem spaces are inherently parameterized by their initial and desired states. Therefore, it may be that it is not necessary for chunks to create parameterized operators. These operators can come from another source (problem spaces)[25]. Chunks would only be responsible for making these operators more efficient.

In summary, doing method acquisition via chunking in problem spaces looks feasible, at least at the rather cursory level of detail at which it has been

---

[24]One form of parameter independence achievable with the current system is the location-independent recognition of patterns. This can be accomplished by having one goal (or a set of goals) to recognize and relate the components of the pattern via their *relative* locations, and a second goal to determine the absolute location of the entire pattern. Each chunk for the first goal would be a location-independent pattern recognizer.

[25]This of course finesses the issue of where problem spaces come from.

described here. If it does pan out, we hope to be able to formulate a number of the other difficult learning problems within this paradigm. The complications would appear as problem-solving in problem spaces, while the chunking mechanism would remain simple, merely recording the results generated by the problem solving system.

8 CONCLUSION

At the beginning of this investigation we set out to develop a generalized, task-independent model of practice, based on chunking, and to use it as the basis (and a source of constraint) for a production-system practice mechanism. All of this has been accomplished. The generalized model is based on a goal-structured representation of reaction-time tasks; each task has its own goal hierarchy, representing an initial performance algorithm.

When a goal is successfully completed, a three-part chunk can be created for it. The chunk is based on the parameters and results of the goal. The encoding component of the chunk encodes the parameters of the goal, yielding a new symbol representing their combination. The connection component of the chunk ties the encoded parameter symbol to an encoded symbol for the results of the goal. The decoding component of the chunk decodes the new result symbol to the results out of which it is composed.

The chunk improves the performance of the system by removing the need to fully process the goal. The chunk takes care of it. The process of chunking proceeds bottom-up in the goal hierarchy. Once chunks are created for all of a goal's subgoals in a specific situation, it is possible to create a chunk for the goal. This process proceeds up in the hierarchy until there is a chunk for the top-level goal for every situation that it could face.

This model has been analyzed analytically, and through simulations. The analytical model predicts that power-law practice curves can be obtained. However, the form of the curve depends on a function relating the number of possible situations a goal can face to the height of the goal in the hierarchy. For several reasonable assumptions about the form of this function, non-power-law curves are yielded. Some assumptions even yield exponential curves.

The simulations were run in a new production-system architecture (*Xaps3*), designed for this purpose. This architecture meets the constraints developed by Rosenbloom and Newell (1982a) for a production-system architecture in which chunking occurs. It also meets two new constraints that were developed in the course of the current research.

Included in the *Xaps3* architecture is the understanding of how to process goals, and the task-independent chunking mechanism. The architecture is capable of both parallel and serial execution of productions. Encoding and decoding productions fire in parallel, because they are variable free (they are also goal free), while connection productions fire serially (when their goal is desired). The result is fast encoding and decoding, and deliberate connection.

Simulations were run for four different experiments (Duncan, 1977; Fitts & Seeger, 1953; Morin & Forrin, 1962; Seibel, 1963) — a total of 15 different experimental conditions. The practice curves so produced were a mixture of power-law and exponential functions. Whenever the general power-law function could be fit to the data, it provided the best fit, though it could not always be fit, and there was no strong trend in the comparison of the exponential and simple power-law fits. However, the human practice data available for the three stimulus-response compatibility experiments (Duncan, 1977; Fitts & Seeger, 1953; Morin & Forrin, 1962) shows this same ambivalence, indicating that the issue may not rest with our basic model, but instead be an indication that practice is not everywhere power law.

In addition to providing practice data for these experiments, the simulations provide the information needed to make between-condition reaction-time comparisons. This is particularly of interest for the three compatibility experiments. Compatibility has been studied for at least 30 years, but these simulations provided the first cross-experimental metric model of the phenomena. The times produced by the simulations provide an excellent fit to the data. We have also shown how similarly good predictions can be obtained more simply by counting the number of operations executed in task-programs written in a simple algorithmic language. These algorithms allow compatibility conditions to be compared via straightforward back-of-the-envelope style calculations.

In summary, we have developed and implemented general models for two related phenomena — practice and compatibility. There are three principal paths along which this work should be pushed in the future. Of most interest within AI, the model must be applied to practice in more complex tasks (such as chess and solitaire), and extended to handle other aspects of learning, such as method acquisition, and generalization. Of most interest to psychologists, the model must be extended to handle other related reaction-time phenomena, such as errors, choice, and sequential dependencies. Of most interest to human-factors researchers, the algorithmic theory of stimulus-response compatibility needs to be shown to apply more widely over the range of compatibility tasks, and integrated into the model human processor (Card, Moran, & Newell, 1983).

ACKNOWLEDGMENT

This part has been based almost exactly on my Ph.D. dissertation completed in 1983 while I was a graduate student in the Carnegie-Mellon University Computer Science Department. What follows is the slightly modified acknowledgment from that dissertation.

My family and friends have provided invaluable support throughout my years of graduate training (and before). I'd especially like to thank my father who inspired me at the age of four to decide to get a Ph.D.; my mother who has always had more confidence in me than I have had myself; Elaine Lee who has helped to keep me sane and happy; and John Laird for many conversations about this material and other topics over the years.

I owe an enormous debt to Allen Newell, my advisor through most of my graduate career. He has shown me a vision of what science in general, and artificial intelligence in particular, can and should be. If I have learned to be a scientist during these years, it is mainly because of his example, and because of his always thought-provoking advice and comments on my work. It goes without saying that many of the ideas in this work either started with him, or benefited greatly from his comments. I would also like to thank the other members of my thesis committee — John Anderson, Jaime Carbonell, and Geoff Hinton — for their time and comments.

Any acknowledgement for this work would be incomplete without mentioning the assistance given by the incomparable people and facilities of the Carnegie-Mellon University Computer Science Department. In addition, I would like to thank Donald Norman, and the rest of the LNR research group at the University of California, San Diego for introducing me to the possibilities of cognitive psychology.

This research was primarily sponsored by the Defense Advanced Research Projects Agency (DOD), ARPA Order No. 3597, monitored by the Air Force Avionics Laboratory Under Contract F33615-81-K-1539. Support during my graduate years was also provided by the National Science Foundation and IBM.

The views and conclusions contained in this document are those of the authors and should not be interpreted as representing the official policies, either expressed or implied, of the Defense Advanced Research Projects Agency, the National Science Foundation, the US Government, or IBM.

REFERENCES

Aho, A. V., Hopcroft, J. E., and Ullman, J. D. *The Design and Analysis of Computer Algorithms.* Reading, MA.: Addison-Wesley, 1974.

Anderson, J. R. *Language, Memory, and Thought.* Hillsdale, N.J.: Lawrence Erlbaum Associates, 1976.

Anderson, J. R. Private communication. 1980.

Anderson, J. R. Acquisition of cognitive skill. *Psychological Review,* 1982, *89,* 369-406.

Anderson, J. R. Private communication. 1982.

Anderson, J. R. *The Architecture of Cognition.* Harvard Press, 1983.

Anderson, J. R., Farrell, R., and Sauers, R. *Learning to plan in Lisp* (Tech. Rep.). Carnegie-Mellon University Department of Psychology, 1982.

Baron, J. Intelligence and general strategies. In G. Underwood (Ed.), *Strategies of Information Processing.* London: Academic Press, 1978.

Bower, G. H. Perceptual groups as coding units in immediate memory. *Psychonomic Science,* 1972, *27,* 217-219.

Bower, G. H., & Springston, F. Pauses as recoding points in letter series. *Journal of Experimental Psychology,* 1970, *83,* 421-430.

Bower, G. H. & Winzenz, D. Group structure, coding, and memory for digit series. *Journal of Experimental Psychology Monograph,* 1969, *80,* 1-17. (May, Pt. 2).

Brebner, J. S-R compatibility and changes in RT with practice. *Acta Psychologica,* 1973, *37,* 93-106.

Brebner, J., Shephard, M., & Cairney, P. Spatial relationships and S-R compatibility. *Acta Psychologica,* 1972, *36,* 1-15.

Broadbent, D. E., & Gregory, M. On the interaction of S-R compatibility with other variables affecting reaction time. *British Journal of Psychology,* 1965, *56,* 61-67.

Card, S. K., English, W. K. & Burr, B. Evaluation of mouse, rate controlled isometric joystick, step keys, and text keys for text selection on a CRT.

Ergonomics, 1978, *21,* 601-613.

Card, S. K., Moran, T. P, & Newell, A. *The Psychology of Human-Computer Interaction.* Hillsdale, NJ: Lawrence Erlbaum Associates, 1983.

Chase, W. G., & Ericsson, K. A. Skilled memory. In J. R. Anderson (Ed.), *Cognitive Skills and Their Acquisition.* Hillsdale, NJ: Lawrence Erlbaum Associates, 1981.

Chase, W. G. & Simon, H. A. Perception in chess. *Cognitive Psychology,* 1973, *4,* 55-81.

Cooper, E. H. & Pantle, A. J. The total-time hypothesis in verbal learning. *Psychological Bulletin,* 1967, *68,* 221-234.

Crossman, E. R. F. W. Entropy and choice time: The effect of frequency unbalance on choice-response. *Quarterly Journal of Experimental Psychology,* 1953, *5,* 41-51.

Crossman, E. R. F. W. The measurement of discriminability. *Quarterly Journal of Experimental Psychology,* 1955, *7,* 176-195.

Crossman, E. R. F. W. A theory of the acquisition of speed-skill. *Ergonomics,* 1959, *2,* 153-166.

DeGroot, A. D. *Thought and Choice in Chess.* The Hague: Mouton, 1965.

Deininger, R. L., & Fitts, P. M. Stimulus-response compatibility, information theory, and perceptual-motor performance. In H. Quastler (Ed.), *Information Theory in Psychology.* Glencoe, Illinois: Free Press, 1955.

Drazin, D. H. Effects of foreperiod, foreperiod variability, and probability of stimulus occurrence on simple reaction time. *Journal of Experimental Psychology,* 1961, *62*(1), 43-50.

Duncan, J. Response selection rules in spatial choice reaction tasks. In S. Dornic (Ed.), *Attention and Performance VI.* Hillsdale, NJ: Lawrence Erlbaum Associates, 1977.

Ellis, H. *Critical Issues in Psychology Series. The Transfer of Learning.* New York: MacMillan, 1965.

Ernst, G. W. & Newell, A. *GPS: A Case Study in Generality and Problem Solving.* New York: Academic Press, 1969. (ACM Monograph).

Filbey, R. A., and Gazzaniga, M. S. Splitting the normal brain with reaction time. *Psychonomic Science,* 1969, *17,* 335-336.

Fitts, P. M., & Deininger, R. L. S-R compatibility: Correspondence among paired elements within stimulus and response codes. *Journal of Experimental Psychology,* 1954, *48,* 483-492.

Fitts, P. M., & Seeger, C. M. S-R compatibility: Spatial characteristics of stimulus and response codes. *Journal of Experimental Psychology,* 1953, *46,* 199-210.

Forgy, C. L. *OPS4 User's manual* (Tech. Rep. CMU-CS-79-132). Carnegie-Mellon University Department of Computer Science, July 1979.

Garvey, W. D., & Knowles, W. B. Response time patterns associated with various display-control relationships. *Journal of Experimental Psychology*, 1954, *47*, 315-322.

Hale, D. The relation of correct and error responses in a serial choice reaction task. *Psychonomic Science*, 1968, *13*(6), 299-300.

Hawkins, H. L., & Hosking, K. Stimulus probability as a determinant of discrete choice reaction time. *Journal of Experimental Psychology*, 1969, *82*, 435-440.

Hawkins, H. L., Thomas, G. B., & Drury, K. B. Perceptual versus response bias in discrete choice reaction time. *Journal of Experimental Psychology*, 1970, *84*, 514-517.

Hayes, J. R., and Simon, H. A. Understanding written problem instructions. In L. Gregg (Ed.), *Knowledge and Cognition.* Potomac, Md.: Lawrence Erlbaum Assoc., 1974.

Hellyer, S. Stimulus-response coding and amount of information as determinants of reaction time. *Journal of Experimental Psychology*, 1963, *65*(5), 521-522.

Hick, W. E. On the rate of gain of information. *Quarterly Journal of Experimental Psychology*, 1952, *4*, 11-26.

Hyman, R. Stimulus information as a determinant of reaction time. *Journal of Experimental Psychology*, 1953, *45*, 188-196.

Johnson, N. F. Organization and the concept of a memory code. In Melton, A. W. & Martin, E. (Eds.), *Coding Processes in Human Memory.* Washington, D.C.: Winston, 1972.

Kao, D-L. Plateaus and the curve of learning in motor skill. *Psychology Monographs*, 1937, Vol. *49*(219).

Knuth, D. E. *The Art of Computer Programming.* Reading, MA.: Addison-Wesley, 1968.

Kolers, P. A. Memorial consequences of automatized encoding. *Journal of Experimental Psychology: Human learning and memory*, 1975, *1*(6), 689-701.

Laberge, D. & Tweedy, J. R. Presentation probability and choice time. *Journal of Experimental Psychology*, 1964, *68*, 477-481.

Laird, J. E., and Newell, A. A universal weak method: Summary of results. In *Proceedings of the Eighth IJCAI.*, 1983.

Laird, J. E., and Newell, A. *A Universal Weak Method* (Tech. Rep. #83-141). Carnegie-Mellon University Computer Science Department, June 1983.

Leonard, J. A. Tactual choice reactions: I. *Quarterly Journal of Experimental Psychology*, 1959, *11*, 76-83.

Lewis, C. H. *Production system models of practice effects.* Doctoral dissertation, University of Michigan, 1978.

Marsh, D. Memo functions, the graph traverser, and a simple control situation. In B. Meltzer & D. Michie (Ed.), *Machine Intelligence 5.* New York: American Elsevier, 1970.

McDermott, J. R1: A rule-based configurer of computer systems. *Artificial Intelligence,* September 1982, Vol. *19.*

Merkel, J. Die zeitlichen Verhaltnisse der Willensthatigkeit. *Philos. Stud.,* 1885, *2,* 73-127.

Michie, D. "Memo" functions and machine learning. *Nature,* 1968, *218,* 19-22.

Miller, G. A. The magic number seven plus or minus two: Some limits on our capacity for processing information. *Psychological Review,* 1956, *63,* 81-97.

Moran, T. P. *Compiling cognitive skill* (AIP Memo 150). Xerox PARC, 1980.

Morin, R. E., & Forrin, B. Mixing two types of S-R associations in a choice reaction time task. *Journal of Experimental Psychology,* 1962, *64,* 137-141.

Morin, R. E., & Grant, D. A. Learning and performance of a key-pressing task as a function of the degree of spatial stimulus-response correspondence. *Journal of Experimental Psychology,* 1955, *49,* 39-47.

Mowbray, G. H., & Rhoades, M. V. On the reduction of choice reaction times with practice. *Quarterly Journal of Experimental Psychology,* 1959, *11,* 16-23.

Neisser, U., Novick, R., Lazar, R. Searching for ten targets simultaneously. *Perceptual and Motor Skills,* 1963, *17,* 427-432.

Neves, D. M. & Anderson, J. R. Knowledge compilation: Mechanisms for the automatization of cognitive skills. In Anderson, J. R. (Ed.), *Cognitive Skills and their Acquisition.* Hillsdale, NJ: Erlbaum, 1981.

Newell, A. Heuristic programming: Ill-structured problems. In Aronofsky, J. (Ed.), *Progress in Operations Research, III.* New York: Wiley, 1969.

Newell, A. Production systems: Models of control structures. In Chase, W. G. (Ed.), *Visual Information Processing.* New York: Academic Press, 1973.

Newell, A. Harpy, production systems and human cognition. In Cole, R. (Ed.), *Perception and Production of Fluent Speech.* Hillsdale, NJ: Erlbaum, 1980. (Also available as CMU CSD Technical Report, Sep 1978).

Newell, A. Reasoning, problem solving and decision processes: The problem space as a fundamental category. In R. Nickerson (Ed.), *Attention and Performance VIII.* Hillsdale, N.J.: Erlbaum, 1980. (Also available as CMU CSD Technical Report, Aug 79).

Newell, A. & Rosenbloom, P. S. Mechanisms of skill acquisition and the law of practice. In J. R. Anderson (Ed.), *Cognitive Skills and Their Acquisition.* Hillsdale, NJ: Erlbaum, 1981.

Newell, A. & Simon, H. A. *Human Problem Solving.* Englewood Cliffs: Prentice-Hall, 1972.

Nicoletti, R., Anzola, G. P., Luppino, G., Rizzolatti, G., & Umilta, C. Spatial compatibility effects on the same side of the body midline. *Journal of Experimental Psychology: Human Perception and Performance,* 1982, *8*(5), 664-673.

Nilsson, N. J. *Problem-Solving Methods in Artificial Intelligence.* New York: McGraw-Hill, 1971.

Rosenbloom, P. S., & Newell, A. *Learning by chunking: A production-system model of practice* (Tech. Rep. #82-135). Carnegie-Mellon University Computer Science Department, September 1982.

Rosenbloom, P. S., & Newell, A. Learning by chunking: Summary of a task and a model. In *Proceedings of AAAI-82, National Conference on Artificial Intelligence.* American Association for Artificial Intelligence, 1982.

Samuel, A. L. Some studies in machine learning using the game of checkers. *IBM Journal of Research and Development,* 1959, *3,* 210-229.

Samuel, A. L. Some studies in machine learning using the game of checkers, II - Recent progress. *IBM Journal of Research and Development,* November 1967, *11*(6), 601-617.

Sauers, R., and Farrell, R. *Grapes user's manual* (Tech. Rep.). Carnegie-Mellon University Department of Psychology, 1982.

Seibel, R. Discrimination reaction time for a 1,023-alternative task. *Journal of Experimental Psychology,* 1963, *66*(3), 215-226.

Shepard, R. N. Role of generalization in stimulus-response compatibility. *Perceptual and Motor Skills,* 1961, *13,* 59-62.

Shortliffe, E. H. *Computer-Based Medical Consultations: MYCIN.* New York: American Elsevier, 1976.

Simon, H. A., and Hayes, J. R. The understanding process: Problem isomorphs. *Cognitive Psychology,* 1976, Vol. *8.*

Simon, J. R., Hinrichs, J. V., & Craft, J. L. Auditory S-R compatibility: Reaction time as a function of ear-hand correspondence and ear-response-location correspondence. *Journal of Experimental Psychology,* 1970, *86,* 97-102.

Smith, E. E. Choice reaction time: An analysis of the major theoretical positions. *Psychological Bulletin,* 1968, *69,* 77-110.

Smith, G. A. Studies of compatibility and a new model of choice reaction time. In S. Dornic (Ed.), *Attention and Performance VI.* Hillsdale, NJ: Lawrence Erlbaum Associates, 1977.

Snoddy, G. S. Learning and stability. *Journal of Applied Psychology,* 1926, *10,* 1-36.

Sternberg, S. High-speed scanning in human memory. *Science,* 1966, *153,* 652-654.

Thorndike, E. L. *Educational Psychology. II: The Psychology of Learning.* New York: Bureau of Publications, Teachers College, Columbia University, 1913.

VanLehn, K. *On the representation of procedures in repair theory* (Tech. Rep. CIS-16). Xerox PARC, October 1981.

Wallace, R. J. S-R compatibility and the idea of a response code. *Journal of Experimental Psychology*, 1971, *88*, 354-360.

Welford, A. T. Choice reaction times: Basic concepts. In A. T. Welford (Ed.), *Reaction Times*. London: Academic Press, 1980.

Winston, P. H. Learning structural descriptions from examples. In Winston, P. H. (Ed.), *The Psychology of Computer Vision*. New York: McGraw Hill, 1975.

PART III

TOWARDS CHUNKING
AS A GENERAL
LEARNING MECHANISM

John E. Laird
Paul S. Rosenbloom
Allen Newell

1. Introduction

Chunking was first proposed as a model of human memory by Miller (1956), and has since become a major component of theories of cognition. More recently it has been proposed that a theory of human learning based on chunking could model the ubiquitous power law of practice (Newell and Rosenbloom, 1981). In demonstrating that a practice mechanism based on chunking is capable of speeding up task performance, it was speculated that chunking, when combined with a general problem solver, might be capable of more interesting forms of learning than just simple speed ups (Rosenbloom & Newell, 1983). In this paper we describe an initial investigation into chunking as a general learning mechanism.

Our approach to developing a general learning mechanism is based on the hypothesis that all complex behavior — which includes behavior concerned with learning — occurs as search in problem spaces (Newell, 1980). One image of a system meeting this requirement consists of the combination of a performance system based on search in problem spaces, and a complex, analytical, learning system also based on search in problem spaces (Mitchell, 1983). An alternative, and the one we adopt here, is to propose that all complex behavior occurs in the problem-space-based performance system. The learning component is simply a recorder of experience. It is the experience that determines the form of what is learned.

Chunking is well suited to be such a learning mechanism because it is a recorder of goal-based experience (Rosenbloom, 1983; Rosenbloom & Newell, 1983). It caches the processing of a subgoal in such a way that a chunk can substitute for the normal (possibly complex) processing of the subgoal the next time the same subgoal (or a suitably similar one) is generated. It is a task-independent mechanism that can be applied to all subgoals of any task in a system. Chunks are created during performance, through experience with the goals processed. No extensive analysis is required either during or after performance.

The essential step in turning chunking into a general learning mechanism is to combine it with a general problem-space problem solver. One candidate is *Soar*, a reflective problem-solving architecture that has a uniform representation and can create goals to reason about any aspect of its problem-solving behavior (Laird, 1983). Implementing chunking within *Soar* yields four contributions towards chunking as a general learning mechanism.

1. Chunking can be applied to a general problem solver to speed up its performance.
2. Chunking can improve *all* aspects of a problem solver's behavior.

3. Significant transfer of chunked knowledge is possible via the implicit generalization of chunks.
4. Chunking can perform strategy acquisition, leading to qualitatively new behavior.

Other systems have tackled individual points, but this is the first attempt to do all of them. Other work on strategy acquisition deals with the learning of qualitatively new behavior (Langley, 1983; Mitchell, 1983), but it is limited to learning only one type of knowledge. These systems end up with the *wandering bottle-neck* problem — removal of a performance bottleneck from one part of a system means that some other locale becomes the bottleneck (Mitchell, 1983). Anderson (Anderson, 1983) has recently proposed a scheme of knowledge compilation to be a general learning mechanism to be applied to all of cognition, although it has not yet been used on complex problem solving or reasoning tasks that require learning about all aspects of behavior.

2. Soar — A General Problem-Solving Architecture

Soar is a problem solving system that is based on formulating all activity (both problems and routine tasks) as heuristic search in problem spaces. A problem space consists of a set of *states* and a set of *operators* that transform one state into another. Starting from an initial state the problem solver applies a sequence of operators in an attempt to reach a desired state. *Soar* uses a production system[1] to implement elementary operators, tests for goal satisfaction and failure, and *search control* — information relevant to the selection of goals, problem spaces, states, and operators. It is possible to use a problem space that has no search control, only operators and goal recognizers. Such a space will work correctly, but will be slow because of the amount of search required.

In many cases, the directly available knowledge may be insufficient for making a search-control decision or applying an operator to a state. When this happens, a *difficulty* occurs that results in the automatic creation of a subgoal to perform the necessary function. In the subgoal, *Soar* treats the difficulty as just another problem to solve; it selects a problem space for the subgoal in which goal attainment is interpreted as finding a state that resolves the difficulty.

---

[1] A modified versions of *Ops5* (Forgy, 1981), which admits parallel execution of all satisfied productions.

Thus, *Soar* generates a hierarchy of goals and problem spaces. The diversity of task domains is reflected in a diversity of problem spaces. Major tasks, such as configuring a computer, will have a corresponding problem space, but so also will each of the various subtasks. In addition, problem spaces will exist in the hierarchy for performing tasks generated by problems in the system's own behavior, such as the selection of an operator to apply, the application of an operator to a state, and testing for goal attainment. With such an organization, all aspects of the system's behavior are open to problem solving when necessary. We call this property *universal subgoaling* (Laird, 1983).

Figure 1 shows a small example of how these subgoals are used in *Soar*. This is the subgoal/problem-space structure that gets generated while trying to take steps in a task problem space. Initially (A), the problem solver is at State1 and must select an operator. If search control is unable to uniquely determine the next operator to apply, a subgoal is created to do the selection. In that subgoal (B), a *selection* problem space is used that reasons about the selection of objects from a set. In order to break the tie between objects, the selection problem space has operators to evaluate each candidate object.

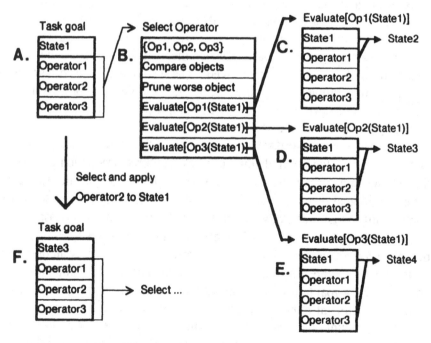

Figure 1: Eight Puzzle subgoal/problem space structure.

Evaluating an operator, such as Operator1 in the task space, is a complex

problem requiring a new subgoal. In this subgoal (C), the original task problem space and state (State1) are selected. Operator1 is applied, creating a new state (State2). The evaluation for State2 is used to compare Operator1 to the other operators. When Operator1 has been evaluated, the subgoal terminates, and then the whole process is repeated for the other two operators (Operator2 and Operator3 in D and E). If, for example, Operator2 creates a state with a better evaluation than the other operators, it will be designated as better than them. The selection subgoal will terminate and the designation of Operator2 will lead to its selection in the original task goal and problem space. At this point Operator2 is reapplied to State1 and the process continues (F).

3. Chunking in Soar

Chunking was previously defined (Rosenbloom & Newell, 1983) as a process that acquires chunks that generate the results of a goal, given the goal and its parameters. The parameters of a goal were defined to be those aspects of the system existing prior to the goal's creation that were examined during the processing of the goal. Each chunk was represented as a set of three productions, one that encoded the parameters of a goal, one that connected this encoding in the presence of the goal to (chunked) results, and a third production that decoded the results. These chunks were learned bottom-up in the goal hierarchy; only terminal goals — goals for which there were no subgoals that had not already been chunked — were chunked. These chunks improved task performance by substituting efficient productions for complex goal processing. This mechanism was shown to work for a set of simple perceptual-motor skills based on fixed goal hierarchies (Rosenbloom, 1983).

At the moment, *Soar* does away with two of the features of chunking that existed for psychological modeling purposes: the three production chunks, and the bottom-up nature of chunking. In *Soar*, single-production chunks are built for every subgoal that terminates. The power of chunking in *Soar* stems from *Soar*'s ability to automatically generate goals for problems in any aspect of its problem-solving behavior: a goal to select among alternatives leads to the creation of a production that will later control search; a goal to apply an operator to a state leads to the creation of a production that directly implements the operator; and a goal to test goal-satisfaction leads to a goal-recognition production. As search-control knowledge is added, performance improves via a reduction in the amount of search. If enough knowledge is added, there is no search; what is left is a *method* — an efficient algorithm for a task. In addition to reducing search within a single problem space, chunks can completely eliminate the search of entire subspaces whose function is to make a search-control decision, apply an operator, or recognize goal-satisfaction.

The conditions of a chunked production need to test everything that was used in creating the results of the subgoal and that existed before the subgoal was invoked. In standard problem solvers this would consist of the name of the goal and its parameters. However, in *Soar* there are no fixed goal names, nor is there a fixed set of parameters. Once a subgoal is selected, all of the information from the prior goal is still available. The problem solver makes use of the information about why the subgoal was created and any of the other information that it needs to solve the problem.

For each goal generated, the architecture maintains a *condition-list* of all data that existed before the goal was created and which was *accessed* in the goal. A datum is considered accessed if a production that matched it fires. Whenever a production is fired, all of the data it accessed that existed prior to the current goal are added to the goal's condition-list. When a goal terminates (for whatever reason), the condition-list for that goal is used to build the conditions of a chunk. Before being turned into conditions, the data is selectively variablized so that the conditions become tests for object descriptions instead of tests for the specific objects experienced. These variables are restricted so that two distinct variables can not match the same object.

The actions of the chunk should be the results of the goal. In traditional architectures, a goal produces a specific predefined type of result. However, in *Soar*, anything produced in a subgoal can potentially be of use in the parent goal. Although the potential exists for all objects to be relevant, the reality is that only a few of them will actually be useful. In figuring out the actions of the chunk, *Soar* starts with everything created in the goal, but then prunes away the information that does not relate directly to objects in any supergoal.[2] What is left is turned into production actions after being variablized in accordance with the conditions.

At first glance, chunking appears to be simply a caching mechanism with little hope of producing results that can be used on other than exact duplicates of tasks it has already attempted. However, if a given task shares subgoals with another task, a chunk learned for one task can apply to the other, yielding *across-task* transfer of learning. *Within-trial* transfer of learning can occur when a subgoal arises more than once during a single attempt on a task. Generality is possible because a chunk only contains conditions for the aspects that were accessed in the subgoal. This is an *implicit generalization*, by which many aspects of the context — the irrelevant ones — are automatically ignored by the

---

[2]Those that are pruned are also removed from memory because they are intermediate results that will never be used again.

chunk.

4. Demonstration

In this section we describe the results of experiments on three tasks: the Eight Puzzle, Tic-Tac-Toe, and computer configuration (a part of the *R1* expert-system implemented in *Soar* (Rosenbloom, Laird, McDermott, Newell, & Orciuch, 1984)). These tasks exhibit: (1) speed ups with practice; (2) within-trial transfer of learning; (3) across-task transfer of learning; (4) strategy acquisition (the learning of paths through search spaces); (5) knowledge acquisition in a knowledge-intensive system; and (6) learning of qualitatively different aspects of behavior. We conclude this section with a discussion of how chunking sometimes builds over-general productions.

4.1. Eight Puzzle

The states for the Eight Puzzle, as implemented in *Soar*, consist of different configurations of eight numbered tiles in a three by three grid; the operators move the blank space up (U), down (D), left (L) and right (R) (Laird, 1983). Search-control knowledge was built that computed an evaluation of a state based on the number of tiles that were moved in and out of the desired positions from the previous state.[3] At each state in the problem solving, an operator must be selected, but there is insufficient search-control knowledge to intelligently distinguish between the alternatives. This leads to the selection being made using the set of selection and evaluation goals described in Section 2. The first column of Figure 2 shows the behavior of *Soar* without chunking in the Eight Puzzle problem space. All of the nodes off the main path were expanded in evaluate-operator subgoals (nodes on the main path were expanded once in a subgoal, and once after being selected in the top goal).[4]

When *Soar* with chunking is applied to the task, both the selection and evaluation subgoals are chunked. During this run (second column of Figure 2),

---

[3]To avoid tight loops, search-control was also added that avoided applying the inverse of the operator that created a given state.

[4]At two points in the search the correct operator had to be selected manually because the evaluation function was insufficient to pick out the best operator. Our purpose is not to evaluate the evaluation function, but to investigate how chunking can be used in conjunction with search-control knowledge.

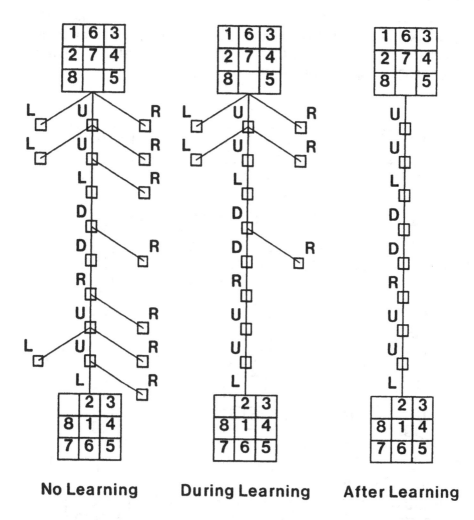

No Learning   During Learning   After Learning

Figure 2: Within-trial transfer and speed-up with practice in the Eight Puzzle.

some of the newly created chunks apply to subsequent subgoals in the search. This within-trial transfer of learning speeds up performance by dramatically reducing the amount of search. The third column in the figure shows that after one run with learning, the chunked productions completely eliminate search.

To investigate across-task learning, another experiment was conducted in which *Soar* started with a learning trial for a different task — the initial and final states are different, and none of the intermediate states were the same (the second column in Figure 3). The first task was then attempted with the productions learned from the second task, but with chunking turned off so that there would be no additional learning (the third column). The reduced search is caused by across-task transfer of learning — some subgoals in the second trial were identical in all of the relevant ways to subgoals in the first trial. This happens because of the interaction between the problem solving only accessing information relevant to the result, and the implicit generalization of chunking only recording the information accessed.

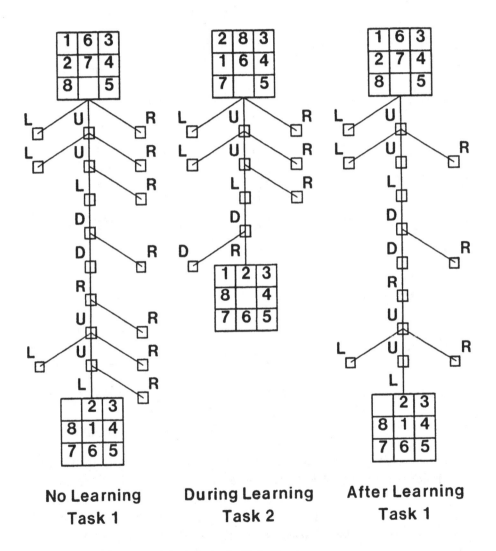

Figure 3: Across-task transfer in the Eight Puzzle.

4.2. Tic-Tac-Toe

The implementation of Tic-Tac-Toe includes only the basic problem space — the state includes the board and who is on move, the operators make a mark on the board for the appropriate player and change who is on move — and the ability to detect a win, loss or draw (Laird, 1983). With just this knowledge, *Soar* searches depth-first through the problem space by the sequence of: (1) encountering a difficulty in selecting an operator; (2) evaluating the operators in a selection subgoal; (3) applying one of the operators in an evaluation subgoal; (4) encountering a difficulty in selecting an operator to apply to the resulting state; and (5) so on, until a terminal state is reached and evaluated.

Chunking in Tic-Tac-Toe yields two interesting results: (1) the chunks detect board symmetries, allowing a drastic reduction in search through within-trial transfer, (2) the chunks encode search-control knowledge so that the correct moves through the space are remembered. The first result is interesting because there is no knowledge in the system about the existence of symmetries, and without chunking the search bogs down terribly by re-exploring symmetric positions. The chunks make use of symmetries by ignoring orientation information that was not used during problem solving. The second point seems obvious given our presentation of chunking, however, it demonstrates the *strategy acquisition* (Langley, 1983; Mitchell, 1983) abilities of chunking. Chunking acquires strategic information on the fly, using only its direct experience, and without complex post-processing of the complete solution path or knowledge learned from other trials. The quality of this path depends on the quality of the problem solving, not on the learning.

4.3. R1

Part of the *R1* expert system (McDermott, 1982) was implemented in *Soar* to investigate whether *Soar* can support knowledge-intensive expert systems (Rosenbloom, Laird, McDermott, Newell, & Orciuch, 1984). Figure 4 shows the subgoal structure that can be built up through universal subgoaling, including both subgoals that implement complex operators (heavy lines) and subgoals that select operators (thin lines to Selection subgoals). Each box shows the problem-space operators used in the subgoal. The actual subgoal structure extends much further wherever there is an ellipsis (...). This subgoal structure does not pre-exist in *Soar*, but is built up as difficulties arise in selecting and applying operators.

Table 1 presents statistics from the application of *R1-Soar* to a small configuration task. The first three runs (Min. S-C) are with a minimal system that

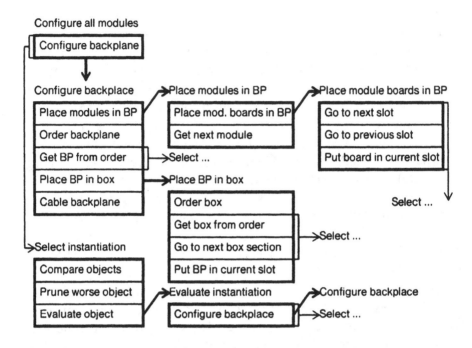

Figure 4: Subgoal Structure in *R1-Soar*.

has only the problem spaces and goal detection defined. This base system consists of 232 productions (95 productions come with *Soar*, 137 define *R1-Soar*). The final three runs (Added S-C) have 10 additional search-control productions that remove much of the search. In the table, the number of search-control decisions is used as the time metric because decisions are the basic unit of problem-solving.[5]

The first run shows that with minimal search control, 1731 decisions are needed to do the task. If chunking is used, 59 productions are built during the 485 decisions it took to do this task. No prior chunking had occurred, so this shows strong within-trial transfer. After chunking, rerunning the same task takes only 7 decisions.

When *Soar* is run with 10 hand-crafted search-control rules, it only takes 150 decisions. This is only little more than three times faster than *Soar* without those rules took when chunking was used. When chunking is applied to this

---

[5]On a Symbolics 3600, *Soar* usually runs at 1 second per decision. Chunking adds an overhead of approximately 15%, mostly to compile new productions. The increased number of productions has no affect on the overall rate if the chunked productions are fully integrated into the existing production-match network.

Run Type	Initial Prod.	Final Prod.	Decisions
Min. S-C	232	232	1731
Min. S-C with chunking	232	291	485
Min. S-C after chunking	291	291	7
Added S-C	242	242	150
Added S-C with chunking	242	254	90
Added S-C after chunking	254	254	7

Table 1: Run Statistics for *R1-Soar*.

situation — where the additional search control already exists — it still helps by decreasing to 90 the number of decisions for the first trial. A second trial on this task once again takes only 7 decisions.

4.4. Over-generalization

The within-trial and across-task transfer in the tasks we have examined was possible because of implicit generalization. Unfortunately, implicit generalization leads to over-generalization when there is special-case knowledge that was *almost* used in solving a subgoal. In *Soar* this would be a production for which most but not all of the conditions were satisfied during a problem-solving episode. Those conditions that were not satisfied, either tested for the absence of something that is available in the subgoal (using a negated condition) or for the presence of something missing in the subgoal (using a positive condition). The chunk that is built for the subgoal is over-general because it does not include the *inverses* of these conditions — negated conditions for positive conditions, and positive conditions for negated conditions. During a later episode, when all of the conditions of a special-case production would be satisfied in a subgoal, the chunk learned in the first trial bypasses the subgoal. If the special-case production would lead to a different result for the goal, the chunk is over-general and produces an incorrect result.

Figure 5 contains an example of how the problem solving and chunking in *Soar* can lead to over-generalization. Consider the situation where **O** is to move in state 1. It already has the center (E), while **X** is on a side (B). A tie arises between all the remaining moves (A, C, D, F, G, H, I) leading to the creation of a subgoal. The Selection problem space is chosen in which each of the tieing moves are candidates to be evaluated. If position I is evaluated first, it leads to a line of play resulting in state 2, which is a win for **O** because of a fork. On return to the Selection problem space, move I is immediately chosen as the best move, the original tie-subgoal terminates, move I is made, and **O** goes on to win.

When returning from the tie-subgoal, a chunk is created, with conditions sensitive to all aspects of the original state that were tested in productions that fired in the subgoals. All positions that have marks were tested (A, B, C, E, I) as well as those positions that had to be clear for **O** to have a fork (G, F). However, positions D and H were not tested. To see how this production is over-general consider state 3, where **O** is to move. The newly chunked production, being insensitive to the X at position D, will fire and suggest position I, which leads to a loss for **O**.

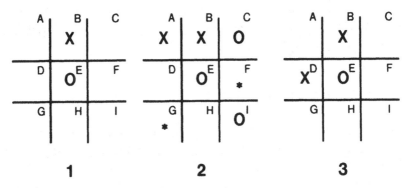

Figure 5: Over-generalization in Tic-Tac-Toe.

Over-generalization is a serious problem for *Soar* if we want to encode real tasks that are able to improve with experience. However, over-generalization is a problem for any learning system that works in many different environments and it leads to what is called *negative transfer* in humans. We believe that the next step in handling over-generalization is to investigate how a problem solver can recover from over-general knowledge, and then carry out problem-solving activities so that new chunks can be learned that will override the over-general chunks. This would be similar to Anderson's work on discrimination learning using knowledge compilation (Anderson, 1983).

5. Conclusion

In this paper we have taken several steps towards the establishment of chunking as a general learning mechanism. We have demonstrated that it is possible to extend chunking to complex tasks that require extensive problem solving. In experiments with the Eight Puzzle, Tic-Tac-Toe, and a part of the **R1** computer-configuration task, it was demonstrated that chunking leads to performance improvements with practice. We have also contributed to showing how chunking can be used to improve many aspects of behavior. Though this is only partial, as not all of the different types of problem solving arose in the tasks we demonstrated, we did see that chunking can be used for subgoals that involve selection of operators and application of operators. Chunking has this generality because of the ubiquity of goals in *Soar*. Since all aspects of behavior are open to problem solving in subgoals, all aspects are open to learning. Not only is *Soar* able to learn about the task (chunking the main goal), it is able to learn about how to solve the task (chunking the subgoals). Because all aspects of behavior are open to problem solving, and hence to learning, *Soar* avoids the wandering bottle-neck problem.

In addition to leading to performance speed ups, we have shown that the implicit generalization of chunks leads to significant within-trial and across-task transfer of learning. This was demonstrated most strikingly by the ability of chunks to use symmetries in Tic-Tac-Toe positions that are not evident to the problem solving system. And finally, we have demonstrated that chunking, which on first glance is a limited caching function, is capable of strategy acquisition. It can acquire the search control required to turn search-based problem solving into an efficient method.

Though significant progress has been made, there is still a long way to go. One of the original goals of the work on chunking was to model human learning, but several of the assumptions of the original model have been abandoned on this attempt, and a better understanding is needed of just why they are necessary. We also need to understand better the characteristics of problem spaces that allow interesting forms of generalization, such as use of symmetry to take place. We have demonstrated several forms of learning, but others, such as concept formation (Mitchell, 1978), problem space creation (Hayes and Simon, 1976), and learning by analogy (Carbonell, 1983) still need to be covered before the proposal of chunking as a general learning mechanism can be firmly established.

Acknowledgment

This research was sponsored by the Defense Advanced Research Projects Agency (DOD), ARPA Order No. 3597, monitored by the Air Force Avionics Laboratory Under Contract F33615-81-k-1539. The views and conclusions contained in this document are those of the authors and should not be interpreted as representing the official policies, either expressed or implied, of the Defense Advanced Research Projects Agency or the US Government.

References

Anderson, J. R. Knoweldge compilation: The general learning mechanism. In R. S. Michalski, J. G. Carbonell, & T. M. Mitchell (Eds.), *Proceedings of the 1983 Machine Learning Workshop.* , 1983.

Carbonell, J. G. Learning by analogy: Formulating and generalizing plans from past experience. In R. S. Michalski, J. G. Carbonell, & T. M. Mitchell (Eds.), *Machine Learning: An Artificial Intelligence Approach.* Palo Alto, CA: Tioga, 1983.

Forgy, C. L. *OPS5 Manual.* Computer Science Department, Carnegie-Mellon University, 1981.

Hayes, J. R. and Simon, H. A. Understanding complex task instructions. In Klahr, D. (Ed.), *Cognition and Instruction.* Hillsdale, NJ: Erlbaum, 1976.

Laird, J. E. *Universal Subgoaling.* Doctoral dissertation, Computer Science Department, Carnegie-Mellon University, 1983. (Also appears as Part I of this book).

Langley, P. Learning Effective Search Heuristics. In *Proceedings of IJCAI-83.* IJCAI, 1983.

McDermott, J. R1: A rule-based configurer of computer systems. *Artificial Intelligence*, 1982, *19*, 39-88.

Miller, G. A. The magic number seven, plus or minus two: Some limits on our capacity for processing information. *Psychological Review*, 1956, *63*, 81-97.

Mitchell, T. M. *Version Spaces: An approach to concept learning.* Doctoral dissertation, Stanford University, 1978.

Mitchell, T. M. Learning and Problem Solving. In *Proceedings of IJCAI-83.* IJCAI, 1983.

Newell, A. Reasoning, problem solving and decision processes: The problem space as a fundamental category. In R. Nickerson (Ed.), *Attention and Performance VIII.* Hillsdale, NJ: Erlbaum, 1980.

Newell, A. and Rosenbloom, P. Mechanisms of skill acquisition and the law of practice. In Anderson, J. A. (Ed.), *Learning and Cognition.* Hillsdale, NJ: Erlbaum, 1981.

Rosenbloom, P. S. *The Chunking of Goal Hierarchies: A Model of Practice and Stimulus-Response Compatibility.* Doctoral dissertation, Carnegie-Mellon University, 1983. (Also appears as Part II of this book).

Rosenbloom, P. S., and Newell, A. The chunking of goal hierarchies: A generalized model of practice. In R. S. Michalski, J. G. Carbonell, & T. M. Mitchell (Eds.), *Proceedings of the 1983 Machine Learning Workshop.* , 1983. (To appear in R. S. Michalski, J. G. Carbonell, & T. M. Mitchell (Eds.), *Machine Learning: An Artificial Intelligence Approach, Volume II.*

Los Altos, CA: Morgan Kaufmann, In press.).

Rosenbloom, P. S., Laird, J. E., McDermott, J., Newell, A., & Orciuch, E. R1-Soar: An experiment in knowledge-intensive programming in a problem-solving architecture. In *Proceedings of the IEEE Workshop on Principles of Knowledge-Based Systems.* IEEE Computer Society, 1984. (To appear in *IEEE Transactions on Pattern Analysis and Machine Intelligence,* In press.).

AUTHOR INDEX

302

SUBJECT INDEX

PART I

PART II

PART III